Problems in Price Theory

Problems in Price Theory

DAVID de MEZA
MICHAEL OSBORNE

The University of Chicago Press

The University of Chicago Press, Chicago 60637
Philip Allan, Deddington, Oxford

89 88 87 86 85 84 83 82   2 3 4 5 6

Library of Congress Cataloging in Publication Data

De Meza, David.
  Problems in price theory.

  1. Microeconomics — Problems, exercises, etc.
I. Osborne, Michael, 1952 — joint author. II. Title.
HB171.5.D46   338.5'076   80-16597
ISBN 0-226-14293-0 (cloth)
        0-226-14294-9 (paper)

*In memory of
my mother, Cecile*
D. de M.
To my mother, Margaret
M.O.

Contents

PART II

Foreword

The role of micro theory in the study of economics is probably more central now than it has been for the last forty years. Not only is micro analysis being extended to deal with a whole range of new problems — crime, the family, job search, and so on — but, more and more, the boundaries between microeconomics and macroeconomics are becoming hazy indeed. Many major advances in the macro-economics field over the last ten years have involved establishing or strengthening the microeconomic foundations of macroeconomic relationships. More than ever, then, the student who wishes to master economics as a discipline must master microeconomics.

At the same time, microeconomic theory is frequently found by students to be the most difficult area of the subject. The reason for this is surely that to master micro theory requires the active participation of the student. Simply to sit in lectures and take notes or to read through other people's expositions of the subject is not enough. The student must work at micro problems himself in order to become proficient in the area; and not just from time to time when preparing for an examination, but on a regular ongoing basis.

This book by David de Meza and Michael Osborne therefore fills an enormous gap in the existing textbook literature. It contains a set of structured problems which the student must work through for himself, applying as he goes the analysis that he will find set out in any number of more orthodox textbooks. These problems are carefully graded. They begin at an elementary level, but progress in difficulty, and in subject matter, to tackle areas that as often as not will be found in first-year level graduate courses. Moreover, when more advanced topics that are not always dealt with in orthodox textbooks are taken up, the problems are supplemented by brief but clear expositions of the analysis they exploit. The book will thus be invaluable to students studying economics at all levels in universities and colleges, and is so organised that the student can work through it by himself if he so wishes. However, it is also an ideal source of questions for formal classroom discussion or for informal student-organised study sessions.

I have had a great deal of fun reading through the manuscript, and I have learned a few things from doing so as well. I am sure the authors must have enjoyed themselves in writing the book, and I hope that students will get equal pleasure from it. In making the learning of micro theory enjoyable, David de Meza and Michael Osborne will have earned the gratitude of everyone who works through this book.

David Laidler
University of Western Ontario

Introduction

Economic theory should attempt to explain the world about us. When successful it yields intellectual order out of the chaos of seemingly unrelated events, and thus the theorist not only proves his or her social worth by answering questions that are of practical importance but achieves an intellectual kick by doing so. It follows that economics seriously pursued is, like all sciences, essentially a problem solving enterprise. But whatever your motivation for studying theory, you will only fully understand it by meeting the challenge of trying to apply it.

This book contains many problems with which a practising economist may be confronted. Whilst some of the questions do concern the internal logic of the theory, we have made every effort to include questions which potentially have relevance to everyday events. We are not offering a manual of applied economics, but hope that working through this book will give you sufficient feel for the economic approach to be able to tackle the many different problems you may actually face as a working economist. With this aim in mind we have chosen questions and answers which emphasise basic economic logic rather than esoteric technical detail. For this reason the book is intended to be useful to all students from second year undergraduates to university professors.

Part I of the book covers the basic ingredients of most intermediate microeconomics courses. We hope the questions and answers provided here show how useful the tools acquired on such courses can be. The topics in Part II are generally dealt with only in advanced courses, but we feel they are interesting, and can usefully be studied using no more than the tools of Part I. As the subject matter of Part II is not covered in a comprehensive fashion in most textbooks, each chapter contains an outline of the basic theory. But only by thinking through the implications of the abstract theory will you appreciate its meaning, and the questions which follow the exposition are intended to give the opportunity to do just that. Finally, we have included references which enable you to follow up our discussion.

We believe all our answers are at least logically correct. However, we invite you to make us look idiots, though we sincerely hope you don't succeed. Further, we have no doubt that even if there are no glaring errors it would be a useful exercise for you to think what improvements could be made both to our questions and answers.

In various ways all the following have contributed to the book, sometimes unknowingly, for which we thank them, whilst absolving them from all errors: George Assaf, David Blake, Bob Gould, Eve Harris, Richard Layard, Alan Marin, Anita McLeod, Chris Pissarides, Avner Shaked, Margaret Sharp, John Sutton, Thomas von Ungern Sternberg, Nigel Wellard, Toni Zabalza. We owe a particular debt to all those students who over a number of years have greatly refined both our questions and answers.

Our especial thanks go to David Laidler who has given immense help and encouragement in the preparation of the book and without whom it would be a great deal worse.

Finally, we apologise to anyone to whom inadvertently we have not given proper acknowledgement for a question.

Operating Instructions

The first part of each chapter is intended to contain the more straight-forward problems, and these are followed by some which are tougher and occasionally call for elementary calculus. Most of the problems are in the form of propositions that are to be assessed as true, false or uncertain. For example, the proposition 'all commodity demand curves must be downward sloping' is false, for consumer theory permits of exceptions. However, the empirical proposition 'no upward sloping demand curves have ever existed' is uncertain for conflicting evidence exists.

We strongly recommend you think out your own answers before looking at ours and hope you find the book provides some stimulation, enjoyment and insight.

1982 Reprint

In the reprint of May 1982, misprints, errors and omissions found in the first printing have been corrected.

References

The market for microeconomics textbooks is perhaps a good example of monopolistic competition in action. We have chosen a few of the many books available to serve as references to the material of Part I and at the start of each chapter the relevant sections of these textbooks are cited. Any of these books will provide sufficient background to answer the questions which follow, as will many others we have not listed.

Becker, Gary, *Economic Theory*, Alfred Knopf 1971.

Ferguson C.E. and Gould J.P., *Microeconomic Theory*, 4th Edition, Irwin 1975.

Friedman, Milton, *Price Theory*, Aldine 1976.

Hirshleifer, Jack, *Price Theory and Applications*, Prentice-Hall 1976.

Laidler, David, *Introduction to Microeconomics*, Philip Allan 1974.

Lancaster, Kelvin, *Introduction to Modern Microeconomics*, 2nd Edition, Rand McNally 1974.

Layard, Richard and Walters, Alan, *Microeconomic Theory*, McGraw-Hill 1978.

Mansfield, Edwin, *Microeconomic Theory and Applications*, 2nd Edition, Norton 1975.

Stigler, George, *The Theory of Price*, Macmillan 1966.

PART I

1

Basic Consumer Theory

References

Becker Chapters 2 and 3. Ferguson Part I. Friedman Chapter 2. Hirshleifer Chapters 3 and 6. Laidler Chapters 2 to 6. Lancaster Chapter 7. Layard Chapter 5. Mansfield Chapters 2 and 3. Stigler Chapters 3 and 4.

A textbook entirely devoted to consumer theory and covering Chapters 1 to 4 and parts of Chapter 12 of this book is H. John Green's *Consumer Theory* (Macmillan 1976).

Questions

Q1.1 The table below shows various combinations of X and Y which yield a consumer the indicated levels of cardinal utility. (On the distinction between cardinal and ordinal utility see Laidler p. 49.)

1 UTIL		4 UTILS		16 UTILS	
X	Y	X	Y	X	Y
1	1	1	2	1	4
2	½	2	1	2	2
4	¼	4	½	4	1

(a) The marginal utility of Y diminishes as Y consumption increases holding X constant.

(b) The marginal utility of X diminishes as X consumption increases holding Y constant.

(c) The marginal rate of substitution of X for Y diminishes as X rises.

(d) These preferences give rise to indifference curves which are convex to the origin.

(e) An increase in the amount of X consumed increases the marginal utility of Y.

3

Q1.2 Propositions 1.1(a) to (e) hold for the preferences shown below.

5 UTILS		6 UTILS		6.5 UTILS	
X	Y	X	Y	X	Y
1	24	1	27	1	33
2	21	2	24	2	29
3	16	3	19	3	24

Q1.3 A good is inferior only if quantity demanded falls as price falls.

Q1.4 If we observe an individual to demand less of a good as its price falls, we may conclude that it is an inferior good for him.

Q1.5 If a man is offered a second-hand car for $3000 he will buy it. But if he is offered the same car for only $300 he becomes suspicious that all is not as it seems and refuses to buy. The car is therefore an inferior good.

Q1.6 As the price of coffee rises I drink less tea. Hence my income elasticity of demand for tea is negative.

Q1.7 An individual's demand curve for a particular good cannot be upward sloping at all prices.

Q1.8 Suppose a consumer's uncompensated price elasticity of demand for good X, one of the many goods he buys, is less than one. A rise in the price of X will reduce both his demand for X and for at least one of the other goods he buys.

Q1.9 The price of food rises by 10% and disposable income by 5%. A man initially spending half his income on food would be neither better nor worse off as a result of these changes.

Q1.10 A housewife buys 2 lb of steak per week. Its price rises by 50p per lb. The compensating variation associated with this price change must be less than or equal to + £1.

Q1.11 The equivalent variation for the price change in the previous question must exceed or equal minus £1.

Q1.12 If a consumer spends all his income then the simple average of the income elasticities of demand of all the goods he buys is unity.

Further Questions

Q1.13 A consumer buys one unit of a good when its price is £2 and two units when its price is £1. Hence he would rather pay £2.80 for two units of the good than go without it altogether.

Q1.14 A consumer buys from two shops, each selling a different type of good. Visiting one of these shops involves a bus journey. If the bus fare rises he must decrease his purchases from the other shop as long as neither good is inferior and both goods continue to be bought.

Q1.15 During a war, food and clothing are rationed. In addition to a money price a certain number of ration points must be paid to obtain a good. Each consumer has an allocation of ration points which may be used to purchase either good and also has a fixed money income. Suppose the money income of a consumer is raised and he buys more food and less clothing. It follows that clothing is an inferior good.

Q1.16 Goods i and j are net complements if a compensated (i.e. removing the income effect) fall in the price of i leads to an increase in the amount of j consumed. If the consumer buys only two goods they cannot both be net complements but in the case of three or more they may all be net complements.

Q1.17 In order to aid the poor the government introduces a scheme whereby the first 2 lb of butter a family buys is subsidised and the remaining amounts are taxed. Consider a family which consumes butter and is made neither better nor worse off as a result of this scheme. The total amount of tax it pays cannot exceed the subsidy it receives.

Q1.18 When price changes it is sometimes claimed that the quantity demanded of a good varies by more in the long run than the short run. As one approach to this problem suppose there are two types of goods. For good Y, say housing, it is not feasible to change the quantity at all in the short run (in effect, transaction costs are pro-hibitive). On the other hand, consumption of goods of type X can be immediately varied. If type X goods are normal it does follow that demand for them will be more elastic in the long run than in the short run.

Q1.19 Students can buy a travel pass which entitles them to a percentage reduction in the price of all British Rail tickets.

   (i)   If a student is indifferent between buying the pass or paying the standard fare he will never spend less and in general will spend more on rail travel if he does buy the pass.
   (ii) The introduction of such a pass scheme can never reduce the number of rail journeys a student makes.

Q1.20 A consumer has a fixed money income. There is a rise in the price of one of the goods he buys. The consequent absolute increase in his cost of living as measured by a Laspeyres income variation (i.e. the change in the cost of buying the original commodity bundle) will exceed the Hicks compensating variation associated with the price increase whether or not the good is normal.

Q1.21 For the consumer in the previous question the increase in his cost of living as measured by a Paasche income variation (i.e. the change in the cost of buying the final commodity bundle) must be less than the equivalent variation associated with the price rise.

Q.1.22 (a) Suppose, once again, that there is a rise in the price of one of the goods a consumer buys. The increase in the cost of living as measured by a Paasche income variation will exceed that as measured by a Laspeyres income variation if and only if the good is inferior.

   (b) If all goods are normal, the Laspeyres price index must exceed the Paasche price index if the price of one good rises.

   (c) If his Laspeyres price index rises by a proportion equal to or less than his income, an individual must be better off; and if his Paasche price index rises by a proportion equal to or greater than his income, he must be worse off.

Q1.23 A consumer has a fixed money income. There is a rise in the price of one of the goods he buys. If the good is normal an un-ambiguous ranking of the size of Paasche, Laspeyres, compensating and equivalent variations is possible.

Q1.24 If a good is normal, the area underneath a consumer's money income constant demand curve and above the price line is an over-estimate of the sum of money necessary to compensate him for the loss that arises from banning its sale.

Answers

A1.1 (a) **FALSE.** The marginal utility of Y is the additional utility generated by an extra unit of Y consumption. It is diminishing, if, holding X consumption constant, each unit of Y adds a smaller amount to total utility than did the previous unit. In the present case, if X is fixed at 1 then, when Y rises from 1 to 2, utils increase from 1 to 4 and so marginal utility is 3. When Y rises from 2 to 4, utils increase from 4 to 16 and so marginal utility over this interval is 6. In similar fashion the marginal utility of Y can be shown to be increasing if X is held constant at 2 and 4.

(b) **FALSE.** This time hold Y constant at 1.

(c) **TRUE.** The marginal rate of substitution of X for Y is the change in X required to leave the consumer just as well off if he has an extra unit of Y. Given the data in the question, X must fall from 4 to 2 when Y rises from ¼ to ½ if the consumer is to remain on the 1 util indifference curve. The marginal rate of substitution is therefore −8. As Y rises from ½ to 1, X falls from 2 to 1 and thus the marginal rate of substitution is −2. It therefore diminishes as X increases.

(d) **TRUE.** A diminishing marginal rate of substitution means that successive increases in Y require the loss of smaller and smaller amounts of X to keep the individual on the same indifference curve. This defines an indifference curve which is convex to the origin.

(e) **TRUE.** When Y changes from 1 to 2 and $X = 1$, 3 utils are added. When Y changes from 1 to 2 and $X = 2$, 12 utils are added. It is a general rule that if marginal utility is increasing and the marginal rate of substitution is diminishing, more of one good raises the marginal utility of the other (can you prove this?).

Note: The message of this question and answer is that diminishing marginal utility is not a necessary condition for standard convex indifference curves.

A1.2 (a) **TRUE.**

(b) **TRUE.**

(c) **FALSE.**

(d) **FALSE.**

(e) **FALSE.**

Note: The message of this question and answer is that diminishing marginal utility is not sufficient to ensure convex indifference curves.

A1.3 FALSE. A good is inferior if demand for it falls as income rises. Since a cut in price increases real income it is possible in the case of an inferior good that the income effect outweighs the substitution effect and demand falls. If so the good is Giffen. But inferiority does not guarantee that the substitution effect will be swamped by the income effect.

A1.4 FALSE. Quantity demanded may move in the same direction as price for reasons other than that a negative income effect offsets the standard substitution effect along a conventional demand curve. Suppose utility depends on price as well as quantity. Thus if the price of a fur coat falls and everyone can afford it, it no longer serves as a status symbol and a rich woman may cease to buy. However, at the original price it is quite possible that only when her income exceeded a certain level would the woman buy the coat, so making it a normal good. Similar results may occur with durable goods, where a present fall in price is taken as a signal that prices will fall further in the future (extrapolative expectations), and also with goods for which price is taken as an indicator of quality (see next question).

A1.5 FALSE. Once again there is no reason why at any price the man's demand for the car does not increase with his income. However, the fall in price changes his perception of the good. (The implications of this kind of behaviour are taken up in Chapter 14.)

A1.6 FALSE. The substitution effect of an increase in the price of coffee will induce more tea consumption. Real income will fall. This will cut demand for tea only if it is a normal good (positive income elasticity). We assume that coffee drinking is not a 'snob' activity and that coffee and tea are net substitutes.

A1.7 TRUE. If a rise in price induces more consumption of a good, total expenditure on it must increase with price. Unless the demand curve eventually took on the conventional negative slope, it would follow that at sufficiently high prices expenditure on the good must exceed income, which is of course impossible.

A1.8 FALSE. The quantity demanded of good X falls by a smaller percentage than the rise in price. Thus money expenditure on it rises. With a fixed money income it follows that expenditure on the other goods the consumer buys must fall. Since the money price of all these goods is unchanged, consumption of at least one of them must fall. But the twist is that the question does not rule out X being a Giffen good (negative price elasticity) and thus the consumption of X itself may not fall.

A1.9 **FALSE.** Without loss of generality suppose the man has an initial income of £100 of which he spends £50 on food. If he purchases the same quantity of food after the 10% price rise it will cost him £55. Thus the 5% rise in income to £105 will allow him to purchase his original bundle of goods, therefore he cannot be worse off. But apart from the extreme case of a right-angled indifference curve, he will not choose to consume the original mix of goods. Thus he must consider himself to be better off. This is illustrated in figure 1.1 where AB is the original budget constraint and CD the new one.

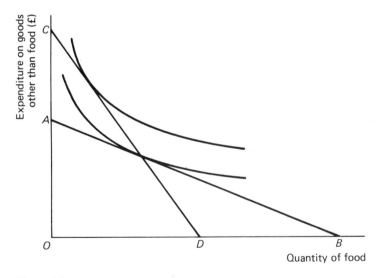

Figure 1.1

A1.10 **TRUE.** To purchase the original commodity bundle the housewife requires an additional £1 of income. If given this £1 she will either buy the same quantity of steak as before or, in response to the higher relative price of steak, buy less (the diagram is similar to that in the previous question). In the case that a new commodity bundle is chosen, since the old is still available, the housewife is better off and the £1 is overcompensation. Otherwise it exactly compensates for the price change.

A1.11 FALSE. The equivalent variation is the change in income that has the same effect on welfare as the price change. In figure 1.2 (a), AB is the original budget constraint and AC is the budget constraint after the price rise. A fall in income of AD puts the housewife on the same indifference curve as does the price rise. Since by construction the distance FH is £1 and FG is shorter, it follows that the equivalent variation is greater than $-£1$. Note that as income rises from DE to AB demand for steak rises and it is therefore a normal good. In figure 1.2 (b) the analysis is repeated. But this time steak is an inferior good and the equivalent variation is less than $-£1$. (You should be able to check that when income elasticity is zero $EV = -CV > -1$, and so if $EV < -1$ the good must both be strongly inferior and have a high substitution effect. An alternative demonstration of this makes use of the fact that the EV is the area between the two price lines and the Hicks real income demand curve associated with the final level of utility (see A1.24 for a method of proof). For an inferior good this curve is less steep than the money income constant demand curve.)

A1.12 FALSE. Consider an individual with an initial income of £100 and who spends £20 on good X and £80 on good Y. When his income rises to £110 he spends £25 on X and £85 on Y. Thus the income elasticity of X is $(5/20)/(10/100) = 2.5$ and of Y is $(5/80)/(10/100) = 0.625$. The average income elasticity is 1.56, not unity. But there is a relationship:

The expenditure pattern when income is M^0 is

$$p_1 q_1^0 + p_2 q_2^0 + \ldots + p_n q_n^0 = M^0 \tag{1}$$

The expenditure pattern when income is M^1 is

$$p_1 q_1^1 + p_2 q_2^1 + \ldots + p_n q_n^1 = M^1 \tag{2}$$

Subtracting (1) from (2)

$$p_1(q_1^1 - q_1^0) + p_2(q_2^1 - q_2^0) + \ldots + p_n (q_n^1 - q_n^0)$$

$$= M^1 - M^0 \tag{3}$$

or

$$\left(\frac{p_1 q_1^0}{M^0}\right)\left[\left(\frac{q_1^1 - q_1^0}{M^1 - M^0}\right)\left(\frac{M^0}{q_1^0}\right)\right] + \ldots + \left(\frac{p_n q_n^0}{M^0}\right)\left[\left(\frac{q_n^1 - q_n^0}{M^1 - M^0}\right)\left(\frac{M^0}{q_n^0}\right)\right] = 1 \tag{4}$$

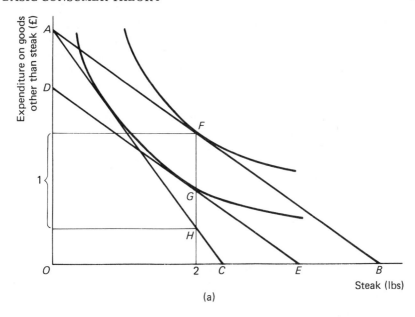

(a)

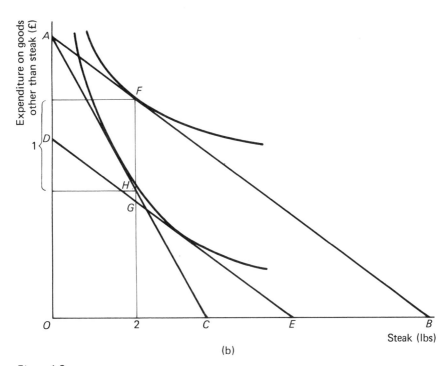

(b)

Figure 1.2

Equation (4) states that the sum of income elasticities of demand weighted by the percentage of total expenditure spent on the good at the initial level of income sums to unity. This is simply another way of saying that the budget constraint must hold at all levels of income. Check equation (4) by means of the numerical example given above.

A1.13 FALSE. In figure 1.3, the budget constraint when X costs £1 is YA and YB when X costs £2. Since C is on a lower indifference

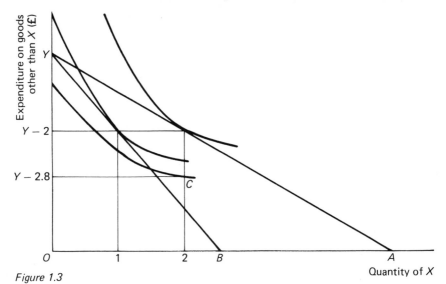

Figure 1.3

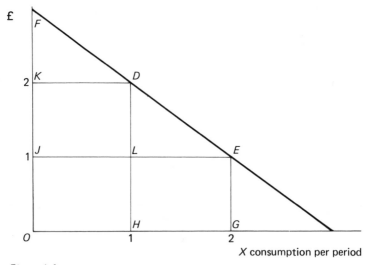

Figure 1.4

curve than Y the all-or-nothing offer of 2 units for £2.80 will be rejected if the consumer has the preference map shown. (Note this answer does not depend on X being inferior.)

Can you see where the fallacy lies in the following? Given the information in the question the demand curve for X must pass through points D and E in figure 1.4. The value the consumer places on 2 units of the good is the area $FEGO$, under the demand curve. Since $KDHO + LEGH = 2 + 1 = 3$, it follows that two units of the good are worth more than £2.80 to the consumer who will therefore definitely accept the all-or-nothing offer. As a hint to error in this line of reasoning consider the properties of the constant real income demand curve through F.

A1.14 TRUE. The bus fare constitutes a fixed cost in obtaining goods from one of the shops (say Y). The initial budget constraint is therefore ABC (figure 1.5) where AB is the bus fare and the slope of BC embodies the relative prices set by the two shops.

When the bus fare is increased the budget constraint becomes ADE. If the indifference map is $U_1 U_2$ the increase in bus fare only has income effects and less Y is purchased if it is a normal good. If the consumer's preferences were different, as shown by the alternative indifference map $U_1 U_2'$, the rise in bus fare will eliminate all purchases of X. This is because the tangency point F lies on a lower indifference curve than is achieved if only Y is consumed. More Y will therefore be bought if the indifference map is $U_1 U_2'$.

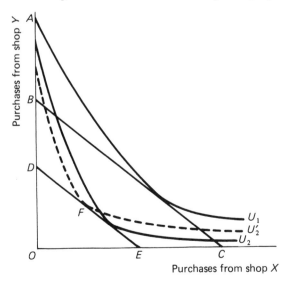

Figure 1.5

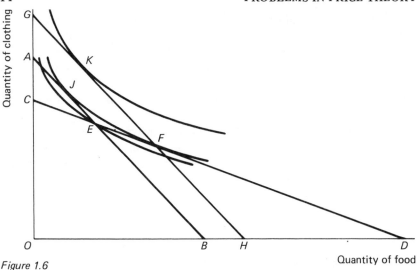

Figure 1.6

Quantity of food

A1.15 **FALSE.** In the figure 1.6, *AEB* shows the conventional income constraint of the consumer. The ration constraint is *CED* which is derived from the linear equation $P_F F + P_C C = R$, where P_F is the number of ration points that must be paid per unit of food consumed, F is total consumption of food and P_C and C have similar interpretations for clothing. R is the number of ration points available. The feasible consumption set satisfying both income and ration constraints is therefore *OCEB*. Given the particular preferences shown here the consumer maximises utility at the kink point E where all of his money income and points allocation is used up. (Note that, in general, a consumer can be in equilibrium leaving either some of his ration points unused or some of his money income unspent.) Now suppose the consumer's income is raised to *GH*. His consumption shifts from E to F involving less clothing and more food. But if income were the only constraint his consumption would change from *J* to *K* and it can therefore be seen that clothing is a normal good.

A1.16 **FALSE.** A compensated fall in the price of good i increases the amount of i consumed. If every other good is a complement, their consumption also rises. But this means the individual would end up consuming more of all goods and must therefore be better off. This is inconsistent with a compensated price fall. Note that we have not proved that the own substitution effects for a compensated price change is negative. However, even if the consumption of good i fell (which can in fact be shown to be impossible — see the Revealed Preference Appendix) the same reasoning implies that not all goods can be complements since then the consumer would be worse off.

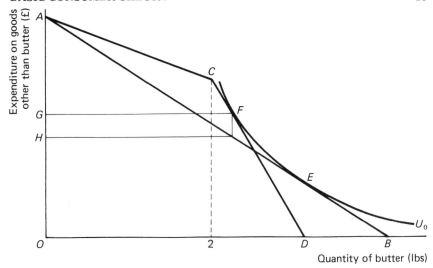

Figure 1.7

A1.17 TRUE. Before the introduction of the scheme the family faces budget constraint AB in figure 1.7. When the scheme is in operation the subsidy reduces the effective price of the first 2 lb of butter so, assuming the market price of butter remains unchanged, the new budget constraint lies above and has a gentler slope than AB. For quantities in excess of 2 lb the cost per pound has risen, and so the new budget constraint is steeper than AB. Overall, the new budget constraint is shown as ACD. If the family is to be just as well off with or without the scheme the same indifference curve must be tangential to both new and old budget constraints. As can be seen from figure 1.7, this therefore is only possible if consumption of butter falls, in this case from E to F. Since F lies above AB, the expenditure required to purchase this amount of butter is GH less than before the introduction of the government scheme. The net subsidy received is therefore GH.

A1.18 FALSE. In figure 1.8 let the initial budget constraint be AB along which commodity bundle Y_0, X_0 is chosen. The price of X then falls, yielding budget constraint AC. Since in the short run Y is fixed at Y_0, after the fall in price X consumption expands to X_1'. The question is whether in the long run X consumption could fall below X_1'. Such a case is illustrated. The substitution effect of the price fall leaves consumption less than X_1' and although the income effect will cause a further expansion in demand to X_1, the total effect is nevertheless that X consumption is lower in the long run than the short run.

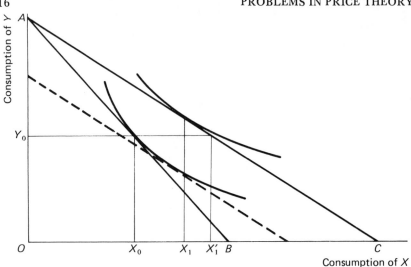

Figure 1.8

A1.19 (i) **TRUE.** On the vertical axis of figure 1.9 expenditure on goods other than rail travel is measured and on the horizontal axis the number of rail journeys taken. (Since journeys may be to different destinations there is an aggregation problem here. However this is a presentational problem and does not affect the result, thus rail journeys are here assumed to be a homogeneous good.) Given an income of OA, AF is the conventional budget constraint when no pass is bought. If a pass is bought then, even if no journeys are made, expenditure on other goods is reduced by the pass cost of AC. But when the pass is bought the cost of each rail journey is lower than before, so the slope of the constraint is gentler. Thus when the pass is bought the constraint is ACE. Since the student is indifferent between the two options his indifference curve must, as shown, be tangential to both constraints. If no pass is bought, OB is spent on other goods and so AB is spent on rail travel. With the pass, OD is spent on other goods and hence AD is spent on rail travel. It can be seen that when the pass is bought expenditure on rail travel is higher by BD and the number of journeys also rises. Only if the indifference curves are right-angled will there be no change.

(ii) **FALSE.** As illustrated in figure 1.10, when the pass is superior to the standard fare, and rail travel is an inferior good, rail travel may fall. This latter condition is not very likely for rail but may explain why coach companies are less inclined to offer such schemes than British Rail. However, a more plausible explanation is that British Rail is a monopoly practising price discrimination by offering lower

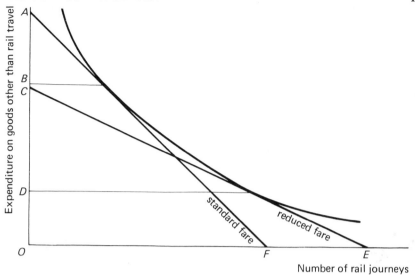

Figure 1.9

prices to students, who as a group have a higher price elasticity of demand than other rail travellers such as businessmen. On the other hand the coach industry is more competitive and has greater difficulty enforcing discriminatory schemes, and in any case the price elasticity of demand is probably rather similar for all groups of coach travellers, and so special discount schemes are less advantageous.

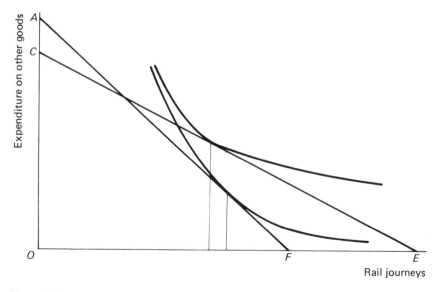

Figure 1.10

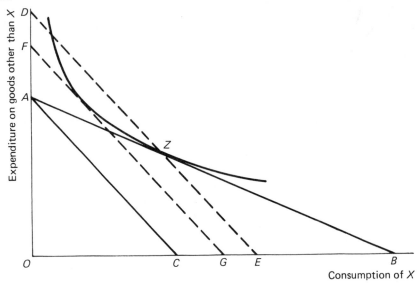

Figure 1.11

A1.20 TRUE. The consumer is initially in equilibrium at Z in figure 1.11. After the price rise his budget constraint becomes AC. To purchase his original commodity bundle after the price rise his income would have to rise by AD which is therefore the increase in the cost of living as measured by the Laspeyres income variation. But the budget constraint DE allows the consumer to reach a higher indifference curve than his original one. It must therefore represent an over-compensation. The change in income that would leave the consumer just as well off after the price rise as before it (the compensating variation) is the smaller amount FA. Since income effects are not involved in ranking these measures the result is true whether or not the good is normal.

A1.21 TRUE. After the price rise the consumer purchases the commodity bundle at W in figure 1.12. Before the price rise this commodity bundle could have been purchased if his income had been lower by JL. Thus the increase in the cost of purchasing the new commodity bundle after the price rise is JL, which is the Paasche income variation. But the change in income that would have an equivalent effect on utility to the rise in price (i.e. bring the consumer to the same indifference curve) is JN, which exceeds JL.

A1.22 (a) FALSE. Using superscripts 0 and 1 to denote base and current prices and quantities purchased, if the Paasche income variation

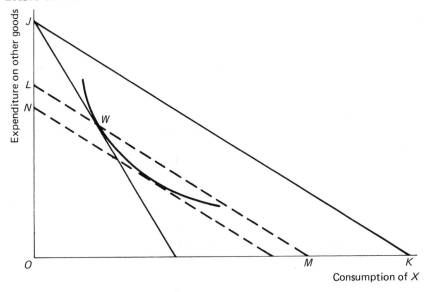

Figure 1.12

(P) exceeds the Laspeyres (L) it follows that;

$$P = \Sigma p_i^1 q_i^1 - \Sigma p_i^0 q_i^1 > \Sigma p_i^1 q_i^0 - \Sigma p_i^0 q_i^0 = L \tag{1}$$

Rearranging;

$$\Sigma \, (p_i^1 - p_i^0) \, (q_i^1 - q_i^0) > 0 \tag{2}$$

But the price of only one good, call it j, has risen. Thus (2) reduces to

$$(p_j^1 - p_j^0) \, (q_j^1 - q_j^0) > 0 \tag{3}$$

Now (3) is only positive if, when the price of j rises, the quantity of j demanded also increases. Thus $P > L$ if and only if the good is Giffen. Inferiority is not enough.

(b) **FALSE.** This is so, despite the previous answer and the assertions of some textbooks. Consider the following example. Let the initial prices of goods X and Y be £1 and a consumer buy 50 units of each. The price of X then rises to £2 and the consumer buys 40 units of X and 20 of Y, which is consistent with both goods being normal. At the original prices the cost of the initial commodity bundle is £100 and at the new prices it is £150. Hence the Laspeyres (base weighted) price index stands at 1.5. The cost of the new bundle at the old prices is £60 and at the new prices is £100. Hence the Paasche (current weighted) index stands at 1.66. It is therefore false to claim that if all goods are normal the Laspeyres price index over-estimates the rise in the cost of the original standard of living and the Paasche price index underestimates it.

(c) **TRUE.** If the Laspeyres index rises by a proportion no higher than the rise in income $\Sigma\, p_i^1\, q_i^0 / \Sigma\, p_i^0\, q_i^0 \leqslant \Sigma\, p_i^1\, q_i^1 / \Sigma\, p_i^0\, q_i^0$ and hence $\Sigma\, p_i^1\, q_i^0 \leqslant \Sigma\, p_i^1\, q_i^1$. This last inequality means that in the second period the individual could have purchased his first period commodity bundle and so must be better off.

For the Paasche price index to rise by a proportion at least as high as income requires $\Sigma\, p_i^1\, q_i^1 / \Sigma\, p_i^0\, q_i^1 \geqslant \Sigma\, p_i^1\, q_i^1 / \Sigma\, p_i^0\, q_i^0$ and so $\Sigma\, p_i^0\, q_i^0 \geqslant \Sigma\, p_i^0\, q_i^1$. This last inequality means that in the first period the individual could have purchased the second period consumption bundle. As he chose not to, he must regard it as inferior and so be worse off in the second period.

In these answers we have assumed that preferences are the same in both periods and that all income is spent.

A1.23 **TRUE.** From the answers to questions 1.19 and 1.20 we know that independently of whether the good is normal $L > CV$ and $EV > P$. From questions and answers 1.10 and 1.11 it follows that for a normal good $CV > EV$, where both are measured in absolute terms. Finally, from question 1.21, $L > P$. Thus since $L > CV$, $EV > P$, $CV > EV$ and $L > P$ then $L > CV > EV > P$ is the only ordering satis-fying all conditions. Can you show that for a Giffen good $EV > P > L > CV$, but that for an inferior but non-Giffen good no definite ranking is possible? The simplest method is probably to use areas under compensated and uncompensated demand curves, but the interpretation of such areas must first be proved (see A1.24).

A1.24 **FALSE.** In figure 1.13 AC is the money income constant demand curve. The good is sold at price P_1. The question is whether area ABP_1 correctly measures the sum of money which if paid to the consumer when sale of the good is banned would be just sufficient to compensate him for its loss. In terms of the indifference curve diagram (figure 1.14), in which FJ is the budget constraint when price is P_1, this compensating variation is measured as GF. The issue is whether $GF = ABP_1$.

The indifference curve itself may be regarded as showing a func-tional relationship between S (expenditure on goods other than X) and X such that $S = U_0(X)$. The slope of the indifference curve is given by $dS/dX = U_0'(X)$. We know that in equilibrium the slope of the indifference curve equals minus the price ratio. A unit of expendi-

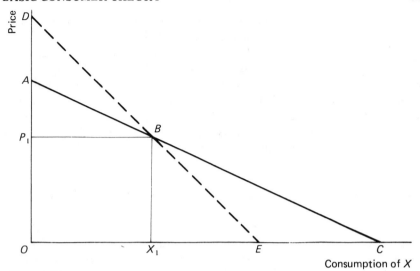

Figure 1.13

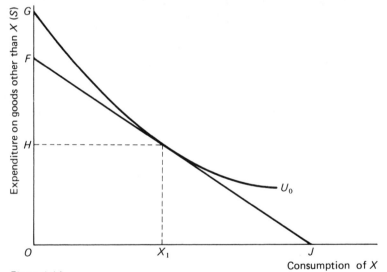

Figure 1.14

ture on S of course costs 1, so if the price of X is P, then $- U_0'(X)$ $= P$. This equation defines the real income constant demand curve. As P varies it shows how much X will be demanded if the consumer achieves the level of utility U_0. It is plotted as DE in figure 1.13. At prices below P_1 the consumer is able to reach a higher indifference curve than U_0 with his fixed money income, and so if X is normal more of it will be bought than along the real income constant demand curve. The reverse is true at prices higher than P_1.

Now something definite can be said about the area under the real income constant demand curve. Area $ODBX_1$ in figure 1.13 is, by definition of an integral, $-\int_0^{X_1} U_0'(X)dX$. This is evaluated as $U_0(X_1) - U_0(0)$. In the indifference curve diagram $U_0(X_1)$ is OH and $U_0(0)$ is OG. Thus $U_0(X_1) - U_0(0) = GH$ which equals area $ODBX_1$ under the real income constant demand curve. Further, $FH = OP_1BX_1$ is simply the cost of buying X_1 units of X at price P_1. Thus the required compensating variation appearing as GF in figure 1.14 is DBP_1 in figure 1.13. It therefore exceeds ABP_1.

APPENDIX: THE REVEALED PREFERENCE APPROACH

All the standard propositions of consumer theory may be derived using revealed preference analysis. This has the disputable merit of banishing indifference curves and utility functions from the scene, though revealed preference also provides a method of constructing indifference curves from observed behaviour (see e.g. Stigler pp. 68—71). It does not yield any new results but is generally considered to provide a more elegant derivation of those already known. We give a brief exposition of the method below and recommend the reader to try using revealed preference analysis where previously indifference curves have been employed.

Samuelson (*Economica* February 1938) introduced revealed preference analysis and Sen (*Economica*, August 1973) gives a clear and critical review of the implicit assumptions behind it.

Geometry

The rationale of revealed preference analysis is easily seen from the geometry of the two-good case. In figure 1.15 AB is the initial budget constraint. A good is defined to have the characteristic that more is preferred to less and so the consumer will choose a commodity bundle which lies on AB rather than inside it. Suppose Z is the chosen commodity bundle. A compensated fall in the price of X which just permits the consumer to purchase his original commodity bundle (a Slutsky compensation) is shown by budget constraint CD. At the new price ratio consumption between C and Z will never be observed. For example, point E was a feasible choice when the budget constraint was AB and yet Z was revealed preferred. E and Z remain feasible choices when the budget constraint is CD. But assuming preferences are independent of prices, Z must still be preferred to E. Thus E will never be a chosen commodity bundle. Either consumption stays at Z or shifts to a point between Z and D.

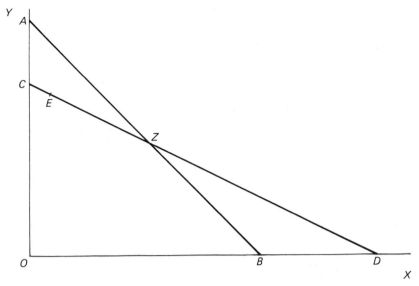

Figure 1.15

Less X is never consumed. This is the basic result of consumer theory. The own substitution effect is non-positive.

Algebra

Suppose at initial prices $p_1 \ldots p_n$ an individual spends all his income, M, in buying the bundle of goods $q_1 \ldots q_n$. Thus $p_1 q_1 + p_2 q_2 \ldots + p_n q_n = M$. Prices then change to $\bar{p}_1 \ldots \bar{p}_n$ and at the same time the consumer receives a compensating change in income which just allows him to buy his original bundle of goods. Writing this new income $\bar{M}$ it follows that $\bar{M} = \bar{p}_1 q_1 + \bar{p}_2 q_2 \ldots + \bar{p}_n q_n$. But at the new levels of income and prices the consumer does not necessarily buy the old commodity bundle. If he chooses $\bar{q}_1 \ldots \bar{q}_n$ and this is different from $q_1 \ldots q_n$, he has revealed the new bundle preferred to the old. Assuming his preferences are independent of prices, the only reason $q_1 \ldots q_n$ was chosen originally must be that at prices $p_1 \ldots p_n$ the bundle $\bar{q}_1 \ldots \bar{q}_n$ was more expensive.

Thus

$$p_1 \bar{q}_1 + p_2 \bar{q}_2 + \ldots + p_n \bar{q}_n \geqslant p_1 q_1 + p_2 q_2 + \ldots + p_n q_n \quad (1)$$

The equality holds if $q_1 = \bar{q}_1$, $q_2 = \bar{q}_2$, $\ldots$, $q_n = \bar{q}_n$, in which case the new bundle is the same as the old. We have already noted that

$$\bar{p}_1 \bar{q}_1 + \bar{p}_2 \bar{q}_2 + \ldots + \bar{p}_n \bar{q}_n = \overline{M} = \bar{p}_1 q_1 + \bar{p}_2 q_2 + \ldots + \bar{p}_n q_n \qquad (2)$$

Subtracting (2) from (1) yields

$$(p_1 - \bar{p}_1)\bar{q}_1 + (p_2 - \bar{p}_2)\bar{q}_2 + \ldots + (p_n - \bar{p}_n)\bar{q}_n \geqslant$$

$$\qquad (p_1 - \bar{p}_1) q_1 + (p_2 - \bar{p}_2) q_2 + \ldots + (p_n - \bar{p}_n) q_n \qquad (3)$$

or

$$(p_1 - \bar{p}_1)(\bar{q}_1 - q_1) + (p_2 - \bar{p}_2)(\bar{q}_2 - q_2) + \ldots$$

$$\qquad + (p_n - \bar{p}_n)(\bar{q}_n - q_n) \geqslant 0 \qquad (4)$$

which is known as the *general law of demand*. Take the special case when only the price of good 1 changes. Since $p_i - \bar{p}_i = 0, i = 2 \ldots n$, it follows from (4) that $(p_1 - \bar{p}_1)(\bar{q}_1 - q_1) \geqslant 0$. If price falls, $p_1 - \bar{p}_1 > 0$ and so to preserve inequality (4) $\bar{q}_1 - q_1 \geqslant 0$. Consumption of good 1 either remains the same or rises. The own substitution effect is non-positive.

Question

Q1.25 What is rather grandly known as the weak axiom of revealed preference has already been stated. If commodity bundle q is once chosen when $\bar{q}$ was available, $\bar{q}$ will only be chosen when q is not available. In symbols this amounts to:

If $\qquad p_1 q_1 + p_2 q_2 + \ldots + p_n q_n \geqslant p_1 \bar{q}_1 + p_2 \bar{q}_2 + \ldots + p_n \bar{q}_n$

then $\qquad \bar{p}_1 \bar{q}_1 + \bar{p}_2 \bar{q}_2 + \ldots + \bar{p}_n \bar{q}_n < \bar{p}_1 q_1 + \bar{p}_2 q_2 + \ldots + \bar{p}_n q_n$

Of course, the test must also hold in the reverse direction. If

$$\Sigma \bar{p}\bar{q} \geqslant \Sigma \bar{p}q \quad \text{then} \quad \Sigma pq < \Sigma p\bar{q}$$

The choices made by two individuals are as follows. When the prices of both X and Y are £1, individual A buys 6 units of X and 4 of Y, and individual B buys 4 units of X and 6 of Y. The price of X then rises to £2 and that of Y falls to £0.5. At the same time the income of A falls and that of B rises. A now buys 3 units of X and 5 of Y, and B buys 8 units of X and 3 of Y.

(a) Does consumer A violate the weak axiom of revealed preference (WARP)?
(b) Does consumer B?
(c) Do the aggregated choices of A and B violate the weak
axiom of revealed preference?

Answer

A1.25 (a) **NO.** The cost of the original bundle of goods at base
prices is $\Sigma \, pq = (6 \times 1) + (4 \times 1) = 10$. The cost of the new bundle
at the old prices is $\Sigma \, p\bar{q} = (1 \times 3) + (1 \times 5) = 8$. Hence q is revealed
preferred to $\bar{q}$. The cost of the new bundle at the new prices is
$\Sigma \, \bar{p}\bar{q} = (2 \times 3) + (0.5 \times 5) = 8.5$ and the cost of the old bundle at
the new prices is $\Sigma \, \bar{p}q = (2 \times 6) + (0.5 \times 4) = 14$ and so it must now
be unavailable. $\Sigma \, pq > \Sigma \, p\bar{q}$ and $\Sigma \bar{p}\bar{q} < \Sigma \, \bar{p}q$. WARP is satisfied.

(b) **NO.** $\Sigma pq = (4 \times 1) + (6 \times 1) = 10$. $p\bar{q} = (8 \times 1) + (3 \times 1) = 11$.
As q is initially cheaper than $\bar{q}$ there is no way of knowing which is
the preferred bundle by means of this comparison. However $\Sigma \, \bar{p}\bar{q} =$
$(2 \times 8) + (0.5 \times 3) = 17.5$ and $\Sigma \, \bar{p}q = (2 \times 4) + (0.5 \times 6) = 11$. Thus
$\bar{q}$ is revealed preferred to q. Since $\Sigma \, p\bar{q} > \Sigma \, pq$ the initial choice
does not conflict with the final one.

(c) **YES.**
$\Sigma \, pq = 1(6 + 4) + 1(4 + 6) = 20, \ \Sigma \, p\bar{q} = 1(3 + 8) + 1(5 + 3) = 19$
$\Sigma\bar{p}\bar{q} = 2(3 + 8) + 0.5(5 + 3) = 26, \ \Sigma\bar{p}q = 2(6 + 4) + 0.5(4 + 6) = 25$
$\Sigma pq > \Sigma p\bar{q}$ and $\Sigma\bar{p}\bar{q} > \Sigma\bar{p}q$.

The WARP is violated.

2

Labour Supply

References

Becker Chapter 9. Ferguson pp. 69—73 and pp. 377—381. Friedman pp. 54—56 and Chapter 11 and parts of Chapter 13. Hirshleifer Chapter 15. Laidler Chapters 7 and 19. Lancaster pp. 210—214. Layard Chapter 11. Mansfield pp. 364—370.

Questions

Q2.1 If leisure is a normal good, a rise in the wage rate must lead to an increase in the number of hours that an individual wishes to work.

Q2.2 For an individual with a fixed money wage rate an increase in the price of the goods that he consumes will increase hours of work if the supply curve of labour is backward bending.

Q2.3 If leisure is a normal good the marginal rate of substitution of income for leisure must increase as income is raised with hours of leisure held constant.

Q2.4 A man who receives half of his income from work and half from dividends will always prefer a 10% increase in dividends to a 10% increase in the wage rate.

Q2.5 If leisure is a normal good a man who receives half his income from work and half from dividends will always work longer hours if there is a 10% increase in the wage rate than if there is a 10% rise in dividends.

Q2.6 Suppose jobs A and B require equal hours, but to compensate for its less pleasant work conditions job A offers a higher wage than B. If an individual is initially indifferent between the two jobs, then he will remain so if the rate of income tax is raised.

Q2.7 An overtime premium commencing at fewer hours per week than an individual was previously working will increase the number of hours he wishes to work.

Q2.8 All the workers in an industry have identical preferences and all the firms offer the same fixed wage rate. If one of the firms were to offer a lower basic rate and a higher overtime rate such that the new wage structure is just as attractive to the workers as the old, it could reduce the average cost of its labour input.

Q2.9 A firm offers a wage rate of w and requires that its workers put in a 45-hour week. At this wage rate these are longer hours than the workers would prefer. If another firm were to enter the industry it could obtain its labour input at lower unit cost.

Q2.10 The first £800 a man earns is tax free and all income in excess of this amount is taxed at 30%. Assuming leisure is a normal good, an increase in tax free income will never increase hours of work.

Q2.11 The conventional analysis of the income—leisure choice assumes that at the margin work is unpleasant. However, some people enjoy even the last hour of the day they work. Hence the theory is invalid.

Q2.12 Pigou was right in arguing that 'for a rise in income tax, since income is taken away from taxpayers, the marginal utility of money (income) is raised but the marginal disutility of work is unchanged. Hence, unless they are somehow impeded they will increase the amount of work done.'

Q2.13 A worker 'moonlights' when he takes a second job because he is limited in the hours he can work on his primary job. If leisure is a normal good, an increase in the wage rate offered on his primary job will reduce the number of hours he 'moonlights'.

Q2.14 As the wage increases an individual supplies more labour. Eventually, income effects dominate, and further rises in the wage rate reduce his labour supply. Given uniform wage rates the maximum amount of labour he will supply is L_0, at wage W_0. Some combination of a basic rate below W_0 and a higher overtime rate would definitely increase labour supply beyond L_0.

Q2.15 Other things equal, the total benefits of a given training programme are negatively related to the age of the trainee whilst its costs will be positively related.

Q2.16 Given that entry to an occupation requires formal training, occupational mobility will be negatively related to age.

Q2.17 The wage elasticity of labour supply to an occupation tends to be lower the greater the amount of psychic relative to money income it offers.

Q2.18 The fact that the average income of doctors exceeds that of pop musicians can only be explained by the non-pecuniary advantages of the latter occupation.

Q2.19 Women are less likely to acquire skills that are specific to particular jobs than skills which are general to a number of occupations because they are more risk averse than men.

Further Questions

Q2.20 An individual is free to work as many hours as he chooses at a wage rate of £2 per hour and earns £4000 per annum. The first £800 is tax free but every pound earned in excess of this amount is taxed at 30%. The tax system is then reformed so that the threshold below which no tax is paid is lowered to £600 whilst the tax rate on income above this level is reduced just sufficiently to leave the individual as well off as before.
  (i)   Hours of work will rise.
  (ii) He will pay more tax in total.
  (iii) A marginal tax rate of 25% under the reformed scheme is inconsistent with the other information in the question.
  (iv) Since the second tax scheme yields more tax revenue than the first, increases hours of work and does not reduce utility, no government would be sensible to choose the first scheme.

Q2.21 A firm operates one work shift per day. It has to decide how many hours it should last. Production requires two activities. Job I is the more arduous. The minimum daily income that must be paid to induce a worker to accept shifts of various lengths is shown below. To produce a unit of output selling at £10 requires 4 man-hours of job I and 1 man-hour of job II.

Length of shift (hrs):		8	9	10
Minimum daily wage:	Job I	9.5	11	14
	Job II	8.8	10	12

(i)   What length of shift will the firm choose if it wishes to maximise profits?

(ii) Will workers on job I feel that they are required to put in longer hours than they would choose if freely allowed to vary their hours of work at the implicit hourly wage rate?

Answers

A2.1 **FALSE.** An increase in the wage rate has both an income effect and a substitution effect. As the relative price of leisure has risen, the substitution effect will be in favour of more work and less leisure. However, the increase in the wage rate makes the individual better off. If leisure is a normal good more of it will be consumed. The income effect therefore induces fewer hours of work and may more than offset the substitution effect. This is illustrated in figure 2.1. AB is the original budget constraint along which L_1 hours of leisure are chosen. When the wage rate increases the budget constraint becomes BC. Compensating the individual to allow him to remain on his original indifference curve whilst facing the new wage rate would require a move to budget constraint DE. The substitution effect is a fall in hours of leisure from L_1 to L_2. Moving from budget constraint DE to CB yields the income effect which results in an increase in hours of leisure from L_2 to L_3. The total effect of the wage increase is to raise hours of leisure from L_1 to L_3 and correspondingly reduce hours of work, despite leisure being a normal good.

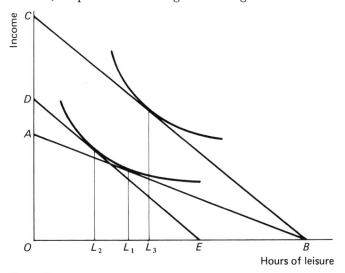

Figure 2.1

A2.2 TRUE. A backward bending labour supply curve means that a fall in the real wage increases labour supply (because the income effect dominates the substitution effect). A rise in the price of goods lowers the real wage rate. Therefore, given the backward bending supply curve hours of work increase.

A2.3 FALSE. The marginal rate of substitution of income for leisure is the change in income required to compensate for an extra hour of leisure. As can be seen from figure 2.2, if leisure is a normal good the higher the level of income the more income must be given up to compensate for a unit increase in leisure. Thus the marginal rate of substitution of income for leisure falls along a vertical (i.e. it has become more negative).

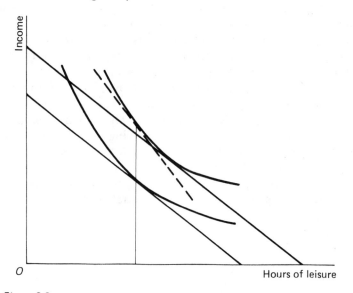

Figure 2.2

A2.4 FALSE. In figure 2.3, *ABC* is the initial budget constraint along which point *G* is chosen. If dividend income rises by 10% the budget constraint becomes *ADE*. The 10% rise in the wage rate changes the budget constraint to *ABF,* which must intersect *DE* vertically above *G*. This is because if the individual chooses to work the same number of hours as before, the 10% increase in the wage rate will increase his total income by 5%, just as will a 10% increase in dividends. Given the solid indifference map, the wage increase is preferred to the dividend increase and with the broken map the dividend rise is preferred.

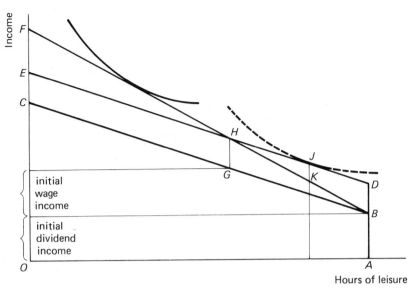

Figure 2.3

A2.5 TRUE. The diagram is as for answer 2.4. As the dividend increase represents a pure income effect, the chosen consumption point must lie along *DE* to the right of *H*. In the case of the broken preference map it lies at *J*. If preferences are such that when the wage increases consumption takes place along *FB* to the left of *H*, hours of work must be higher than at *J*. Should consumption take place between *H* and *B* it can be proved as follows that the chosen point must be to the left of *K*. Since *HB* lies below *HD* the individual must be worse off than at *J*. Thus the income effect will induce less leisure than at *J*. But along *HB* the relative price of leisure is also higher than along *HD*. The substitution effect will, therefore, also lead to less leisure being taken with the wage increase. Whatever the shape of the indifference curves it follows that hours of work will be higher with the wage increase than with the dividend rise.

A2.6 FALSE. A higher tax rate makes the individual worse off. This will normally mean that the monetary income he is prepared to forego to 'purchase' the non-pecuniary benefits of job B will fall. So he will tend to prefer job A.

A2.7 FALSE. In figure 2.4, *ABC* is the original budget constraint and *ABDE* is the budget constraint when the overtime rate is paid. It can be seen that there are the usual income and substitution effects. If leisure is a normal good it is quite possible hours of work will fall.

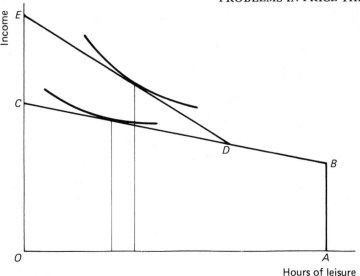

Figure 2.4

A2.8 FALSE. In figure 2.5, AB is the initial wage rate and each worker achieves utility level U_0. The firm introducing the new contract must be able to offer at least as high a level of utility if it is to get any labour at all. Budget constraint BCD does so by means of a lower basic wage than along AB but a higher overtime rate. The individual is induced to move from E to F and supply more hours. But since F lies above AB, the firm is paying on average more per

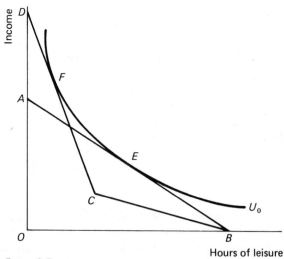

Figure 2.5

hour than it was previously. This is because the slope of a straight line through *B* and *F* measures average labour costs, which have risen since this line is steeper than *AB*. Note, however, that this answer assumes the firm faces no fixed costs of employment, such as training costs.

A2.9 **TRUE.** Point *A* in figure 2.6 shows the income—leisure package offered by the first firm. If the second firm were to offer the package shown at *B,* or one with marginally higher income than at *B,* workers would accept it since it yields the same utility as does working for the first firm. However, the hourly wage rate is lower for the second firm. This suggests that firms operating in competitive markets do offer contracts which reflect the desires of workers with respect to hours required. But note that if there is a fixed cost to employing each man (national insurance contributions, training costs, etc.) then, when these are averaged over the greater number of hours per employee at *A*, this contract may minimise average total labour cost.

A2.10 **FALSE.** In figure 2.7, the initial budget constraint is *ABC*. After the increase in tax-free income the budget constraint becomes *ADE*. If the individual was previously in equilibrium along *CB* (earning more than £800) he enjoys a pure income effect and will reduce hours of work. If he was in equilibrium between *B* and *A*

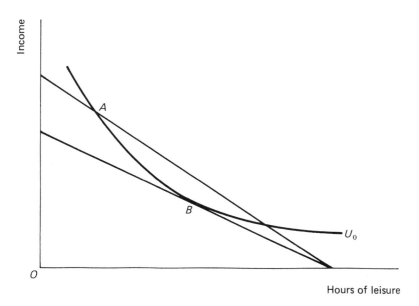

Figure 2.6

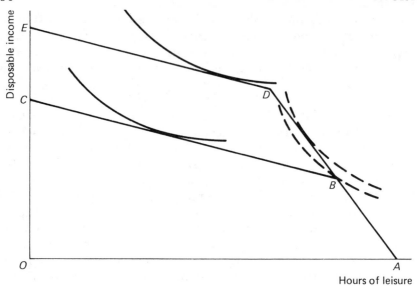

Figure 2.7

the change in his budget constraint will not affect his income–
leisure choice. But if the individual was previously at the kink
point *B* it is possible that the increase in tax free income will increase
hours of work. This case is shown by the dashed indifference map.

A2.11 FALSE. The conventional analysis assumes that the indifference curves between income and leisure are downward sloping and
convex to the origin in the region of equilibrium. This is quite consistent with the individual liking his work but enjoying leisure even
more. Thus an additional hour of leisure yields a net benefit and the
indifference curves between income and leisure are downward sloping.
Further, the less leisure the individual has, the more he values an
additional hour of leisure and the less he values another hour of
work. Thus the marginal rate of substitution between income and
leisure is diminishing.

   The argument is perhaps more clearly stated as follows. The true
utility function is $U = U(Y, H_L, H_W)$, where Y is income, H_L is hours
of leisure and H_W is hours of work. Assuming 8 hours sleep are
needed per day (but are hours of sleep really a choice variable?),
$H_L + H_W = 16$, and thus the utility function can be written
$U = U(Y, H_L, 16 - H_L)$. It is this function which is used to plot the
indifference curves between income and leisure. Leisure is a 'good'
if $(\partial U/\partial H_L) - (\partial U/\partial H_W) > 0$ but this is consistent with $\partial U/\partial H_W > 0$
and so with work being enjoyable.

A2.12 **FALSE.** Pigou argues that a rise in tax will have an income effect which will increase hours of work. He ignores the fact that the relative price of leisure has fallen. Robbins pointed out that a change in the real wage rate will have both an income and a substitution effect.

A2.13 **TRUE.** The initial rate of pay on the primary job is represented by the slope of AEP in figure 2.8. The rate of pay on the secondary job is represented by the slope of ES. Given the restrictions on hours of work, the actual budget constraint will be AES. Only AA' hours are spent at the primary job while $A'B$ are spent on the secondary job. If the individual was prevented from 'moonlighting', he would be forced to accept the lower level of welfare U_0 (he would get even less utility if he chose the secondary job).

A rise in the wage rate on the primary job to AF has only an income effect if the individual is in an initial equilibrium to the left of the vertical at A'. After the wage increase, the budget constraint is AFZ, given no change in the wage rate on the secondary job. This represents a pure income effect. As leisure is a normal good, hours of work must fall, reducing time spent on the secondary job.

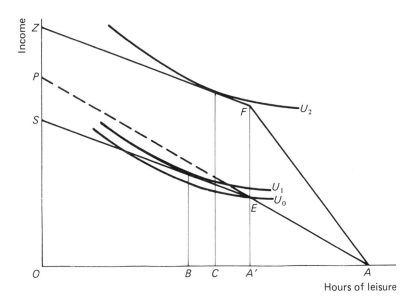

Figure 2.8

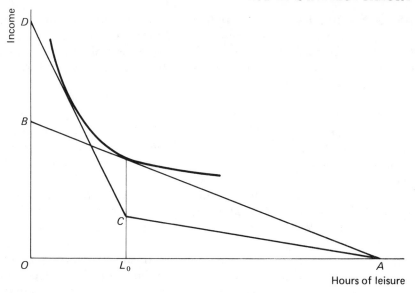

Figure 2.9

A2.14 TRUE. In figure 2.9, AB shows the uniform wage rate W_0 and the wage schedule ACD satisfies the requirement of increasing hours of work.

A2.15 TRUE. People undertake a training programme because it raises their earning capacity. The benefit from any period of training will depend upon the length of the working life over which the services of the worker can be sold. As the worker grows older so the length of his remaining working life declines and with it the benefits of training. The cost of training will be positively related to age because in general the wage rate increases with age. Thus the opportunity cost of the time input into training rises.

A2.16 TRUE. From the answer to question 2.15, it follows that the net returns to training decline with age. Thus we will observe less occupational mobility amongst older workers.

A2.17 TRUE. Suppose occupation A offers psychic benefits equal in value to the wage it pays, whilst occupation B pays a wage twice as high but has no psychic benefits. A 10% increase in the wage offered by job A will increase its attractiveness by 5%, but a 10% increase in the wage offered by job B increases its attractiveness by 10%. Assuming the supply of labour rises as the net return to an occupation increases, the wage elasticity for B will be higher than for A, other things equal.

A2.18 FALSE. The issue raised by this question was discussed by Adam Smith in 1776. Marshall, agreeing with Smith, argued 'It is true that an advantageous occupation, such as gold-mining, has special attractions for some people: the deterrent force of risks of loss in it is less than the attractive force of chances of great gain, even when the value of the latter estimated on the actuarial principle is much less than that of the former; and as Adam Smith pointed out, a risky trade, in which there is an element of romance, often becomes so overcrowded that the average earnings in it are lower than if there were no risks to be run.' (Principles, 1920, Book V, Chapter 7, para 4.) Thus, according to Smith's explanation, non-pecuniary differences do offer a possible explanation. However, we would also want to take into account the relative costs of entering the two occupations. To be a doctor one needs a long period of training which is not the case for pop musicians. It could be the case that the observed wage differential is simply a compensating differential to take account of the different training costs.

There may also be the influence of non-competing groups. In this case we would argue that the occupations open to an individual depend upon his innate abilities or his family background. The number of those with the ability to be doctors may be far less than those with the ability to be pop musicians, relative to the demand for each group.

In practice, of course, all these factors and others will influence the choice of occupation.

A2.19 UNCERTAIN. This is a possible but not very plausible explanation. If we assume that firms pay for specific training while workers pay for general training, the difference between the skills acquired by men and women may be due to the high quit rates of women. That is, women have a very high probability of leaving the labour force to get married which reduces the expected return to a firm investing in their training. On the other hand, a woman who knows she will be permanently in the labour force has her incentive to undertake general training undiminished.

A2.20 (i) and (ii) TRUE. In figure 2.10 (not drawn to scale) *AB* is the budget constraint if no tax is levied and *AEF* is the budget constraint under the initial tax scheme. Total tax paid (the difference between pre-tax and post-tax income) is *GH*. Under the revised scheme utility remains the same and the new budget constraint is *ACD*. Total tax paid is now *JK*, which exceeds *GH*. This is because the new budget constraint lies below the old one at the original hours of work (if it passed through or above *H* the individual would definitely be better off) and therefore more tax is paid even if hours of work remain unchanged. However, since hours of work actually rise, still more tax is paid on the consequent increase in income.

(iii) **TRUE.** As already noted if the new budget constraint passes above H the individual would be better off. At H, gross income is £4000. His take-home pay is $(1 - 0.3)(4000 - 800) + 800 = £3040$. If under the new scheme the tax rate were to be 25%, take-home pay at the original hours of work would be $(1 - 0.25)(4000 - 600) + 600 = £3150$. The individual would definitely be better off and so the 25% marginal tax rate is impossible if the individual is not to be made better off.

(iv) **FALSE.** The individual in question is no worse off under the second scheme and the government receives more revenue. It would therefore seem to be strictly superior to the first. And, indeed, if all workers are identical and the marginal product of labour at least equals £2, nobody (including employers) is any worse off. As the government has more to spend the scheme is almost unarguably superior to the first. However, not all individuals are the same and the low exemption level means that individuals initially earning less than £4000 will almost certainly be worse off and those earning above this amount better off. The second scheme is more inegalitarian than the first and there is no way of choosing between the two without making ethical judgements.

A2.21 (i) **9 HOURS.** If a shift length of 8 hours is chosen, the cost of another hour of job I input is £1.50 and of job II £1.20. The cost of an additional unit of output is therefore $(4 \times 1.5) + (1 \times 1.2) = £7.20$. It is therefore worth extending the shift length to 9 hours as the unit of output sells for £10. Raising the shift length a further hour to 10 hours means the cost of every additional unit thereby produced is $(4 \times 3) + (1 \times 2) = £14$. This is not worth doing.

(ii) **YES.** Job I workers earn £11 for a 9 hour shift. This averages out to $11/9 = £1.222$ per hour. However, from the information in the question, £1.50 is required to compensate for the last hour of work. Workers on job I would prefer an 8-hour shift if the average wage rate were to remain £1.22. The position is shown in figure 2.11 where U_0 is the level of utility obtained if the workers are employed in their next best job and 8 hours of work and £9.80 of income is definitely preferred to 9 hours and £11.

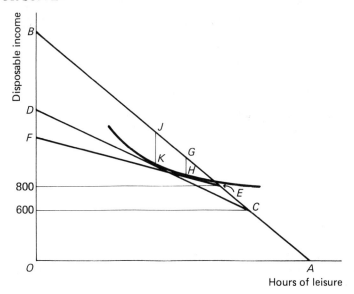

Figure 2.10

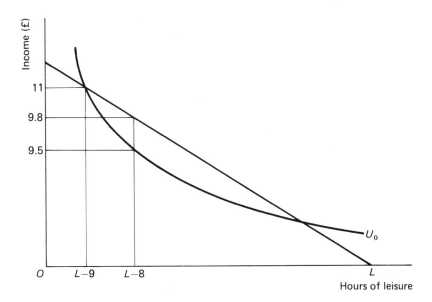

Figure 2.11

3

Intertemporal Choice

References

Becker Chapter 37. Ferguson pp. 75—78. Friedman p. 57—60 and Chapter 17. Hirshleifer Chapter 16. Laidler Chapter 8. Lancaster Chapter 11. Layard Chapter 12. Stigler Chapter 17.

Questions

Q3.1 An individual can only be in intertemporal equilibrium if the marginal utility of an additional dollar of consumption is equal in all periods.

Q3.2 A man has an income of £2000 this year and £3000 next year. To compensate for the loss of £1 this year he requires £2 extra next year. His rate of time preference proper is therefore 100%.

Q3.3 If his rate of time preference proper is equal to the rate of interest then an individual will consume the same amount in each of two periods.

Q3.4 An individual has a zero rate of time preference proper, a two-period time horizon and an income elasticity of consumption in each period of unity. He receives a $100 increase in income in the first period. The absolute change in his consumption in the first period will be greater than that in the second period if the interest rate is positive.

Q3.5 A building society offers a rate of interest of 10% on deposits. Interest payments are taxable at a rate of 30%. During the year prices rise by 7%. For a tax paying saver the real rate of return available on this investment is zero.

Q3.6 In an economy in which non-interest bearing money exists the real rate of interest can be negative in a zero inflation equilibrium as long as individuals have a negative rate of time preference proper.

Q3.7 I can buy a car for £5000 today and at the end of the year expect to be able to sell it for £4400. The car yields services which I should be prepared to forgo if offered a lump sum of £1100 today. I believe prices in general will rise by 10% during the year and am currently earning 15% after tax on my investments. I should buy the car.

Q3.8 A rise in the rate of interest increases the opportunity cost of current consumption. Both borrowers and lenders will in consequence tend to reduce their current consumption. (Assume saving and borrowing is in the form of bank deposits and loans the capital value of which do not change with the rate of interest.)

Q3.9 If a man decides to borrow from a bank he would definitely be worse off if the rate of interest was higher.

Further Questions

Q3.10 In a perfect capital market a change in an individual's intertemporal preferences will not change his decision whether or not to undertake an investment project which costs $X in the current period and pays $Z next period.

Q3.11 Suppose taking a degree at Harvard offers a rate of return of 10% and at Oxford of 20%. If an individual can borrow and lend in a perfect capital market, is only interested in pecuniary gain, and can go to either university he would be irrational to choose Harvard (note that the figures are hypothetical).

Q3.12 In a capital market in which private individuals face a higher borrowing rate than lending rate a change in an individual's preferences may change his decision as to whether to undertake an investment project which costs $X in the current period and pays $Z next period.

Q3.13 The children of rich parents on average receive more higher education than those of poor parents. As the rate of return to higher education is higher for the more intelligent, it follows that on average the children of the rich must be more intelligent than those of the poor.

Q3.14 Assume that for an individual consumption in each period is a normal good. An increase in the tax on income from all sources (including interest income) will lead to a reduction in the absolute amount he saves if the pre-tax interest rate is unchanged.

Q3.15 If instead of the income tax increase in the previous question an expenditure tax is levied which leaves the individual at the same level of welfare he will save more than with the income tax increase.

Q3.16 (i) An economy with zero storage costs of goods cannot be in equilibrium if the rate of time preference of any individual is negative.

(ii) If storage costs of goods are positive then, in an economy with no money, equilibrium is possible with a negative rate of time preference.

(iii) In an economy in which paper money exists the economy cannot be in equilibrium with a negative rate of time preference.

Q3.17 An individual has a choice between two occupations which offer a fixed wage rate in each period but do not yield any psychic income. One of the jobs requires three years of training and so offers a higher wage rate than the other. Training takes the form of a university education for which there are no tuition fees. A given percentage increase in both wage rates will have no effect on behaviour if it is thought to be permanent, but will if it is expected to be temporary. (You should assume that individuals select an occupation on the basis of maximising the present value of lifetime money income.)

Q3.18 It has been observed that individuals work longer hours in those periods of their life in which they earn the highest wage rate. This implies that the substitution effect dominates the income effect which is inconsistent with the observed fall in the hours of work per man since the beginning of the century.

Q3.19 It has been observed that at any moment of time individuals with high rates of pay tend to work longer hours than those with lower pay. But it has also been observed that as average wages have risen through time average hours of work have fallen. These two findings can only be reconciled if those people with the ability to earn high wages have a low preference for leisure.

Answers

A3.1 **FALSE.** An individual is in intertemporal equilibrium when the rate at which he is prepared to substitute present for future consumption is equal to the rate at which he can do so. The outcome specified in the question could only result if the rate of interest is zero, for then a dollar of present consumption does exchange for a dollar of future consumption and so equilibrium is achieved if the individual values an extra dollar equally in the two periods.

A3.2 **FALSE.** The rate of time preference proper is defined as the marginal rate of substitution between present and future income when income is equal in each period, all minus 1. In the question income is not equal in each period. Nothing can be deduced. If in the question income had been equal in the two years the rate of time preference proper would have been 100%.

A3.3 **TRUE.** By definition of the rate of time preference proper, p, if an individual consumes equal amounts in the two periods the slope of his indifference curve is $-(1+p)$. With a rate of interest of r, the slope of the budget constraint is $-(1+r)$ and so with equal consumption in the two periods we have the required tangency between budget constraint and indifference curve.

A3.4 **TRUE.** The income elasticity of unity means that if income in either period rises by 10%, consumption in each period also rises by 10%. Thus the income expansion path is a ray through the origin. A zero rate of time preference proper means the slope of the indifference curve is -1 when consumption is equal in both periods. If the rate of interest is zero the slope of the budget constraint is also -1. Consumption will then be equal in both periods and a rise in income will increase consumption by the same amount in the two periods. This is shown by the move from budget constraint AB to DC in figure 3.1. But if the rate of interest is positive, the increase in income will change the budget constraint from FE to HG. The individual will have a higher consumption in the second period than the first and increases in income will similarly raise consumption in absolute amount by more in the first period than the second.

A3.5 **TRUE.** Suppose £100 is invested. At the end of the year £110 is received. But on the interest income of £10, £3 of tax must be paid leaving a net receipt of £107. However, an article costing £100

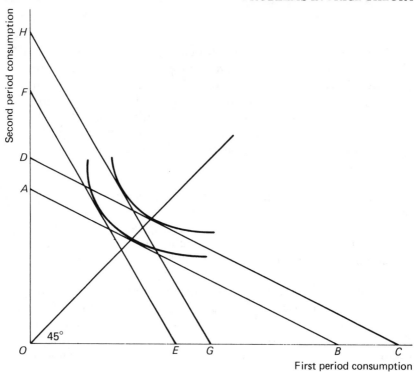

Second period consumption

First period consumption

Figure 3.1

at the start of the year now costs £107. In real terms the investor can buy at the end of the year just what he could at the start. The real return is zero.

A3.6 **FALSE.** By holding cash individuals can end the year with the same purchasing power they started with. No asset with a negative return would ever be held since there is always something better available. The fact that individuals would under some circumstances be prepared to hold an asset with a negative real return, if that were the best return available, is irrelevant.

A3.7 **FALSE.** If prices rise by 10% the real return on my financial investments is 15 − 10 = 5%. Buying the car yields services with a present value of £1100 and costs £5000 today. At the end of the year £4400 is received, but when the rise in prices is taken into account this represents only £4000 of purchasing power at current prices. Thus the present value of buying the car, in terms of current prices, is

$$\pounds 1100 - \pounds 5000 + \frac{\pounds 4000}{1 + 0.05} = -91$$

which being negative means it is not worth buying the car.

A3.8 **FALSE.** A rise in the rate of interest will generate both substitution and income effects. If the individual is a net borrower then a rise in the rate of interest will lead to a fall in real income and a rise in the cost of current consumption relative to future consumption. So both the income and substitution effect will reinforce each other and tend to reduce the level of current consumption compared to future. This is depicted in figure 3.2 for the preference map $\bar{U}_0$, $\bar{U}_1$, where the rise in the rate of interest shifts the budget constraint from AB to CD.

If an individual is a net lender then income and substitution effects work in opposite directions. (This is analytically analogous to the effect of a rise in the wage rate in the analysis of the supply of labour.) The rise in real income generated by the increase in interest payments will tend to increase consumption in all periods. The rise in the rate of interest will also reduce the cost of future consumption relative to current and so reduce current consumption. However, the net effect may go in either direction but the preferences U_0, U_1 in the diagram show a rise in current consumption.

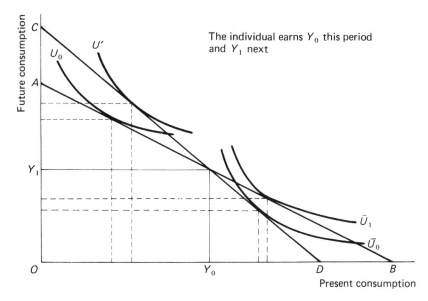

Figure 3.2

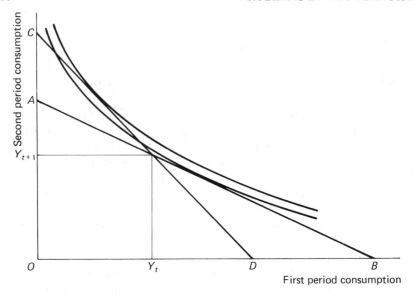

Figure 3.3

A3.9 FALSE. It is possible that at a higher rate of interest the man would become a lender and be better off. This possibility is illustrated in figure 3.3 where the man's income endowment is Y_t Y_{t+1}. AB is the budget constraint at the lower rate of interest and CD that at the higher.

A3.10 TRUE. Suppose the individual has initial income stream Y_1, Y_2. If he does not undertake the project his budget constraint is AB (figure 3.4), the slope of which, as usual, depends upon the interest rate. If the project is undertaken and he neither borrows nor lends, consumption in the first period is now $Y_1 - X$ and in the second is $Y_2 + Z$, as indicated by point C. But having reached C he can borrow or lend as much as he wishes at the same ruling interest as before. Thus his budget constraint becomes DCE. Whatever his preferences this must enable him to reach a higher indifference curve than previously. So if there is a shift in his preferences this will not alter his decision to invest. This result is known as the Fisher Separation Theorem and clearly applies however many investment projects the individual has available, but only as long as he has access to a perfect capital market. Note, if C lay below AB then whatever his preferences he will never undertake the project.

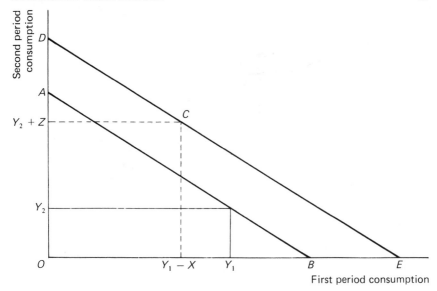

Figure 3.4

A3.11 **FALSE**. To make the general point let us choose some simple figures. Suppose going to Harvard costs £10,000 and yields £1000 per year after graduation. Again, to simplify matters, let the course last one year and the higher income enjoyed after graduation last for ever. It follows that Harvard offers a 10% rate of return. If the market interest rate is 5%, the present value of £1000 for ever is £20,000 (at 5% a bond offering £1000 per year for ever sells for £20,000). Thus the increase in the individual's present value from going to Harvard is £20,000 − £10,000 = £10,000. Now suppose the Oxford course costs £2000 and increases income in every year after graduation by £400. It therefore offers a return of 20%. However, the present value of £400 for ever at a 5% market rate of interest is £8000 and so the increase in the individual's present value from the Oxford degree is £8000 − £2000 = £6000.

If the individual has access to perfect capital markets he will choose the option which has the highest present value since his intertemporal budget constraint will then lie further from the origin and whatever his preferences he must be better off (see the answer to question 3.1). Thus the Harvard degree is preferred. The explanation as to why the project with the lower return is preferred is simply that since it is the 'larger' of two mutually exclusive projects the total gain from undertaking it is greater even though the gain per pound is less.

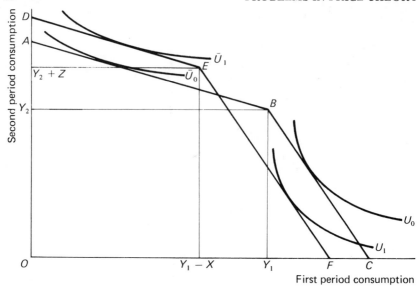

Figure 3.5

A3.12 TRUE. Once again the individual has initial income endowment $Y_1 Y_2$. But since the rate available on loans is lower than that on borrowing, the intertemporal budget constraint must be kinked at the endowment point and is drawn as ABC in figure 3.5. If the project is undertaken, the budget constraint becomes DEF. If the individual is initially a borrower with preferences U_0, U_1, the project is not worth undertaking, but if his preferences are $\bar{U}_1$, $\bar{U}_0$ so that initially he is a lender, the project raises his welfare.

A3.13 FALSE. The obvious counter to the proposition in the question is that the rich are better able to finance their children through higher education than are poor families. Our answer will indeed be broadly along these lines; however developing the reasoning is somewhat tricky. Suppose in figure 3.6 the initial income endowment of a poor family is A, and of a rich family is B. Let us make the extreme assumption that neither family can borrow and that lending rates for both are shown by the equal slopes of AD and BE. The returns from investing in education for the children are shown by AG and BF (the same for both families). We assume that family decisions can be represented by a single consistent utility function. The poor family therefore invests HJ in higher education. If the rich family were to invest the same amount it would arrive at point L at which point the slope of the investment frontier is the same as it is at K for the poor family. But if the income elasticity of

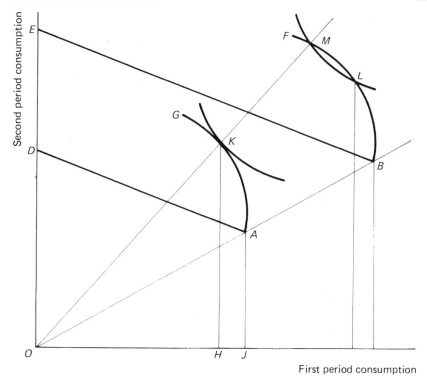

Second period consumption (vertical axis label)

First period consumption

Figure 3.6

consumption in each period is unity (preferences are homothetic) then the slope of the indifference curve at L must be steeper than at K (because the slope at M equals that at K). It can be seen that the rich family would be in equilibrium between L and M, i.e. would invest more in higher education than the poor family. This result has been derived even assuming that rich and poor have the same access to capital markets, the same return to higher education, the same intertemporal pattern of income and the same intertemporal consumption preference pattern.

A3.14 **FALSE.** In figure 3.7 Y_0, Y_1 is the initial disposable income endowment and the individual's budget constraint is ABC (remember that interest income is subject to tax so the effective rate on lending must be less than that on borrowing). Given his preferences the individual will save $Y_0 - G$. When income tax is raised the disposable income endowment point becomes E. If the rate of return to saving remained the same the new budget constraint would be FED and the individual would save $H - J$ (which is consistent with consumption

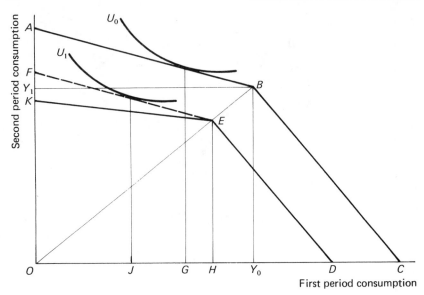

Figure 3.7

in both periods being normal goods since at the lower income less is consumed in both periods). Since $(H - J) > (Y_0 - G)$ saving has increased. However, with the increase in income tax the net return to saving falls (at least assuming that the pre-tax interest rate is unchanged). Thus the actual budget constraint will be something like *KED*. The movement from *FED* to *KED* involves an income and substitution effect which, as we know from question 3.8, may either increase or decrease saving. It is therefore quite possible that the income tax in shifting the budget constraint from *ABC* to *KED* may increase saving.

A3.15 **FALSE.** It may seem that the changeover results in a pure substitution effect and there will necessarily be more saving with the expenditure tax than the income tax. But this is not so. The reason is that it is consumption, not saving, which is the good and although second period comsumption will be higher with the expenditure tax it does not follow saving will be. To be explicit, an increase in expenditure tax reduces the endowment of real purchasing power in both periods by an equal percentage. However, it does not affect the rate at which purchasing power can be transferred through time since it does not tax interest income. Thus if the budget constraint with the income tax is *DEF* that with the expenditure tax is *ABC* (figure 3.8). Under either scheme the individual is equally well off. With the

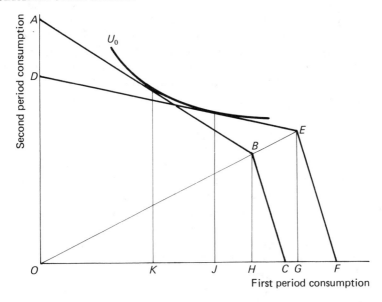

Figure 3.8

income tax saving is *JG* and with the expenditure tax it is *HK*. *HK* < *JG* so there is less saving with the expenditure tax.

A3.16 (i) **TRUE.** If the rate of time preference is negative it means that at the margin individuals prefer consumption tomorrow rather than today. For equilibrium to be achieved with a negative rate of time preference the rate of return on investment must also be negative. But if storage costs are zero, an individual in effect can obtain at least a zero rate of return on investment as he can simply store goods he buys today at a zero cost for tomorrow. It follows that equilibrium cannot be realised with a negative rate of time preference.

(ii) **TRUE.** This follows from (i).

(iii) **FALSE.** At first sight this appears true. An individual can always transfer consumption between periods by using money to store his purchasing power. The rate of return on money is zero so storage costs of money are in effect zero. However, if there is inflation then the rate of return on money is negative. As goods prices rise so purchasing power of a given cash balance falls.

A3.17 **TRUE.** Some people might wish to answer this question as follows. If the rise in the wage rate is permanent, then by choosing the job which requires training a worker will be earning a higher income in a large number of periods while paying the higher costs in terms of forgone income in only a few periods. Thus it must be the case that the present value of a university education has increased and more people will undertake training. To see why this argument is false note that the net present value of a university education is

$$\sum_{i=4}^{n} \frac{W_T}{(1+r)^i} - \sum_{i=1}^{n} \frac{W_U}{(1+r)^i}$$

where n is age of leaving the labour market, W_T is the wage rate in the job requiring training and W_U is the rate on the other job.

Given that individuals are presumed to select occupations on the basis of maximising present value, then only if the net present value is positive will university training be undertaken. If the expression is negative the no-training job is optimal. Suppose wages increase by 10% then all terms in the equation will rise by 10%. But this will have no effect on the individual's choice of occupation as it will not change the sign of the net present value, and it is the sign which is all important in deciding which occupation to enter.

If the increase in wages lasts for three years $\sum_{1}^{n} W_U/(1+r)^i$ must increase whilst $\sum_{4}^{n} W_T/(1+r)^i$ will be unchanged. This will result in a negative net present value from a university education for those who were previously at the margin of decision. Hence there will be a reduction in the number of entrants to university in the current period.

A3.18 **FALSE.** Firstly, let us consider an individual who knows that he will earn the same wage rate in all periods. The number of hours that he works in one period relative to another will not be influenced by the absolute wage rate. This is because the opportunity cost of time is the same in all periods so, *ceteris paribus*, there is no reason, on the basis of relative price, why an individual should consume more leisure in one period compared to another. Secondly, take the case of an individual who faces a higher wage rate in one period of his life than in all the rest (say middle age). In this period it follows that the cost of leisure is higher than in any other period. Thus we would expect an individual to consume less leisure in this period relative to others. At the same time the extra income earned in this period will tend to increase the consumption of all goods, including leisure, in all periods (at least assuming access to a perfect capital market). It follows that in the period in which the wage is high, hours of work will also tend to be relatively high.

It is also the case that over the century wages in general have risen. That is to say in every period of his life a worker now expects a higher wage rate than did workers at the beginning of the century. This rise will tend to have the same effect on work hours in every period of the worker's life since it does not influence relative wages across the life cycle. The evidence is that for this kind of change income effects do dominate substitution effects and so hours of work fall in every period of the life cycle. But this is consistent with the individual working longer hours in those periods when he enjoys his peak wage as compared to other periods.

A3.19 **FALSE.** A possible alternative explanation follows immediately from the previous answer. In the cross-section observation the individuals working longer hours are those enjoying their peak earnings and the substitution effect works in favour of relatively few hours of leisure in those periods. The time series observation reflects the effects of rises in income in all periods of the life cycle and the income effect of this change dominates the substitution effect so leading to a fall in hours worked by everybody in every period of the life cycle. For a different interpretation of the observation in the question see A12.13.

APPENDIX: DEPLETABLE RESOURCES

A depletable (or non-replenishable) resource is a commodity of which there is a fixed stock available and which once consumed cannot be replaced. Obvious examples are oil and other minerals which the earth has in limited total supply.[1] We shall examine how such resources would be depleted over time if privately owned and sold in competitive markets.

For simplicity take the case of an owner who has a fixed stock, Q, of a resource. This can be extracted from the ground at zero cost. Also assume the owner has only a two-period time horizon (the results do generalise in obvious fashion to a many-period model). Let the selling price of the resource be P_0 in the current period and let the owner believe that it will be P_1 next period. The problem he faces is to decide in which period to sell. If he sells a unit of the resource in the current period he receives P_0 and if instead he sells next period he receives P_1.

Suppose he chooses to extract and sell a unit of the resource this

1. Some minerals can be recycled but here we ignore this important possibility.

period. By investing the proceeds at the market interest rate, r, he would receive $P_0 (1 + r)$ next period. It follows that if the owner is to have any incentive to defer extraction until next period he must expect to receive at least this amount. In other words P_1 must be at least equal to $P_0 (1 + r)$. If he is indifferent as to the period in which he extracts then $P_1 = P_0 (1 + r)$ or $P_1 / (1 + r) = P_0$. The term $1/(1 + r)$ is the discount factor at which revenue received next period can be converted into its present value equivalent. Rearranging the equation one last time yields $(P_1 - P_0)/P_0 = r$. That is, if the owner expects prices to rise at the rate of interest he will be indifferent as to whether he extracts in period one or period two.

If price is expected to rise faster than the rate of interest all output will be sold next period and, if slower, this period. It follows that if all owners have the same expectations price must be expected to rise at the rate of interest. If it rose faster, there would be no sales in the current period and price in that period would be bid up until the initial assumption that price would be higher in the second period would obviously be false. Using a similar argument, if everyone expected the resource price to rise at a rate below the rate of interest, it can be seen that no extraction would be planned in the future. This would lead to an expectation of a very high future price, which is inconsistent with the initial assumption. To recapitulate, given the above assumptions, price will be expected to rise through time at a rate equal to the rate of interest.

The seminal reference on the economics of depletable resources is H. Hotelling's 'The economics of exhaustible resources', *Journal of Political Economy*, April 1931. A difficult recent symposium is in *The Review of Economic Studies* 1974.

Questions

Q3.20 Suppose it costs every owner C to extract each unit of a non-replenishable resource. Under competition, price will rise at a faster rate than the rate of interest.

Q3.21 Let the cost of extracting the resource differ between owners. Those with the higher cost deposits will be more likely to extract them in the second period than those with lower cost reserves.

Q3.22 Suppose price this period is known with certainty, but price next period is uncertain. This may be because there is a possibility that a man-made substitute for the resource will be discovered next period. If all resource owners have zero extraction costs and are risk averse the expected price of the resource must rise at a rate exceeding the rate of interest.

Q3.23 When the second period price is known with certainty and extraction costs differ between resource owners then no owner will extract in both periods. When the second period price is uncertain then owners with greatly differing costs will be extracting in both periods.

Q3.24 Suppose the demand curve for the resource is the same in each period and is of constant elasticity greater than unity. If there is no uncertainty and zero extraction costs, monopolisation of a competitive extraction industry will have no effect on price in any period.

Answers

A3.20. **FALSE.** The net value of extracting a unit of the resource in the current period is $P_0 - C$ and deferring extraction to the next period yields a present value of $(P_1 - C)/(1 + r)$. An owner will be indifferent as to the period of extraction if $(P_0 - C) = (P_1 - C)/(1 + r)$ which can be rewritten as

$$(P_1 - P_0)/P_0 = r(1 - C/P_0) \tag{1}$$

Now $P_0 > C$ since otherwise there would be no extraction in the first period. Hence it follows from (1) that, for indifference, and hence market equilibrium, price must rise at a slower rate than the rate of interest.

A3.21 **TRUE.** $(P_1 - P_0)/P_0$ is the same for all owners. However, the right hand side of equation (1) in the previous answer is lower for owners with a high C. When the RHS of (1) exceeds the LHS it pays to defer extraction to the second period, and hence the high cost owners are the ones who will be extracting in the second period.

A3.22 **TRUE.** If expected price rose at the rate of interest then the discounted expected return from extracting in the second period, rather than the first, would be the same. But the return in the second period is uncertain and so a risk averter would definitely prefer first period extraction. With everyone behaving in this way there will be no market sales in the second period and therefore excess demand in that period. Thus, expected period 2 price will rise and as it does this will both reduce period 2 demand and give resource owners an incentive to defer some of their extraction to the second period. It follows that the resource price must, in equilibrium, rise at a rate which exceeds the interest rate.

A3.23 **TRUE.** The first part of the proposition was demonstrated in the answer to question 3.21 where from equation (1) it follows that the owner will extract in the second or first period according to whether C exceeds some threshold. But, when price is uncertain, for at least some owners, period 2 extraction must raise their expected returns (answer 3.22). At the same time it increases the risk of their return. In fact the problem of deciding how to allocate extraction between the two periods is closely analogous to the problem of an investor deciding how to allocate a given wealth portfolio between a safe and a risky asset. Just as in that case a risk averse investor typically holds a diversified portfolio (see Chapter 12), so in this case this result is achieved by extracting some of the resource in both periods. Owners with widely differing extraction costs will be spreading their risks by operating in both periods.

A3.24 **TRUE.** We have seen that in the case of a competitive industry with zero extraction costs price rises at the rate of interest. The monopolist will choose the price path such that the present value of marginal revenue is the same in each period, for otherwise a re-allocation of extraction could increase the present value of his income. Thus the price path must satisfy

$$MR_0 = MR_1 /(1 + r)$$

or

$$P_0 \left(1 - \frac{1}{\eta}\right) = P_1 \left(1 - \frac{1}{\eta}\right)/(1 + r)$$

where η is the constant elasticity of demand. From this last equation $P_0(1 + r) = P_1$. Price therefore grows at the rate of interest. In the case of the two-period model, in which price elasticity exceeds unity and so never pays to leave any of the resource in the ground at the end of the second period, this immediately implies that price in the two periods is the same under competition and monopoly and this conclusion also follows in a many period model. For further elaboration of this point see Stiglitz, J.E., 'Monopoly and the rate of extraction of exhaustible resources', *American Economic Review*, Vol. 66, 1976, pp. 655–61 and subsequent comments in Vol. 69, 1979, pp. 227–32.

4

Choice under Uncertainty

References

Becker Chapter 4. Ferguson p. 80–89. Friedman Chapter 4. Laidler Chapter 9. Layard Chapter 13.

Questions

Q4.1 A person who is averse to risk at all levels of income would never buy a share in a company which offered an uncertain return.

Q4.2 Three individuals have initial wealth W and are offered the opportunity, at a cost of $5, to participate in a gamble with pay-offs of $10 or nothing, each with probability one half. Suppose individual A accepts the gamble, B rejects it and C is indifferent. It follows that A has diminishing marginal utility of wealth, B has increasing and C constant marginal utility of wealth (assume none of the individuals enjoys the experience of gambling as such).

Q4.3 If most people are risk averse then risky occupations will command higher wages than safe jobs.

Q4.4 A man has an income of £1000. He is offered the chance to invest in a project which has a 50% chance of making £200 and a 50% chance of losing £100. The utility he derives from various income levels is shown below.

Income	Utils
900	200
950	210
1000	214
1010	214.5
1100	218.5
1200	220

(i)   He will invest in the project.

(ii)   The cost of the risk associated with a project is defined as the difference between the expected monetary return it offers and the return which, if promised with certainty, would yield the individual the same utility. In the present case the cost of risk is £90.

(iii) Suppose the project in the question is to be equally shared between two investors both with the preferences above. They will wish to invest on this basis.

(iv) The total cost (i.e. summed over the two individuals) of risk is now zero.

Q4.5 The cost of risk for a given project will be greater for a risk averter than for a risk lover.

Q4.6 Suppose a family firm can borrow as much capital as it wants at the ruling market rate of interest. It would then have no incentive to go public and issue stock market traded equity in itself.

Q4.7 A risk averter will save more if the asset he invests in has no risk than if it offers the same expected return but is risky.

Further Questions

Q4.8 A risk-neutral consumer has the choice between:
(i)   ordering supplies of coffee for delivery next period at a price to be paid then of $1 per jar.
(ii)   buying coffee next period at the then current price which, with equal probability, may be either $0.90 or $1.10 per jar.
Bearing in mind that quantity demanded depends on price, which of the two options will he choose? (Let coffee have zero income elasticity.)

Q4.9 In 1732 Bernoulli composed the following game. A coin is tossed until it falls tails. If tails occurs on the first toss the player receives £2 and the game stops. Should the first tail appear on the second throw, £4 is paid and the game stops. If tails appears for the first time after n tosses, £2^n is paid.
(i)   What is the expected monetary value of the pay-off to such a game?
(ii)   Why are people not prepared to pay this much in order to play?
(iii) Show that if the individual has the utility function below and an initial income of £99, the most he will pay to play the game is £3.

Income	Utility
96	195
98	198
99	199.25
100	200
102	201
104	201
.	.
.	.
.	.
∞	201

Q4.10 A ship is overdue in port and a shortage of water develops. The limited supplies available are divided amongst all those on board. One of the crew receives 225 pints which is his supply of water from today, day 1, until the ship docks. His utility function is $U = 600P - 2.5P^2$, where U is utility for the day and P is daily consumption of water (in pints). For simplicity, but not very realistically, today's utility from water is therefore assumed to be independent of yesterday's consumption. Given this utility function, marginal utility is $MU = 600 - 5P$. The probability of making landfall at the end of day 1 is 0.6, at the end of day 2 is 0.3 and at the end of day 3 is 0.1. How many pints of water does he allocate to consumption on each of the three days? [Question based on problem in Jevons *The Theory of Political Economy*, first published in 1871, Penguin edition, pp 123–125.]

Q4.11 A man has the utility function $U = \log Y - C/M$ where Y is expenditure on consumption goods and M is expenditure on medical insurance. C is 1 if the man is ill and 0 if he is well. This utility function thus has the form that the more insurance that is taken out the better the medical care and the less onerous the illness. The probability he will fall ill is ½. If he has an income of $10, how much medical insurance will he take out?

Q4.12 Local government has the problem of attempting to reduce the number of people who park illegally. A perennial question is whether it should increase the probability that illegal parking will result in a conviction, or whether it should raise the fine which is imposed once convicted. If law breakers are risk averse it follows that a 10% rise in the fine will have a greater disincentive effect than a 10% increase in the probability of conviction.

Q4.13 (i) Suppose a manufacturer introduces a new good. If the product lives up to the claims made by the seller a consumer's utility is given by $U = X^{1/2} Y^{1/2}$ where X is the number of units of the new good consumed and Y the number of units of the other good he buys. There is, however, a half chance that the new good X does not live up to expectations and delivers only ¼ of the expected flow of services, in which case utility is given by $U = (¼X)^{1/2} Y^{1/2}$. Assuming both goods cost £1 per unit, that it is impossible to test X before purchase and that no comeback is possible if it performs badly, how much X will be bought if income is £16?

(ii) If the individual believes that each unit of X bought yields a unit of service with certainty how much will he buy? How much does the reduction in uncertainty raise his welfare?

(iii) Suppose the probability that a unit of X will yield only ¼ of a unit of X services remains at ½. To compensate for this, the price of X is reduced to ½ × 1 + ½ × ¼ = 5/8 so that £1 buys an expected quantity of one unit of X services. What will be the quantity of X purchased and will utility be as high as in (ii)?

Q4.14 The utility an individual derives from various income levels next period is shown below.

$$U(260) = 1000$$
$$U(285) = 1500$$
$$U(290) = 1575$$
$$U(310) = 1856$$
$$U(315) = 1926$$
$$U(320) = 1980$$
$$U(330) = 2080$$
$$U(340) = 2170$$

This period he decides to save £200 and next period will receive income from other sources of £100. The £200 of saving can be invested either in a bond which yields 10% with certainty or a company share which yields 20% capital gain with a probability of 0.8 and a 20% loss with probability 0.2. Both shares and bonds are sold in units of £100.

(i)   With no tax on investment income he puts all the £200 in bonds.

(ii) Let us introduce a tax system which does not allow losses to be offset against gains. Thus if an individual loses £20 on a share and gains £20 on a bond he is not allowed to claim that his income is zero. That is, the tax authorities do not allow pooling and therefore tax must be paid on the gain. If a 50% tax is introduced on all investment income whether in the form of capital gains or interest and no loss offset is permitted this will not change the result of (i).

(iii) Let us now consider a tax system which does allow for full loss offset. Thus if one loses £20 on a share, for tax purposes this loss may be offset against any income derived from bonds. If again we assume that all sources of income are taxed at 50%, it follows that our individual will buy both a share and a bond.

Q4.15 The effort of carrying an umbrella reduces my utility by ½ a unit. If it rains and I have no umbrella, my utility falls by 3 units, whilst it only falls by 1 unit if I do have an umbrella. I consider that the probability it will rain is ½. Therefore I carry an umbrella.

Q4.16 (i) A farmer can grow wheat or potatoes or both. If the weather is good, an acre of land yields a profit of $2000 if devoted to wheat, and a profit of $1000 if devoted to potatoes. Should the weather be bad, an acre of wheat yields $1000, and of potatoes $1750. Good and bad weather are equally likely. Assuming the farmer has utility function $U = \log Y$, where Y is income, what proportion of his land should he turn over to wheat?

(ii) Suppose the farmer can buy an insurance policy which for every $1 of premium pays $2 if the weather is bad, and nothing if the weather is good. How much insurance will he take out and what proportion of his land will he devote to wheat?

(iii) What would the answer be if the policy paid only $1.50 to compensate for bad weather?

Q4.17 Arrow defines a state of the world as 'a description of the world so complete that, if true and known, the consequences of every action would be known'. For example, in the previous two questions the two possible states of the world were either it rains or it is fine (Q4.15) or that the weather was good or bad (Q4.16), so states of the world are mutually exclusive. If we know the state of the world we know the utility associated with an income receipt in that particular state. Risk aversion implies that an individual's indifference curves between income in one state of the world and income in another will be convex to the origin.

Q4.18 If insurance is sold at a fair price (i.e. so that the cost of the policy equals its expected payout) then a risk averter will take out insurance such that his income is equal in all states. (For this question assume the utility of income function is the same in all states.)

Q4.19 Investment A offers a ½ probability of paying £10 and a ½ probability of £6. Investment B, for the same cost, has a ½ chance of returning £9 and a ½ chance of £5. An individual would definitely prefer investment A since $\frac{1}{2}U(10) + \frac{1}{2}U(6) > \frac{1}{2}U(9) + \frac{1}{2}U(5)$.

Answers

A4.1 FALSE. An individual who is risk averse would not stake $5 on a gamble which offers a 50% chance of winning $10 and a 50% chance of getting nothing. But obviously this does not mean that he would not accept a gamble with odds in favour of winning.

In figure 4.1 we can see that the expected utility from a gamble which involves giving up a certain income of C for B with probability p and A with probability $1 - p$ is less than the utility of C with certainty. But if the probability of B occurring rises to q, then the gamble is accepted in preference to the certain income C. So, if our individual is given the chance of investing in the company's share, he would accept the offer if he believes the probability of terminal wealth B was q and not if it was p.

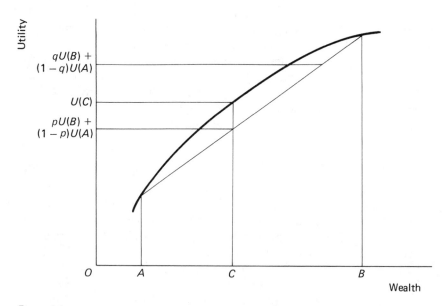

Figure 4.1

A4.2 FALSE. In the case of individual A

$$\tfrac{1}{2}U(W + 5) + \tfrac{1}{2}U(W - 5) > U(W)$$

Rearranging,

$$\tfrac{1}{2}U(W + 5) - \tfrac{1}{2}U(W) > \tfrac{1}{2}U(W) - \tfrac{1}{2}U(W - 5)$$

or

$$U(W + 5) - U(W) > U(W) - U(W - 5)$$

This last inequality shows that the addition of $5 to an initial wealth of W adds more to utility than does the addition of $5 to a wealth of $W - 5$. Hence for this individual, increments to wealth are more valuable the more wealth he has. The marginal utility of wealth is increasing, not decreasing as stated in the question. By similar reasoning, individual C must have constant marginal utility of wealth and B decreasing.

A4.3 **FALSE.** It is true that risk averters will require higher wages if they are to be induced to work in risky jobs and risk lovers will be the reverse. But although there may be fewer risk lovers than risk averters, it is possible that there are even fewer risky jobs. If so, it is the risk-free jobs that will have to command the premium in a competitive market to induce the risk lovers to work in them.

A4.4 (i) **FALSE.** If the man rejects the project, he has a certain income of £1000 and so a utility of 214. Investing yields an expected utility of $(\frac{1}{2} \times 200) + (\frac{1}{2} \times 220) = 210$. Thus he rejects the project.

(ii) **FALSE.** Undertaking the project yields a utility level of 210 which is equal to the utility of £950 with certainty. In other words, the project in question which has an expected return of £50 is equivalent in utility terms to one which is sure to lose £50. Thus the cost of risk, which is the difference between these two amounts, is £100.

(iii) **TRUE.** By undertaking the project on a shared basis each has an income of £1100 with probability $\frac{1}{2}$ and £950 with probability $\frac{1}{2}$. This yields an expected utility of $(\frac{1}{2} \times 218.5) + (\frac{1}{2} \times 210) = 214.25$ and so they would both wish to invest on a shared basis.

(iv) **FALSE.** Each investor would be indifferent between £10 with certainty and the shared project. The expected value of the shared project is $(\frac{1}{2} \times 100) - (\frac{1}{2} \times 50) = £75$ per investor. Thus the cost of risk is £15 each and so £30 in total.

A4.5 **TRUE** — as it must be if the definition of risk aversion is to make sense. The cost of risk is the amount of expected income an individual is willing to give up to exchange an uncertain for a certain prospect. To see how to measure this cost, let us assume that two individuals, A and B, face a gamble which involves a 50/50 chance of losing or gaining some given sum. A is a risk averter, while B is a risk lover. Now, as can be seen from figure 4.2, A would be willing to pay up to π_0 to remove the risk. On the other hand, B would in fact have

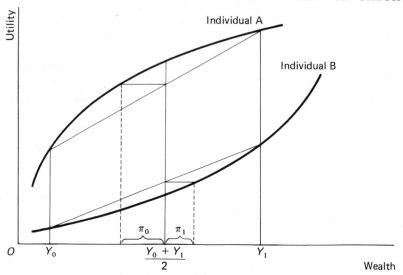

Figure 4.2

to be paid π_1 not to accept the risk. Thus, the cost of risk is positive for a risk-lover and it is negative for a risk averter.

As you can easily check, this result generalises to the proposition in the question which holds for any given prospect faced by both A and B.

A4.6 FALSE. If the company sells equity in itself it has a commitment to share profits with the equity owners in proportion to their holding. On the other hand, borrowing by means of an overdraft, the issue of debentures, or other non-equity debt issue involves undertaking to pay a certain sum at the end of the period no matter what the circumstances of the company. In this case the debt holder does not share in the risks of trade.

If expansion involves projects with uncertain returns a risk averse owner may only be prepared to expand if by means of issuing shares he can share his risks with others. The rationale is as in Q4.4(iii). Hence, even with no capital market constraints the firm's owners may wish to sell equity. Of course, expansion by selling equity does mean sharing ownership and loss of control, which may for various reasons be considered undesirable. Nevertheless, the benefits in terms of risk reduction may exceed the costs.

A4.7 FALSE. Suppose investing £100 in the safe asset yields £110 with certainty next period. However, the risky asset may return £100 or £120 with equal probability. Now if the investor would

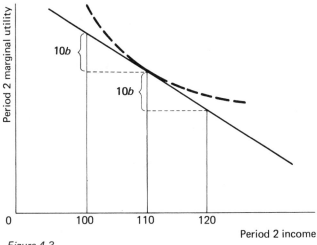

Figure 4.3

save £100 with the certain asset it follows that the last pound saved involves the loss of as much utility this period as it yields expected utility next period. If, with the uncertain asset, £100 were also to be saved then the loss of current utility from the last pound saved would be the same. But what of the expected gain next period? Suppose the marginal utility of income is declining in linear fashion, as in the solid curve in figure 4.3 (linear marginal utility implies a quadratic utility function; i.e. $U = aY - bY^2/2 + c \leftrightarrow dU/dY = a - bY$). As compared to the marginal utility when income in period 2 is £110 with certainty, under uncertainty marginal utility when the asset yields £100 is $10b$ utils higher and when the asset yields £120 marginal utility is $10b$ utils lower. Thus the expected utility yielded by the last pound saved changes by $\frac{1}{2}(10b - 1.2 \times 10b) = -0.1 \times 10b$ utils. Since expected marginal utility is lower, the increase in risk will reduce saving. However, if the marginal utility schedule were of the dashed variety which yields higher marginal utility than the linear, both when income is £100 and when it is £120, then expected marginal utility would be higher with uncertainty and hence saving would rise.

A4.8 **Option (ii) chosen.** It might seem that the two options offer the same expected return and differ only in risk. A risk-neutral consumer knowing his next period preferences with certainty would therefore be indifferent between the two alternatives. This is false. Given the demand curve of figure 4.4, the certain return from alternative (i) equals area $A + B$, which is consumer surplus when price is $1. If alternative (ii) is chosen and price turns out to be $1.10

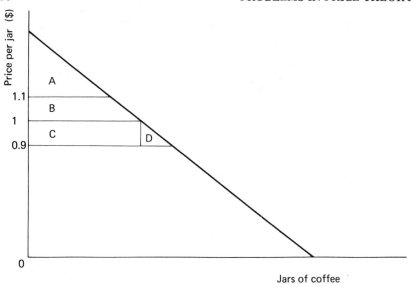

Figure 4.4

then consumer surplus is area A and if price is \$0.90 it is $A + B + C + D$. Since the two prices are equally likely, expected consumer surplus is $A + \frac{1}{2}B + \frac{1}{2}C + \frac{1}{2}D$. As $C > B$, it is clear that expected consumer surplus in this latter case is greater than with the certain price of \$1. Being risk neutral (i.e. having a constant marginal utility of income) the consumer will choose the alternative which yields the highest expected monetary value of consumer surplus, which is option (ii).

A4.9 (i) **INFINITE.** The probability that tails will occur on the first toss of the coin is $\frac{1}{2}$. The probability of obtaining tails for the first time on the nth toss is $(\frac{1}{2})^n$. Since there is no finite number of throws within which we can guarantee that a tail will occur we have for the expected payoff of the game, EP,

$$EP = \sum_{n=1}^{\infty} (\tfrac{1}{2})^n \, 2^n = 1 + 1 + 1 + \dots \, .$$

An individual whose objective is to maximise expected money income should be willing to forgo all his wordly goods in exchange for an offer to play the game.

(ii) Bernoulli suggested that the reason why people would not be prepared to pay their entire income to play such a game is that the

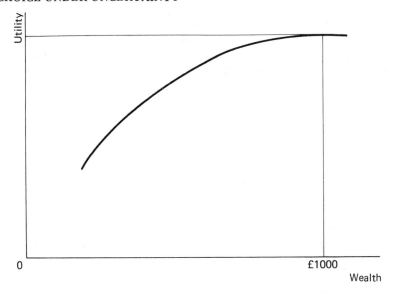

Figure 4.5

marginal utility of income is a declining function of the level of income. Suppose, for example, that marginal utility is zero when income equals £1000 (figure 4.5). It follows that no game can be more valuable to an individual than £1000 with certainty. Thus the maximum amount that our individual would possibly pay to enter the game must be less than £1000.

(iii) This numerical example is illustrative of (ii). As we can see from the table the individual's utility function is bounded at a utility level of 201. Any increase in income beyond £102 adds nothing to the individual's welfare, so beyond this point the marginal utility of income is zero. If the individual does not play the game his utility will be 199.25, given he has an income of £99. But to see whether the game is in fact worth playing we must calculate the expected utility of entering. As it costs £3 to enter, a tail on the first toss will result in an income of 98, while no head on the first toss and one on the second will result in an income of £100 and so on. As we argued in (i), the probability of a tail first occuring on the nth toss is $(\frac{1}{2})^n$, so the expected utility (EU) from playing the game will be

$$EU = \frac{1}{2}(198) + \frac{1}{4}(200) + \frac{1}{8}(201) + \frac{1}{16}(201) + \frac{1}{32}(201) + \ldots$$

$$= \frac{1}{2}(198) + \frac{1}{4}(200) + 201\left[\frac{1}{8} + \frac{1}{16} + \frac{1}{32} + \ldots\right]$$

The expression in square brackets is the probability that a head appears after the second throw. Since there is a ¾ chance that the game terminates before the third throw the square-bracketed term must be ¼, as you can easily check by summing the geometric series. Hence

$$EU = \frac{1}{2}(198) + \frac{1}{4}(200) + \frac{1}{4}(201) = 199.25$$

which equals expected utility if the opportunity to play the game is forgone. Thus at an entrance fee of £3 the individual is indifferent as to whether he plays the game or not. In other words, if the fee rose above £3 he would definitely not play and hence, £3 is the maximum he will pay.

A4.10 **Day 1 consumption 110 pints, day 2 consumption 95 pints, day 3 consumption 20 pints.** If the man maximises his expected utility it must be impossible for him to increase his expected utility by transferring a pint of water from planned consumption on one day to that on another. Thus, the marginal utility of consumption on each day, times the probability the water allocated to that day will actually be consumed, must be equal for all three days. It is certain that the man will be at sea for the first day and so consume the water allocated to day 1. But the chance he will still be at sea during day 2 (the probability of not making landfall on day 1) is only 0.4. The chance of still being at sea and so needing water on day 3 is 0.1. Writing the quantity of water allocation to each of the three days as P_1, P_2 and P_3, the man's consumption programme must satisfy

$$1(600 - 5P_1) = 0.4(600 - 5P_2) \quad [E(MU \text{ day } 1) = E(MU \text{ day } 2)]$$

$$0.4(600 - 5P_2) = 0.1(600 - 5P_3) \quad [E(MU \text{ day } 2) = E(MU \text{ day } 3)]$$

$$P_1 + P_2 + P_3 = 225 \quad [\text{total allocated water equals supply available}]$$

These three linear equations may be solved by simple substitution to give $P_1 = 100, P_2 = 95, P_3 = 20$.

A4.11 **$2 is spent on medical insurance.** Substituting the budget constraint in the expression for expected utility yields

$$E = \frac{1}{2} \log Y + \frac{1}{2} (\log Y - 1/M)$$

Maximising E with respect to Y requires

$$\frac{dE}{dY} = \frac{1}{Y} - \frac{0.5}{(10 - Y)^2} = 0$$

This is solved if $Y = 8$ and hence $M = 2$. The solution involves the expected marginal utility of expenditure on consumption goods and medical services being equal.

Incidentally, you should be able to check that a risk averter, such as the individual here, will indeed cover all medical costs by insurance so long as the policy is offered on actuarily fair terms and the policy avoids moral hazard problems (see Q14.3) perhaps by the company directly providing medical care of the contracted quality, or else paying a lump sum in the event of illness rather than paying a fixed percentage of all medical costs incurred.

A4.12 TRUE. If the individual parks illegally the expected monetary cost changes by the same amount whether the fine rises by 10% or the probability of having to pay it rises by 10%. However, with the increase in the fine, parking illegally is now more of a gamble. There is a smaller chance of a bigger loss. Naturally we should expect a risk averter to be more deterred by this prospect. This is illustrated in figure 4.6 where the individual has an income of Y_0, but if he pays the lower fine his disposable income is reduced to Y_f. When he parks illegally his expected income is $\bar{Y}$ and so his utility is U_0. With the higher fine, if the parker is caught, his disposable income is Y_f' but the lower probability of being caught leaves expected income at $\bar{Y}$. Expected utility now falls to U_0' and so the individual is discouraged more by the higher fine than encouraged by the lower probability of being caught.

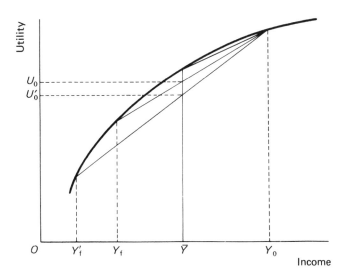

Figure 4.6

A4.13 (i) Let $\bar{X}$ and $\bar{Y}$ be the number of units of the two goods bought. For good Y units consumed, Y, equal units bought so $Y = \bar{Y}$, but for good X there is a 50% probability that $X = \frac{1}{4}\bar{X}$. Hence if $\bar{X}$, $\bar{Y}$ units are bought, expected utility is

$$EU = \frac{1}{2}\bar{X}^{1/2}\ \bar{Y}^{1/2} + \frac{1}{2}(\frac{1}{4}\bar{X})^{1/2}\ \bar{Y}^{1/2} = \frac{3}{4}\ \bar{X}^{1/2}\ \bar{Y}^{1/2}$$

The budget constraint is $\bar{X} + \bar{Y} = 16$. Maximising expected utility therefore amounts to a standard problem of maximising a Cobb—Douglas utility function subject to a conventional budget constraint. However, immediate appeal to symmetry reveals $\bar{X} = \bar{Y}$ and hence $2\bar{X} = 16$ and $\bar{X} = 8$.

(ii) Now utility is $\bar{X}^{1/2}\ \bar{Y}^{1/2}$ with certainty. The budget constraint is as before and again by symmetry $\bar{X} = \bar{Y} = 8$. Thus purchases of $\bar{X}$ remain the same. However, in the presence of uncertainty expected utility was $\frac{3}{4}\bar{X}^{1/2}\bar{Y}^{1/2}$ and is now $\bar{X}^{1/2}\bar{Y}^{1/2}$ and so has increased by a third.

(iii) Expected utility is again $\frac{3}{4}\bar{X}^{1/2}\ \bar{Y}^{1/2}$. With a Cobb—Douglas utility function it is well known and easily checked that expenditure shares equal the ratio of exponents. So in this case $P_X\bar{X} = P_Y\bar{Y} = 8$. Hence if $P_X = \frac{1}{4}$, $\bar{X} = 32$ and with $P_Y = 1$, $\bar{Y} = 8$. Expected utility $= \frac{3}{4} \times 32^{1/2} \times 8^{1/2} = 7.6$. Under certainty in (ii) $\bar{X} = \bar{Y} = 8$ and $U = \bar{X}^{1/2}\ \bar{Y}^{1/2} = 8$. Thus utility is lower in (iii) than (ii). Bearing in mind the utility function exhibits constant marginal utility of income can you work out why this result occurs?

A4.14 (i) **TRUE.** The choice open to the individual is to invest the whole sum in bonds, or in shares, or to divide it equally between the two assets. If two bonds are bought then, next period £100 of non-investment income is received plus £220 from the bonds. The utility achieved is

$U(320) = 1980$

If two shares are bought the expected utility is,

$0.2U(260) + 0.8U(340) = (0.2 \times 1000) + (0.8 \times 2170) = 1936.$

If one bond and one share, expected utility is

$0.2U(290) + 0.8U(330) = (0.2 \times 1575) + 0.8 \times 2080 = 1979$

Thus, as the objective of the individual is to maximise expected utility he will invest the entire sum in bonds.

(ii) **TRUE.** The expected utility from buying the two bonds will now be calculated as follows. The income yield will be £20 on which a tax of 50% is levied so net income is £10; thus the expected utility is

$$U(310) = 1856$$

Proceeding in the same way for two shares, expected utility is

$$0.2U(260) + 0.8U(320) = (0.2 \times 1000) + (0.8 \times 1980) = 1784.$$

For one share and one bond, expected utility is

$$0.2U(285) + 0.8U(315) = (0.2 \times 1500) + (0.8 \times 1926) = 1840.8$$

Thus with no tax loss-offset the individual will continue to invest in the two bonds.

(iii) **TRUE.** With full loss-offset utility is

$$U(310) = 1856 \text{ for the case of two bonds}$$

For the case of one bond and one share, expected utility is

$$0.2U(290) + 0.8U(315) = (0.2 \times 1575) + (0.8 \times 1926) = 1856.8$$

For the case of two shares, expected utility is

$$0.2U(260) + 0.8U(320) = (0.2 \times 1000) + (0.8 \times 1980) = 1784.$$

Thus in this case the individual will buy one share and one bond.

A4.15 **TRUE.** Suppose my utility if it does not rain and no umbrella is carried is $\bar{U}$. If I carry no umbrella my expected utility is therefore $\frac{1}{2}\bar{U} + \frac{1}{2}(\bar{U} - 3) = \bar{U} - 1\frac{1}{2}$. Carrying an umbrella yields expected utility of $\frac{1}{2}(\bar{U} - \frac{1}{2}) + \frac{1}{2}(\bar{U} - 1\frac{1}{2}) = \bar{U} - 1$. Thus, if I am an expected utility maximiser, I carry an umbrella.

A4.16 (i) $\frac{2}{3}$. Suppose the farmer owns L acres of land and devotes a fraction, α, to wheat. His expected utility will then be

$$E(U) = \frac{1}{2} \log [2000\alpha L + 1000 (1-\alpha)] +$$

$$\frac{1}{2} \log [1000\alpha L + 1750 (1-\alpha)L]$$

where the first square-bracketed term shows income if the weather is fine and the second bracketed term is income if the weather is bad. The problem is to choose α so as to maximise $E(U)$. First order conditions are

$$\frac{dE(U)}{d\alpha} = \frac{1}{2} \frac{2000L - 1000L}{2000\alpha L + 1000(1-\alpha)L} +$$

$$\frac{1}{2} \frac{1000L - 1750L}{1000\alpha L + 1750(1-\alpha)L} = 0$$

Cancelling L this equation solves to give $\alpha = \frac{2}{3}$.

(ii) **All land in wheat and $500 of insurance.** Diverting an acre of land from wheat to potatoes reduces income by $1000 if the weather is good and raises income by $750 if the weather is bad. But if instead the land were left in wheat and $1000 of insurance taken out the fall in income if the weather is good is unchanged at $1000, but now the rise is $1000 when the weather is bad. It is therefore better for the risk averse farmer to put all his land in wheat, which offers the higher expected return, and offset the risk by insuring, rather than growing both wheat and potatoes. Since the insurance policy allows the farmer to trade-off income dollar for dollar between the two equally likely states of the world he will equalise marginal utility in the two states, and hence income. To do this requires that he takes out $500 (per acre) of insurance for then each acre of land will earn him $1500 whatever the weather.

(iii) $\frac{2}{3}$ **to wheat and no insurance.** Potatoes are now clearly superior to insurance as a means of risk avoidance. Thus the farmer reverts to his original strategy.

A4.17 TRUE. Let $U_1(Y_1)$ be the utility of consuming an income of Y_1 in state of the world 1 and $U_2(Y_2)$ that of consuming Y_2 in state of the world 2. If p is the probability of state 1 occuring and $1-p$ the probability of state 2, the expected utility of the income combination Y_1, Y_2 is

$$E(U) = p\, U_1(Y_1) + (1-p)U_2(Y_2) \tag{1}$$

The indifference curves plot combinations of Y_1 and Y_2 which preserve a constant level of expected utility. Differentiation of (1) holding $E(U)$ constant yields

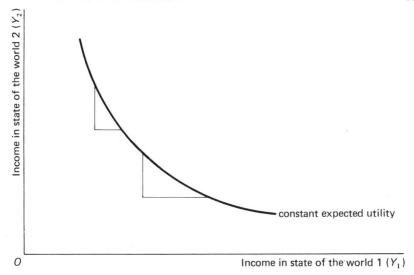

Figure 4.7

$$\frac{dY_2}{dY_1} = -\frac{p \; dU_1/dY_1}{(1-p)dU_2/dY_2} \tag{2}$$

which is the slope of the indifference curve between income in the two states. Suppose Y_1 is increased; it follows from the RHS of (2) being negative that Y_2 must be reduced. We have also assumed risk aversion which is equivalent to diminishing marginal utility. Thus with Y_1 higher, dU_1/dY_1 must be lower. Also Y_2 lower means that dU_2/dY_2 is higher. Hence with Y_1 higher (2) is less negative and the slope of the indifference curve flattens out as Y_1 increases. This is illustrated in figure 4.7.

A4.18 **TRUE.** An individual will be in equilibrium when the slope of his inter-state budget constraint is equal to that of his inter-state indifference curve. We know that the slope of the indifference curve is given by equation (2) of A4.17. (Note that since the utility function is now assumed to be the same in both states we drop the subscripts 1 and 2.)

Now let us find the slope of the budget constraint. If insurance is sold at a price such that the cost of the policy equals the expected payout, then it will be the case that the rate at which income can be transferred from state II to state I is the ratio of the probabilities of the two states occurring. To see this let us define π to be the insurance premium (cost) of a policy paying y if state I occurs and nothing otherwise. The expected net return from selling the policy is therefore

$$EP = (1-p)\pi + p(y-\pi)$$

If $EP = 0$

$$\frac{p}{1-p} = -\frac{\pi}{(y-\pi)}$$

$\pi/(y-\pi)$ is simply the rate at which we can transfer income out of state 2 into state 1. Therefore, we require for equilibrium that

$$\frac{p}{1-p} = \frac{dU/dY_1}{dU/dY_2} \frac{p}{1-p}$$

where the RHS of the equation is the slope of the indifference curve (see equation (2) of A4.17). This in turn requires

$$\frac{dU(Y_1)}{dY_1} = \frac{dU(Y_2)}{dY_2}$$

which can only hold if income is equalised in both states.

A4.19 FALSE. The answer suggested in the question implicitly assumes that the two investments yield their high and low returns in the same state of the world. But this does not follow. Investment B may yield its £9 payoff in the state of the world in which asset A yields £6. If the individual is short of income in this state of the world (say a state associated with crop failure) or if the utility of income in this state is particularly high, he may well prefer asset A. The mistake is that the inequality in the question does not specify in which states the various payoffs occur.

5

Production and Cost Theory

References

Becker Chapter 7. Ferguson Part II. Friedman Chapters 5 and 6. Hirshleifer Chapter 9. Laidler Chapters 11 and 12. Lancaster Chapters 4 and 5. Layard Chapters 9 and 10. Mansfield Chapters 5, 6 and 7. Stigler Chapters 6 to 9.

Questions

Q5.1 The production function shows how much output is obtained from given quantities of inputs.

Q5.2 To produce a given output at minimum cost the marginal rate of technical substitution should equal the wage—interest ratio.

Q5.3 If the production function exhibits increasing returns to scale everywhere, a firm's long-run average cost curve must be declining.

Q5.4 If capital and labour must be combined in fixed proportions to produce a good, marginal products are undefined.

Q5.5 A firm uses 10 units of labour and 20 units of capital to produce 10 units of output. The marginal product of labour is 0.5. If there are constant returns to scale the marginal product of capital must be 0.25.

Q5.6 Short-run average total cost is never less than long-run average total cost.

Q5.7 Short-run marginal cost is never less than long-run marginal cost.

Q5.8 If the average product of labour is at a maximum it must equal the marginal product.

Q5.9 Only if the average and marginal products of a factor are equal is the elasticity of output with respect to the particular input equal to one.

Q5.10 If over time the percentage of labour cost to capital cost in a particular industry increases, the ratio of units of labour to units of capital must be rising.

Further Questions

Q5.11 A firm has available three constant returns production techniques. Technique 1 requires the use of two men and two machines to produce one unit of output per hour; technique 2 requires one man and six machines to produce one unit of output per hour and technique 3 needs two men and four machines to yield one unit of output per hour. The wage rate is £1 per hour and the cost of a machine hour is £2.

(a) What is long run average cost?
(b) Suppose in the short run the firm has 18 machines available. Draw the marginal product schedule of labour and the short-run marginal cost of output per hour curve.
(c) If the firm sells in a competitive market and the price of output is £1.25 how much will it produce per hour? (Again assume 18 machines are available.)

Q5.12 If the wage rate falls, marginal production costs must also fall.

Q5.13 A multinational company (MNC) operates two plants both of which are subject to the same smooth constant returns to scale production function. One plant is sited in a less developed country (LDC) and the other in a developed country (DC). Machines can be transported between the two countries at zero cost as can output. In the DC labour is in perfectly elastic supply at the ruling wage rate but in the LDC the MNC enjoys a degree of monopsony power and the more labour it hires the higher the wage it must pay. The MNC seeks to produce a given output at minimum cost.

(a) It will adopt a more machine intensive production technique in the DC.
(b) It will pay a higher wage in the DC than the LDC.

Q5.14 An MNC operates two plants, one in an LDC and one in a DC. Machines can be transported at zero cost between the two countries as can output. The MNC produces two goods, both subject to fixed proportion production processes. Good A requires one machine, together with an hour of unskilled labour and an hour of skilled labour to produce one unit. Good B requires a machine of a different type, two hours of unskilled labour and one hour of skilled labour. The wage of unskilled labour converted to a common currency is $1 per hour in the LDC and $2 per hour in the DC and that of skilled labour is $2 and $4 respectively. Unskilled labour is freely available to the multinational in both countries but it can hire no more than 250 hours of skilled labour per week in the LDC. It wishes to produce 100 units of A and 100 units of B per week at minimum cost. Supposing the fixed costs of setting up facilities to produce each good in each location is $170, how should it organise its production?

Q5.15 A firm uses inputs A and B to produce output. The price of A is known with certainty but the price of B next period may with equal probability be $P + 1$ or $P - 1$. This period, B is available at price P. It can be stored at zero cost until next period but cannot easily be resold. Assuming the firm is risk neutral it will be indifferent between buying the input this period at the known price or waiting until next period (assume that there is no lag in implementing production decisions and no interest costs).

Q5.16 A machine requires one man to operate it and produces 10 units of output per hour. The marginal labour cost of additional hours of operation rises after 7 hours, and again after 10 hours, either because existing workers must be paid a high overtime rate or because a second work shift must be organised and paid for 'unsocial' hours. If the purchase price of a machine rises what will happen to daily hours of operation of the machine?

Q5.17 In the case of a production function subject to constant returns to scale diminishing marginal productivity implies that more of one input raises the marginal product of the other.

Q5.18 If the wage of labour rises relative to the cost of capital the share of labour costs in total production costs will rise if and only if the elasticity of factor substitution is less than unity.

Q5.19 Given constant returns to scale in production, isoquants can nowhere be concave to the origin.

Answers

A5.1 **FALSE.** The production function shows the *maximum flow* of output (e.g. shoes per year) that can be obtained from given flows of inputs (e.g. man years and machine years). It presupposes that a technological efficiency problem has already been solved.

A5.2 **FALSE.** The marginal rate of technical substitution should be equated to the ratio of the wage rate and the user cost of capital. The interest rate does not measure this latter amount. This is obviously so since the interest rate is a pure number and the wage rate is a money amount and hence the ratio of the two can never equal a pure number such as the MRS. The ratio of two money amounts is a pure number however, and it is the money cost of using a machine for the relevant period that represents the cost of capital. Suppose, for example, that a machine costs £100, its value at the end of the year is expected to be £80 and the interest rate is 10%. The cost of using the machine for that year (in terms of end of the year purchasing power) is therefore £30 and is composed of £10 of forgone interest income which the £100 could otherwise have earned, plus the depreciation of the machine. In deciding whether to substitute a machine for a man it is this cost which should be compared with the cost of the labour saved over the year.
   There is a further dimension to machine costs that should be mentioned. Typically a machine is bought and installed for a long period of calendar time, say a year. What is the long-run hourly cost of using the machine which is to be compared to the hourly wage rate? At first sight it seems this cost will depend on the number of hours in the year it is planned to use it. For whilst it is true that depreciation may depend in part on the rate of usage, some depreciation is a function of age alone. Hence it appears that the hourly cost of a machine varies with the number of hours in the year the machine will be operated. However, the length of the working day is often fixed and so therefore is the number of hours each machine can be operated in a year. Consequently, in order to increase the number of effective machine hours, it is not possible to run existing machines for more hours in a year. Rather, new machines must be bought. Under these circumstances a well defined hourly machine cost exists. Of course, the length of the working day may be a variable under the control of the firm. Question 5.16 explores this possibility. However, unless explicitly mentioned, we shall assume a fixed length of working day and therefore an unambiguous hourly machine cost. (On these issues see also Laidler, p. 200–201.)

A5.3 **FALSE.** Average costs depend both on technology and market opportunities. If 10% more labour and 10% more capital are employed, output may rise by more than 10%. But so may total costs. In order to obtain 10% more labour and 10% more capital a firm operating in imperfect factor markets may find it has to offer increased wage and rental rates as output expands, with the result that total production costs are more than 10% higher. Thus it is quite possible that average costs may rise even though the production function exhibits increasing returns.

A5.4 **FALSE.** Suppose each unit of output requires one machine hour and one hour of labour. Given there are 10 machines available, the first 10 workers each add one unit to total output. Hence their marginal product is 1. An 11th worker would add nothing and therefore his marginal product is zero.

A5.5 **TRUE.** From the constant returns assumption a 10% increase in capital input together with a 10% rise in labour input increases output by 10%. Thus an extra 2 units of capital and 1 unit of labour produces 1 more unit of output. However, by definition of a marginal product an extra unit of labour applied on its own raises output by 0.5. The contribution of the 2 units of capital is therefore to add another 0.5 units output. Its marginal product must therefore be 0.25. This is clearly an approximate procedure since we have averaged marginal product over 2 units of capital and evaluated it at a slightly higher output than 10. However, it so happens that in this instance the answer obtained is exactly correct. To see this, Euler's theorem may be used. This states that for a constant returns production function

$$X = MP_L L + MP_K K$$

(see Laidler p. 187). In our case $X = 10$, $K = 20$, $MP_L = 0.5$; it therefore follows that $MP_K = 0.25$.

A5.6 **TRUE.** The relationship between short and long-run average cost curves is as shown in figure 5.1. To produce any given level of output it is always possible to do in the long run what you can do in the short run. Thus production costs could not be greater in the long run. But in the long run it is possible, if desired, to vary all inputs. Hence in the long run production costs may, and in general will, be lower, since opportunities are taken which are not available in the short run.

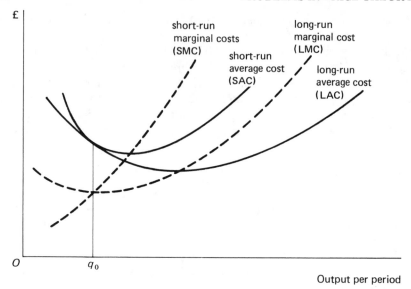

Figure 5.1

A5.7 FALSE. At points to the left of q_0 in figure 5.1 short-run marginal cost is less than long-run marginal cost. The reason is that the capital plant needed for an output of q_0 is excessive when output is below this. However, the extra plant tends to mean that less of the variable input is required, as it is a substitute for the fixed capital stock. Hence SMC (which comprises only the cost of the variable factor) is low.

That short-run marginal cost *must* cut long-run from below at q_0 may be proved as follows. At q_0 we know from answer 5.6 that $dSAC/dq_0 = dLAC/dq_0$ so $d(STC/q_0)/dq_0 = d(LTC/q_0)/dq_0$ or

$$q_0 \frac{dSTC}{dq_0} - STC = q_0 \frac{dLTC}{dq_0} - LTC.$$

Since at q_0 short-run total cost equals long-run total cost ($STC = LTC$), it follows that $SMC = dSTC/dq_0 = dLTC/dq_0 = LMC$. At q_0 we also know that since STC is tangent to LTC from above

$$\frac{d^2(STC/q_0)}{dq_0^2} = \frac{dSTC}{dq_0} + q_0 \frac{d^2 STC}{dq_0^2} > \frac{dLTC}{dq_0} + q_0 \frac{d^2 LTC}{dq_0^2}$$

$$= \frac{d^2(LTC/q_0)}{dq_0^2}$$

From this last inequality it follows that $d^2 STC/dq_0^2 > d^2 LTC/dq_0^2$, i.e. short-run marginal cost cuts long-run from below at q_0.

A5.8 **TRUE.** Let $Q = f(K,L)$. The average product of labour is Q/L. If average product is at a maximum we must have $\partial(Q/L)/\partial L = 0$. Now

$$\frac{\partial(Q/L)}{\partial L} = \frac{f_L}{L} - \frac{Q}{L^2} = \frac{1}{L}\left(f_L - \frac{Q}{L}\right) = \frac{1}{L}(MP_L - AP_L)$$

For average product to be at a maximum the expression in brackets must equal zero, i.e. marginal product must equal average product.

A5.9 **TRUE.** The elasticity of output with respect to labour input is

$$\frac{\partial Q}{\partial L}\frac{L}{Q} = \frac{f_L}{Q/L} = \frac{MP_L}{AP_L}$$

Clearly if $MP_L = AP_L$ the elasticity is equal to unity.

A5.10 **FALSE.** To measure the technological labour intensity of an industry we want to know the number of units of labour employed relative to capital. As such data are not usually available researches have tended to use the ratio of total expenditure on labour, wL to total expenditure on capital services, rK. If over time wL/rK increases, it could be because either w/r or L/K rises. To take an extreme example; if the production technology is characterised by fixed proportions, then any rise in the cost ratio can only occur as a result of a rise in w/r. Clearly, the proxy measure suggested in the question does not provide an unambiguous estimate of changes in technological labour intensity.

A5.11 (a) £6. The input combinations required to produce a unit of output by means of the three techniques are shown in figure 5.2 as points (1), (2) and (3). By combining techniques, output can be produced by means of input combinations lying on the straight lines connecting the individual techniques. For example, using one machine hour and one man hour on technique 1, and three machine hours and half a man hour (ignore any indivisibility problems) on technique 2 yields a total output of 1 unit by a total use of four machine hours and one and a half man hours (point C). This dominates the results possible from technique 3 which will therefore never be used. The unit isoquant is A(1)(2)B. Given the factor prices in the question it is

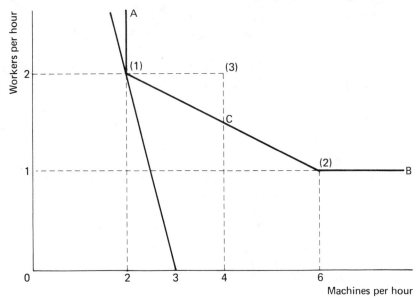

Figure 5.2

the more labour intensive technique 1 that will be chosen and average costs are $2 \times 1 + 2 \times 2 = £6$.

(b) As there are constant returns to scale all isoquants are radial magnifications or reductions of the unit isoquant. From the diagram it is easily seen that if the labour machine ratio is less than or equal to $\frac{1}{6}$ only technique 2 will be used. Since there are 18 machines, the first 3 men will be absorbed on technique 2 and each man therefore adds 1 unit per hour to total output. If the labour machine ratio is between 1 and $\frac{1}{6}$ both techniques 1 and 2 are used. Over this range each machine that is freed from technique 2 reduces labour employment there by $\frac{1}{6}$ of a man hour and lowers output by $\frac{1}{6}$ of a unit. But when the machine is then employed in technique 1, employment rises by 1 and output by 0.5. Thus the net effect of using the machine in technique 1 is that $\frac{5}{6}$ of an hour of extra labour is absorbed and output rises by $\frac{1}{3}$. Hence the marginal productivity of labour is $\frac{1}{3}/\frac{5}{6} = \frac{2}{5}$ and is constant since every machine transferred has this same effect until the overall L/M ratio is raised to 1. Since there are 18 machines, it follows that for inputs between 3 and 18 hours the marginal product of labour is $\frac{2}{5}$. As it is impossible with only 18 machines to absorb more than 18 men per hour, marginal product then becomes zero. This information is presented in figure 5.3.

Obtaining marginal cost is easy. The first 3 men each produce 1 unit of output and as the wage of £1, for the first six units of ouput marginal

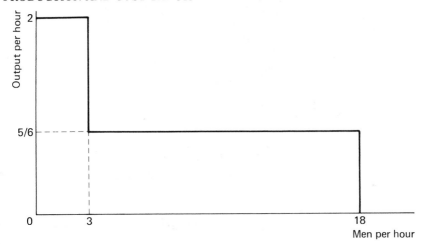

Figure 5.3

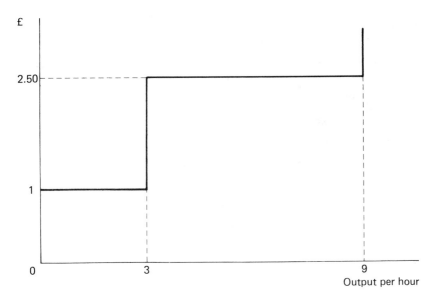

Figure 5.4

cost is £1 (remember that machine costs are now independent of out-put). The next 15 men each yield ⅖ of a unit of output and hence marginal cost is £2.50 for output within the range 3 to 9. This informa-tion is shown in figure 5.4.

(c) If output price is £1.25 it is easily seen from figure 5.4 that price equals marginal cost when 3 units per hour are produced.

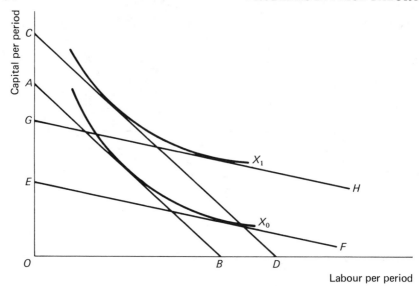

Figure 5.5

A5.12 **FALSE** — contrary to most people's intuition. In figure 5.5 AB and CD show isocost lines given the initial factor prices. The cost of expanding output from X_0 to X_1 is therefore CA in terms of capital. Now suppose the cost of labour falls, as shown by isocost lines GH and EF. Since the absolute price of capital is unchanged production costs can continue to be measured along the capital axis and compared to those at the original higher price of labour. Marginal costs of expanding output from X_0 to X_1 are now EG and higher than before. It should be noted that for this result to occur labour must somewhere be an inferior factor, i.e. given constant factor prices, as output expands less labour is used. Also, because marginal costs rise when the wage falls it is not implied that average costs rise. Quite the reverse is true as can be noted from the fact that $OA > OE$ and $OC > OG$.

A5.13 (a) **FALSE**. Machine intensity will be the same in the two countries. Since machines can be transported at zero cost it follows that to maximise output from a given total quantity of machines (a necessary condition for the minimisation of production costs since if it is not met fewer machines can be used without reducing output) the marginal product of machines must be the same in both plants (if the marginal product is higher in, say, the LDC plant than in the DC, then, by definition, transferring a machine to the LDC adds more to output there than it reduces it in the DC). But with a constant returns

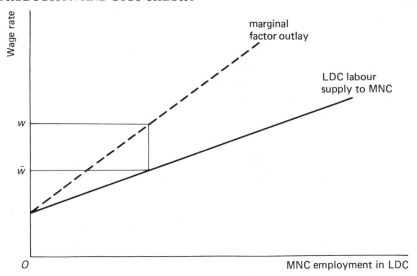

Figure 5.6

production function marginal products depend only on machine $(K)/$ labour (L) ratios.[1] Thus since marginal products of machines are equal so are machine–labour intensities.

(b) **TRUE.** It was shown above that machine intensity is the same in the LDC and the DC. From this it follows that the marginal product of labour is the same. But this in its turn means that the marginal cost of labour must be equalised in the two countries, for unless this were true it would be worthwhile expanding employment and output in the country where marginal labour cost is lower at the expense of employment in the other country. In the DC the supply of labour is perfectly elastic and so the wage equals the marginal cost of labour, but in the LDC the schedule is upward sloping and hence the marginal cost of labour exceeds the wage. If the DC wage is W it can be seen from figure 5.6 that equalisation of marginal costs requires that the LDC wage of $\bar{W}$ be less than W.

A5.14 Produce all B in the LDC and all A in the DC. It is clear that production costs of both goods are lower in the LDC, but not all output can be produced there since only 250 hours of skilled labour are available. However, suppose hypothetically that all output were

1. [If $X = f(K, L)$ is the production function, then by definition of constant returns to scale $\lambda X = f(\lambda K, \lambda L)$, where λ is any positive constant. Set $\lambda = 1/L$ then $X/L = f(K/L, 1)$ or $X = Lf(K/L, 1)$. Thus $\partial X/\partial K = \partial f/\partial(K/L)$, which is a function of K/L only].

produced in the DC. If all production of A is then transferred to the LDC the saving in cost would be $300, whilst if B production were transferred instead $400 would be saved. As both A and B absorb the same quantity of skilled labour there is no doubt that all B should be produced in the LDC. Sufficient labour is then left over to produce 50 units of A as well. This would save $150 of labour costs but involve an extra outlay of $170 on fixed costs. It is therefore not worth dividing production of A between the two countries.

A5.15 FALSE. Suppose the firm does buy B this period at price P, and that at this price the profit maximising level of B usage is $\hat{B}$. Now compare with this plan the alternative feasible strategy of purchasing $\hat{B}$ next period at the then prevailing price. Output and revenue will be the same as under the first scheme whatever happens, but if the price of input B is $P + 1$, profits will fall by $\hat{B}$, and if price is $P - 1$ profits will rise by $\hat{B}$. Thus expected profits are the same under either plan. But now consider a third strategy. Input B is purchased next period but the quantity bought is adjusted in the light of the then current price. If price is high profit maximisation will involve buying less than $\hat{B}$ and if price is low more than $\hat{B}$. Expected profits must then be higher than when the firm is committed to buy $\hat{B}$ whatever happens and so are also higher than when input B is bought this period at price P.

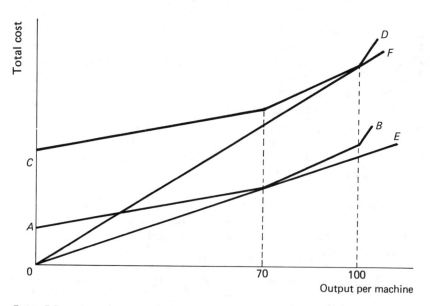

Figure 5.7

A5.16 In figure 5.7 the total cost of output per machine per day is plotted as curve AB where the distance AO is the fixed daily cost of the machine. To find average production costs, draw a ray through the origin which intersects the total cost curve. At the point of intersection the height of the ray measures total cost and the distance on the horizontal axis total output. Thus the ratio of the two distances is average production cost and also measures the slope of the ray. To minimise average production costs per machine day (and thereby total costs) the ray which touches the total cost curve and has the gentlest slope must be chosen. This is ray OE and so each machine produces 70 units per day. When the cost of a machine rises the total cost curve rises at all outputs by the same amount and becomes CD. It can be seen that minimising average production costs now involves economising on the now more expensive machines by producing 100 units from each of them daily.

A5.17 **TRUE.** Let the production function be written as

$$Q = f(K,L)$$

where Q is output, K is capital and L is labour. Assume that the production function is homogeneous of degree 1 (i.e. constant returns to scale), then by Euler's theorem,

$$Q = f_L L + f_K K \tag{1}$$

where f_L is the marginal product of labour and f_K is the marginal product of capital. Let us differentiate both sides of equation (1) with respect to L to obtain

$$f_L = f_L + f_{LL} L + f_{KL} K \tag{2}$$

where f_{LL} is the change in the marginal product of labour with respect to a unit increase in L.

Hence from (2)

$$f_{KL} K = -f_{LL} L \tag{3}$$

Complementarity may be defined as a positive f_{KL} (i.e. an increase in L with K held constant raises the marginal product of capital). If there are diminishing returns to labour input f_{LL} is negative and therefore by (3) labour and capital must be complements in this sense.

A5.18   TRUE. The ratio of capital costs to labour costs is $rK/wL = (K/L)/(w/r)$. To find what happens to this ratio if the relative cost of labour rises we must examine

$$\frac{d\left(\dfrac{K}{L}\Big/\dfrac{w}{r}\right)}{d(w/r)} = \frac{\dfrac{w}{r}\dfrac{d(K/L)}{d(w/r)} - \dfrac{K}{L}}{(w/r)^2} = \frac{K}{L}\left[\frac{w/r}{K/L}\frac{d(K/L)}{d(w/r)} - 1\right]\left(\frac{r}{w}\right)^2 \quad (1)$$

Now the first term in the square bracket shows the percentage rise in the K/L ratio generated by a one percent rise in the w/r ratio, i.e. it is the elasticity of factor substitution. Thus from (1) the share of labour as compared to capital in total cost rises when there is a rise in the relative wage if, and only if, the elasticity of substitution is less than one. (Output has been assumed to be constant, or the production function homothetic.)

A5.19   TRUE. This may be proved by contradiction. Suppose, as in figure 5.8, the reverse. Consider the two techniques at A and B. Technique A requires L_A and K_A to produce an output of X_0. With constant returns using $\tfrac{1}{2}L_A$ and $\tfrac{1}{2}K_A$ it would produce $\tfrac{1}{2}X_0$. But, similarly, using half $\tfrac{1}{2}L_B$ and $\tfrac{1}{2}K_B$ in technique B produces $\tfrac{1}{2}X_0$. Thus, using $\tfrac{1}{2}L_A + \tfrac{1}{2}L_B$ and $\tfrac{1}{2}K_A + \tfrac{1}{2}K_B$ yields output X_0. But this combination of inputs appears half way along the straight line connecting A and B, i.e. at C (this property of linear combinations is proved in the answer to Q11.10 of chapter 11). Since C lies inside

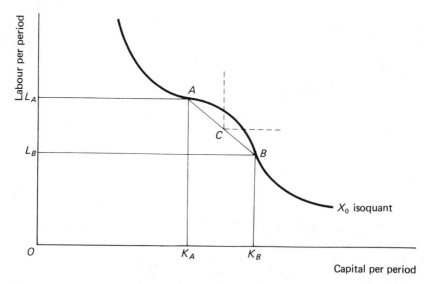

Figure 5.8

the X_0 isoquant it requires less L and less K than do the points indicated by the X_0 isoquant. Isoquants show the maximum output producible from given input quantities. According to the map drawn, using the input combination at C, output must be less than X_0, for C must lie on an isoquant closer to the origin than the X_0 isoquant. However, we have shown that X_0 can be produced using the input combination at C. Hence in reality the X_0 isoquant cannot pass above C. This argument can be used to rule out all isoquants which have any concavities in them since such isoquants cannot show the maximum output from given input combinations. However, note that this proof has been based on the assumption that the firm can run two distinct activities at the same time without them interfering with each other (this is a standard assumption of activity analysis).

6

Labour Demand

References

Becker Chapter 8. Ferguson Part IV. Friedman Chapters 7 and 9, parts of Chapter 13. Hirshleifer Chapter 14. Laidler Chapters 17 and 18. Lancaster pp. 183–184. Layard Chapter 9. Mansfield Chapters 12 and 13. Stigler Chapter 14.

Questions

Q6.1 A competitive firm can be in neither short-run nor long-run equilibrium if the marginal product of labour exceeds the average product.

Q6.2 Unskilled labour receives low wages because its productivity (i.e. average product) is below that of skilled labour.

Q6.3 Define the value added by a firm as the difference between its revenue and the cost of its non-labour and non-capital inputs (that leaves raw material and intermediate input costs to be deducted). If a competitive industry in which all firms are identical experiences a fall in the cost of capital then value added per man in the industry must be higher in the new equilibrium.

Q6.4 If the cost of raw materials rises, value added per man must be unchanged in the new equilibrium.

Q6.5 Anti-neoclassicists are quite correct in arguing that in the real world of monopoly capitalism in product markets labour will not be paid the social value of its marginal product (i.e. price times marginal product). This is also what neoclassical theory concludes.

Q6.6 If a minimum wage is applied to a monopoly it will either cut its employment or leave it unchanged.

Q6.7 If a firm is initially a price taker in a labour market a trade union cannot raise the wage without in the long run reducing employment.

Q6.8 If the elasticity of supply of capital to industry A is greater than that to industry B then, other things being equal, trade unions in A must be in a weaker bargaining position than those in B.

Q6.9 The demand for labour by an industry must fall if technological change increases the capital intensity of the production process; i.e. is labour saving.

Q6.10   If industry A is more capital intensive than industry B, the wage of labour in A will be correspondingly higher.

Q6.11 The wage differential between skilled and unskilled labour has narrowed over time. This is because the education level of workers has increased, thereby raising the relative supply of skilled workers.

Q6.12 Highly concentrated industries (i.e. those with few firms) tend to pay higher wages. Hence the labour market cannot be fully competitive.

Further Questions

Q6.13 Suppose a firm pays for the specific training of its workforce (specific skills are those which are of value to that particular firm alone). The marginal revenue product of labour will then normally exceed the wage rate.

Q6.14 The assumption that firms are profit maximisers is clearly inconsistent with a level of labour employment at which the wage rate exceeds the marginal product of labour.

Q6.15 In mild depressions it is to be expected that most of the lay-offs will be of unskilled workers.

Q6.16 Suppose a firm pays the specific training costs of its workforce. Also assume that the number of years which an average employee stays with the firm is higher the greater the wage that is paid. If training costs rise, the wage the firm offers will also tend to rise.

Q6.17 If the government increases employers' contributions to social security schemes we would expect to observe both a rise in unemployment and in overtime working (ignore any aggregate demand effects of this change).

Q6.18 Just as Giffen goods can appear in consumer theory, it follows analogously that in producer theory a factor may be sufficiently inferior for the industry demand curve for it to be upward sloping.

Q6.19 A fall in the wage rate may lead to a greater expansion in labour demand in the short run than in the long run.

Answers

A6.1 TRUE. The average product of labour, AP_L, is Q/L where Q is total output and L is total labour input. For a firm to be in profit-maximising equilibrium $P.MP_L = w$, where P is output price, MP_L is the marginal product of labour and w is the wage rate. The statement in the question implies,

$$\frac{w}{P} = MP_L > AP_L = \frac{Q}{L} \qquad \text{(i.e. } wL > PQ)$$

Thus, total labour cost exceeds total revenue and in the long run the firm cannot survive. On the conventional assumption that labour is a variable factor, the firm cannot be in short-run equilibrium either, since, if it were to close down immediately, the saving in the labour costs would exceed the loss of sales revenue. This is the familiar proposition that a firm will only stay in business if it can cover its variable costs.

A6.2 FALSE. To take a specific example, a firm may employ 10 skilled workers and 5 unskilled workers. The average product of the skilled will therefore be only half that of the unskilled. The point is that the marginal product of the unskilled labour is equated to the lower wage rate they receive. Wages equal marginal, not average, product.

A6.3 FALSE. In competitive equilibrium normal profits are made and hence $PQ - wL - rK - cM = 0$, where M is the input of raw materials and c is their unit cost. Value added is therefore $PQ - cM = wL + rK$ and value added per man is $(wL + rK)/L = w[1 + (rK/wL)]$. If the cost of capital, r, increases, value added per man will rise only if the ratio of capital costs to labour costs rises. But if the increase in

r resulted in a substantial substitution away from K in favour of L, then the ratio of capital to labour costs may fall. Value added per man would then also fall (if the production function were Cobb—Douglas, value added per man would be unchanged).

A6.4 FALSE. As the price of raw materials rises the firm will tend to substitute in favour of labour and capital. If the raw materials were replaced more by labour than capital or vice versa then rK/wL would change and so, therefore, would value added per man.

A6.5 TRUE. The money wage rate of labour will always be equated to the marginal revenue obtained from the sale of the output of the additional labour. In the case of perfect competition the price of output is fixed and the money wage rate is equated to the marginal value product. In the case of monopoly, the price at which additional output can be sold on the market is not a constant, but varies with the level of output. The value of the marginal product must therefore be adjusted for the fall in the price of output in arriving at the marginal revenue obtained from employing an additional unit of labour.

A6.6 FALSE. Suppose in order to hire more labour the firm must offer a higher wage. In other words, the supply curve of labour is upward sloping (i.e. the firm has some monopsony power). It follows

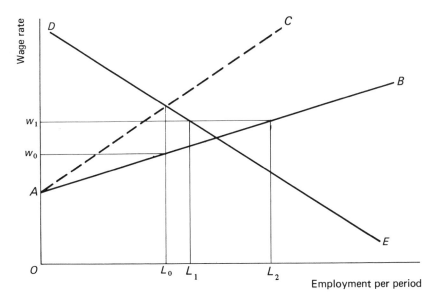

Figure 6.1

that the marginal cost of hiring labour must exceed the wage, since the cost of hiring the last worker is not merely the wage he receives but the higher wage that must in consequence of his employment be paid to everyone. This is shown in figure 6.1 where AB is the labour supply curve, AC is the marginal cost curve and DE the marginal revenue product of labour. Profit maximisation requires that the firm hires L_0 workers at a wage of W_0, for then the marginal cost of an additional worker equals the marginal revenue he generates. But suppose a minimum wage of W_1 is imposed. The marginal cost of labour now becomes horizontal at W_1 over the relevant range, since additional units of labour up to L_2 are now obtained at the unchanging minimum wage. Profit maximisation now requires that L_1 workers are hired, for at this level of employment the new marginal cost schedule intersects marginal revenue. Thus the minimum wage has expanded employment.

A6.7 **FALSE.** A rise in the wage rate will reduce labour demand if the firm is free to vary the quantity of labour it employs. This follows immediately from the downward sloping demand curve for labour (see Question 6.18). However, it is possible that a trade union is strong enough to impose an all or nothing choice on a firm or industry. That is to say the union demands that the firm employs at least a given number of men and pays them a wage of at least a certain level.

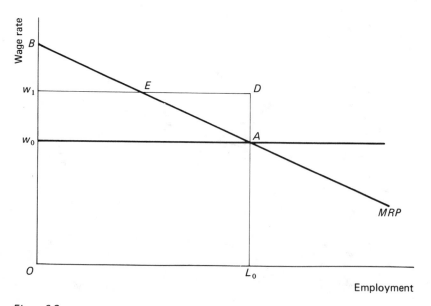

Figure 6.2

Let us illustrate this with the case of a firm which has a monopoly in the product market and which for simplicity uses only labour as an input. Figure 6.2 shows the marginal revenue product of labour schedule and the initial wage rate is W_0. Employment is therefore L_0 and monopoly profits are BAW_0 (total revenue is the area underneath the marginal revenue schedule $OBAL_0$, and wage costs are $OW_0 AL_0$). Now suppose the union demands both a wage of W_1 and that no redundancies be made. If the firm meets this demand its wage bill will rise by $W_0 W_1 DA$ and as long as this is less than its original profit of BAW_0 (i.e. if $W_1 BE \geqslant EDA$) then the firm would meet the union's demands if it believed it would get no labour otherwise (or perhaps face a very prolonged strike). Hence it is possible that a union could raise both employment and wages.

A6.8 **TRUE.** When the price of labour rises all the firms in the industry will tend to substitute capital for labour. But if the cost of capital rises as more of it is used (i.e. capital is in rather inelastic supply) then the degree of substitution away from labour will be limited, and so demand for labour will also be rather inelastic. If demand for labour is inelastic this tends to favour unions since raising the wage rate will not thereby cause much unemployment.

Note, however, that the elasticity of supply of capital to the industry is only one determinant of the elasticity of demand for labour. The elasticity of demand for labour tends to be lower the lower is the elasticity of demand for the final product, the lower the elasticity of substitution between inputs and the lower the percentage of total costs accounted for by labour (though there is an exception to this rule; on all these relationships, known as Marshal's Rules, see Laidler p.180—185). From all this it follows that just because the elasticity of supply of capital to A exceeds that to B, it does not follow that unions in A are in a weaker bargaining position than those in B.

A6.9 **FALSE.** If the capital intensity of the production process has risen then by definition at any given factor price ratio a higher capital—labour ratio will be adopted as compared with the situation before the technological change. (The advance in technology has led to a rise in the marginal product of capital relative to the marginal product of labour.) But this is only a substitution effect. The improvement in technology has permitted any given output to be produced with a smaller total factor input. So production costs and hence output price will fall, given the existing factor prices. This will permit an output effect which could quite possibly swamp any substitution effect tending to reduce the employment of labour.

A6.10 **FALSE.** One can certainly argue that with a given production function, if labour is combined with a greater quantity of capital the marginal product of labour will generally (but not always) rise. But if two industries have different production functions, then to yield the same marginal product of labour different capital intensities will be called for. Furthermore, if labour sells its services in a single market, then the wage rate will be equalised across all employments in that market. Each firm will pay labour the value of its marginal product which will be equated to this wage rate. Thus it is quite possible, and indeed to be expected, that firms in different industries will choose different capital intensities while having the same marginal product of labour.

A 6.11 **UNCERTAIN.** This is a fascinating question over which much debate exists. The question implies that only supply side factors influence relative wage rates. It could equally well be the case that the demand for unskilled workers has increased at a faster rate than supply. One only has to look at the massive growth in industrial processes which require elementary repetition to see why this may be so.

A6.12 **UNCERTAIN.** It may be the case that highly concentrated industries use skilled or other labour in short supply relatively intensively. Thus higher wages paid reflect the usual workings of demand and supply. Alternatively, concentrated industries may offer less attractive working conditions which require monetary compensation for the loss of psychic income. Again this is consistent with competitive labour markets. However, if labour of exactly the same type receives a higher wage in the more concentrated industries this does suggest elements of imperfect competition. For example, trade unions may be better able to organise in concentrated industries and be able to extract a share of monopoly profits there. This situation could only be sustained if the union prevents the entry of workers from other industries bidding down the wage.

A6.13 **TRUE.** For the marginal worker the firm must expect the benefits from employment to equal the costs. Suppose the worker is expected to stay with the firm for n years. It follows that $n (MRP - w)$ = training costs (this equation ignores discounting). Each period the firm gains the difference between the marginal revenue product and the wage which, over the n years, is just sufficient to pay off the training costs. As to why in the question $MRP > w$ was stated to be normal circumstance and hence, by implication, not the only possibility, see the next question and answer.

A6.14 **FALSE**. Suppose a firm invests in workers by providing specific training. It is then subject to a fall in demand which it expects to be of only temporary duration. The result is that the marginal revenue product of labour exceeds the wage rate. It could lay off (discharge) some of its workers. But if it did, when the upswing comes and more workers are required the cost of training the new workers would have to be borne since they would not necessarily be those previously hired. Keeping the same workers over the cycle obviously saves this cost which may well exceed the loss involved when, for a transitory period, the wage exceeds the marginal product. Furthermore, it will prove a more attractive policy for risk averse employees. It is therefore quite consistent that a firm incurs short-run losses if its overall objective is to maximise long-run profits. Hence conventional economic theory permits wage rates to be greater than marginal products in certain periods and for wage rates to remain relatively stable over the cycle as compared with marginal and average products.

Note that if the skills of the workers are specific to the firm this greatly increases the firm's chances of being able to rehire. Consequently, the firm's incentive not to lay off workers is reduced, and this weakens the above argument. Feldstein ('Temporary layoffs in the theory of unemployment' *Journal of Political Economy*, Oct. 1976 and also paper in *A.E.R.*, Dec. 1978) reports that for the US most lay-offs are rehired by the same firm though in the UK such temporary lay-offs are rare, perhaps because of different laws on redundancy payments. However, note that if there is a search cost involved in finding suitable workers this will play exactly the same role as training costs in the above analysis.

It is perhaps also relevant to discuss here why wage rates tend to be sticky over the cycle. One reason has been alluded to. It is costly for workers to change jobs, and so once having accepted a job they have an implicit contract with the firm concerning future pay and conditions. If workers are risk averse they will prefer a steady income and firms will not find it in their interest to compromise their reputation for providing this by cutting wages in slumps. However, if the slump is severe it may prove beneficial (to both parties) to lay off workers who have little current value to the firm but who can claim unemployment benefits.

A perhaps more convincing explanation of wage rigidity combined with lay-offs in slumps is that if the firm cuts wages this may be interpreted as (and may genuinely be) an attempt by the firm to renege on its implicit contract and exploit workers who face heavy fixed costs of moving. However, lay-offs can in general only be motivated by demand deficiencies, for otherwise the firm has nothing to gain from them. It follows that the rigid wage—layoff system may be a more effective method by which workers can monitor whether the terms of the implicit contract are being observed. For discussion of issues in this area see C. Azariadis, 'Implicit contracts and un-employment equilibria', *Journal of Political Economy*, vol. 83, p. 1183 (1975) and B. Klein, R. Crawford and A. Alchian, 'Vertical integration, appropriable rents and the competitive contracting process', *Journal of Law and Economics*, Nov. 1978. p. 297–326, particularly pages 313–319 and footnote 39.

A6.15 TRUE. According to the reasoning of the previous answer firms will be less inclined to lay off those workers for whom the fixed costs of rehiring are the highest. Both because of training and search costs these are most likely to be high for skilled workers, although note the qualification in the previous answer. Furthermore, skilled workers and managers may have the greatest search costs in finding new permanent jobs if dismissed, or in finding short-term alternative employment. Efficient implicit contracts will therefore tend to have less lay-off provision for skilled than unskilled workers.

A6.16 TRUE. Basically, the higher are training costs the greater the incentive the firm has to hold on to its labour force and so avoid the cost of training new workers. More specifically, the expected annual cost of obtaining a skilled worker may be determined from figure 6.3.

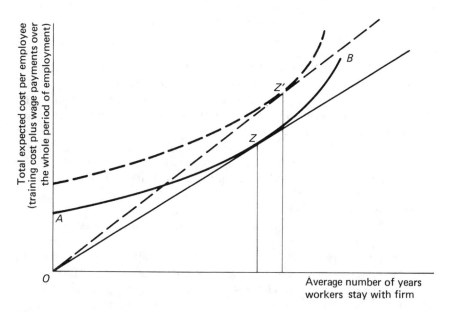

Figure 6.3

OA is the fixed training cost and the curve AB shows the expected total cost of keeping an employee for a given number of years. Its slope becomes steeper as the number of years of employment increase. This reflects the fact that workers are more inclined to stay with the firm the higher the wage rate paid. The average annual cost of trained workers is minimised at Z (this is analogous to the analysis of Chapter 5, question 5.16). When training costs rise the new curves are the dotted ones. Now it is optimal for the firm to induce workers on average to stay with the firm more years which implies that the wage they are offered is higher.

A6.17 **TRUE.** Fixed costs of employment have risen. These costs are independent of the number of hours each man works but not of the number of men employed. Any rise in fixed costs will lead to a reduction in employment because the relative price of men has increased encouraging substitution in favour of hours per man. The extent to which this will take place will depend upon the overtime rate needed to obtain an increase in the supply of hours. This is illustrated in figure 6.4 in which the situation is analogous to that in the previous answer. AB is the initial total cost per man function and hourly labour costs are minimised if each man works H_0 hours. National insurance contributions then rise by CA and each man employed will now work H_1 hours. However, since the minimised

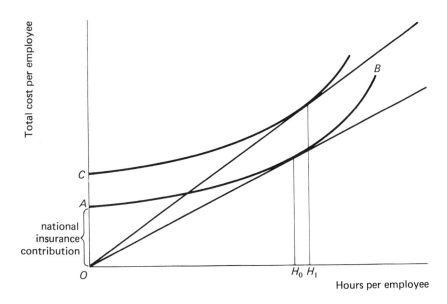

Figure 6.4

hourly cost of labour has risen, fewer hours will be demanded and so the number of men employed must fall.

A6.18 **FALSE** — surprisingly perhaps. First note that the analogy between consumer and producer is not exact. In consumer theory, if the price of good X falls, the consumer in figure 6.5 moves from budget constraint AB to AC and buys less X. But if the price of factor X falls, it is wrong to treat the firm's relevant isocost line as shifting from AB to AC. To do so would imply that the firm spends as much on inputs before and after the wage change. However, there

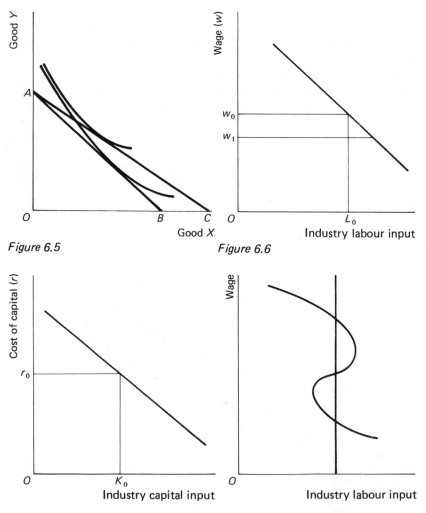

Figure 6.5

Figure 6.6

Figure 6.7

Figure 6.8

is no reason why it should. Factor expenditure will be whatever level maximises profits and is not limited in the same way as is the consumer's.

Now to the proof proper: we shall show that if the wage falls, more labour will always be demanded by a competitive industry. This should be obvious in the short run when capital stock is held fixed, so we shall examine only the long-run case where the analytical problems are much greater. In the first part of the proof it will be demonstrated by contradiction that if the wage rate falls, employment cannot remain the same. Figure 6.6 shows the initial marginal revenue product schedule for labour and figure 6.7 that for capital. If the wage fell from w_0 to w_1 employment could only remain at L_0 if the marginal revenue product of labour schedule shifted to the left. This in turn can only happen if K changes.

Suppose K falls. Since by assumption (ultimately to be shown inconsistent) L is unchanged, output must fall and thus the selling price of output rise. But this means that the marginal revenue product of K would rise (remember that since L is fixed so is the marginal physical product schedule of K) and *more* K would be employed. Hence a new equilibrium with w lower, the same L and K higher is impossible. Now suppose K rises when w falls. If L input is constant, output must rise and so its price falls. But at a lower price of output the marginal revenue product schedule of capital would shift to the left. Since, however, the cost of capital remains at r_0 a new equilibrium with the same L, a lower w and a higher K is impossible. Whether K rises, falls or stays the same, we therefore know that a new equilibrium with w lower and L the same is ruled out. It follows that at a lower wage L demand cannot be unchanged.

To complete the argument, note that the demand curve for labour cannot be upward sloping at all wage rates. This is because it would imply that as the wage rises labour costs tend towards infinity. Hence consumers would be spending an infinite amount on the output of the industry, which is clearly impossible. Incorporating this condition in the labour demand curve of figure 6.8 it can be seen that, assuming continuity, if the curve has any upward sloping portions there must be at least two wage rates at which demand is the same. We have shown this is impossible. Hence the labour demand curve must be downward sloping throughout.

As an alternative demonstration, first note that it is easily shown that the factor demand curve of an individual firm, whether a price taker or price setter, is downward sloping. Suppose that when the wage is w_0 the profit maximising levels of inputs and outputs are L_0, K_0, q_0 and the output price is $P(q_0)$. When the wage is w_1, the optimal production plan is L_1, K_1, q_1 and price is then $P(q_1)$. By

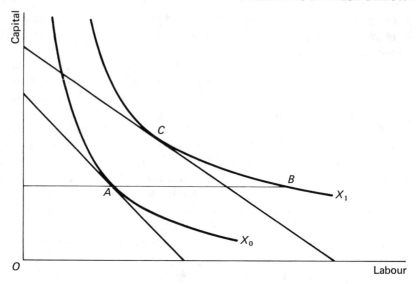

Figure 6.9

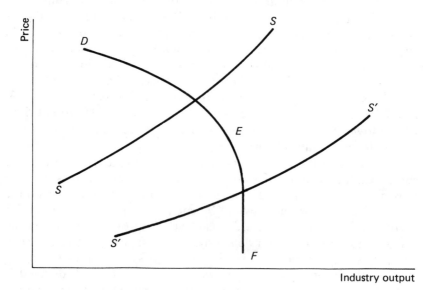

Figure 6.10

definition, at the original wage, profits are no less with the first production plan than the second, i.e.

$$P(q_0)q_0 - w_0L_0 - rK_0 \geqslant P(q_1)q_1 - w_0L_1 - rK_1 \tag{1}$$

Similarly, at the new wage rate,

$$P(q_1)q_1 - w_1 L_1 - rK_1 \geqslant P(q_0)q_0 - w_1 L_0 - rK_0 \qquad (2)$$

From inequalities (1) and (2)

$$w_0 L_1 + rK_1 - w_0 L_0 - rK_0 \geqslant P(q_1)q_1 - P(q_0)q_0 \geqslant$$

$$w_1 L_1 + rK_1 - w_1 L_0 - rK_0 \qquad (3)$$

and hence

$$(w_0 - w_1)(L_1 - L_0) \geqslant 0 \qquad (4)$$

According to (4), if the wage rises, labour demand cannot increase.

Now, the behaviour of a competitive industry parallels that of a multi-plant monopolist in that both achieve productive efficiency. However, for a competitive industry, output is determined by the demand curve rather than the marginal revenue curve. But as these two schedules have the same general properties (at least if the good is non Giffen) and since a monopoly has a downward sloping factor demand curve, so must a competitive industry.

A6.19 **TRUE.** Once again, analogy from consumer theory is misleading. Suppose the wage falls. In the short run more labour is employed with the existing capital stock, output expands from x_0 to x_1 and the firms in the industry move from A in figure 6.9, the original long-run equilibrium, to B. Having had sufficient time to adjust to the new relative factor prices, the higher level of output, x_1, would be produced by the factor combination at C which involves use of less labour and more capital than at B. Even if in the long run output expands beyond x_1, labour demand may be lower than in the short run. To show this unambiguously, suppose in figure 6.10 that the industry demand curve is DEF and its short-run supply curve is SS. After the fall in the wage rate, the short-run supply curve becomes $S'S'$ and output expands. In the long run capital as well as labour can be varied and so the supply curve will fall even more. But since the demand curve has become vertical this will not occasion a further rise in output. Thus, in terms of figure 6.6 the movement is from A to B in the short run and to C in the long run. Elasticity of labour demand is lower in the long run than the short. The intuition behind this result is that in the short run output can only be expanded by using more labour, but in the long run it may become possible and efficient to replace some of the extra labour by capital. It is curious to note that 'perversities' can appear only for finite wage changes and not as the wage change becomes infinitesimally small.

7

Competitive Markets

References

Becker Chapter 6 (lecture 19). Ferguson Chapters 8 and 10. Friedman Chapter 5. Hirshleifer Chapter 10. Laidler Chapters 13 and 14. Lancaster Chapters 2, 3 and 6. Layard Chapter 7. Mansfield Chapter 8. Stigler Chapter 10.

Questions

Q7.1 In a perfectly competitive market firms always operate at the minimum point of their average total cost curve.

Q7.2 In long-run industry equilibrium the marginal firm will produce an output greater than that which minimises its average variable costs.

Q7.3 If a lump sum subsidy (i.e. one independent of output) is granted to every firm in a competitive industry the output of each of the original firms will fall.

Q7.4 If a per unit production tax is levied on a competitive industry in which all firms are identical, some firms will leave the industry but the output of those remaining will be unchanged.

Q7.5 A competitive industry supplies its domestic market and also exports part of its output which is sold at a fixed world price. An export subsidy equal to 10% of selling price will increase output by less than a production subsidy of 10% of selling price.

Q7.6 Suppose a tax is placed on T-bone steak. This will cause its price to rise and so lead to an increase in demand for substitute meat cuts such as sirloin, the output of which will in consequence expand.

Q7.7 If the price of mutton rises so must the cost of woollen suits.

Q7.8 Factor A is competitively supplied and is the only input into good B. If an effective maximum price is imposed on A the price of B will fall.

Q7.9 Industry equilibrium is impossible in the presence of economies of scale.

Q7.10 As the number of trawlers operating in a particular fishery increases so the catch per trawler falls. This is an example of an external pecuniary diseconomy.

Q7.11 Given the circumstances of the previous question a consumption tax on fish could lead to a rise in the total catch.

Q7.12 External pecuniary diseconomies caused by rising factor supply curves may result in a backward bending supply curve of output.

Q7.13 A new invention is discovered which for a particular industry reduces the quantity of all factors required to produce any given output by X per cent (this is known as Hicks neutral technical progress). It is made available free of charge by the government to all firms who wish to use it. If the industry is competititve and all firms are identical, labour demand will rise if and only if the price elasticity of output demand is greater than unity.

Q7.14 Suppose technological progress reduces the production costs of a competitive industry. If on each unit produced each firm must pay a tax equal to 10% of selling price, total tax revenue must rise as a result of the technical progress.

Further Questions

Q7.15 The government wishes to raise the income of dairy farmers. Two schemes are considered. The first is to guarantee them a return above the free market level by paying, for every pound of butter produced, the difference between the market price and the higher level P^* (a deficiency payment system). An alternative is that the government itself can buy butter, in the process building up a butter mountain, and force the market price up until it reaches P^*. Whether the second scheme will cost the government less than the first depends on whether the elasticity of demand exceeds unity.

Q7.16 A firm selling in competitive markets can produce two goods,

X and Y. Good X requires 2.5 man hours and one machine costing £10 per hour of use and occupying 5 sq. ft of floor space. To produce a unit of good Y requires 5 man hours, 2.5 sq. ft of floor space and a machine costing £17.50 per hour of use. The factory owns 1000 sq. ft of floor space which if not used in production cannot in the short run be rented out. The maximum number of man hours it can use is 1000 but as many machines as it wants are available. The wage rate is £1 per hour and the selling price of X is £20 and of Y is £30.

(a) How much X and Y should the firm produce and what will be its level of profits?

(b) Suppose the firm has the opportunity of buying a further 600 sq. ft of floor space at a cost of £700. Should it do so?

(c) Suppose that each unit of X produced also generates 10 units of pollution. The government limits the amount of pollution the firm can cause to 1000 units. By how much do the firm's profits fall?

Q7.17 In the home economy demand for X is given by

$$q_d^h = 100 - P_h \qquad (0 < P_h < 100)$$

and demand in the rest of the world by

$$q_d^f = 200 - 2P_f \qquad (0 < P_f < 100)$$

P_h and P_f are the home and the foreign price of X respectively and both are measured in terms of a common numeraire. The industry is everywhere competitively organised with the home supply function given by

$$q_s^h = 2P_h - 50 \qquad (P_h > 25)$$

and that of the rest of the world by

$$q_s^f = 10P_f - 40 \qquad (P_f > 4)$$

Shipping a unit of the good from one country to the other costs 5.

(a) Find the domestic and foreign price of the good under free trade.

(b) Derive the transport demand equation. Hence find the level of transport cost which will eliminate international trade. Evaluate the elasticity of transport demand with respect to its price when transport costs are 10.

Answers

A7.1 FALSE. In a competitive market all firms are price takers. However, it does not therefore follow that they must operate at minimum average costs. For example, in the short run market price may be as shown below, in which case profit maximising output exceeds that which minimises average costs. Furthermore not all firms need be equally efficient and hence even in the long run non-marginal firms will earn supra-normal profits and be in the situation shown in figure 7.1.

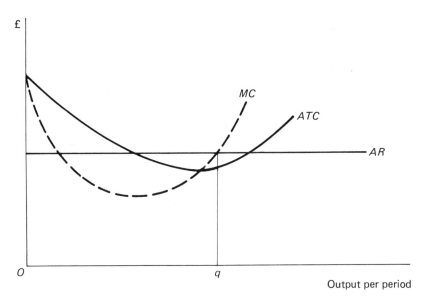

Figure 7.1

A7.2 TRUE. The marginal firm will earn normal profits and so be in the position shown in figure 7.2. Average variable cost, since it excludes fixed costs, must lie below average total cost. Marginal cost cuts both these schedules at their minimum point.[1] Since marginal cost must be rising in the region of equilibrium it follows that as output is determined where ATC is minimised it must exceed that at which AVC is minimised.

1. $dAC/dq = d(TC/q)/dq = [q(dTC/dq) - TC]/q^2 = 0$ at minimum average cost. Thus $dTC/dq = MC = TC/q = AC$ which holds true whichever kind of AC is considered.

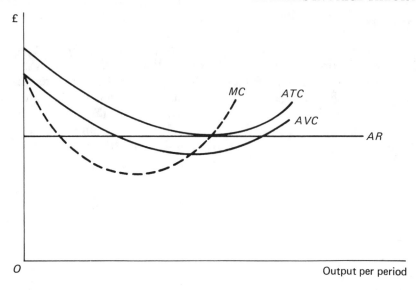

Figure 7.2

A7.3 TRUE – in the long run. A lump sum subsidy lowers average total cost at every output, but by definition leaves marginal cost unchanged. At the original price all firms will therefore continue to produce the same output although their profits will rise by the amount of the subsidy. But this will attract new firms into the industry. The additional output will cause industry price to fall and as it does the original firms will contract output along their marginal cost curve.

A7.4 TRUE. Both average and marginal costs will shift vertically upwards by the amount of the tax. At the original output price firms will therefore make losses and will start to leave the industry. As they do, the fall in industry output will cause output price to rise. This process will continue until each firm is once again just covering its costs. Since all cost curves have shifted vertically upwards the minimum average cost occurs at the same level of output as before and so in the new long-run equilibrium each firm's output will be unchanged.

A7.5 FALSE. The output effect will be the same under either scheme. In figure 7.3 the initial equilibrium with world price W is shown with OB as industry output and AB as exports. The export subsidy raises the effective world price to $1.1W$ and so production expands to OC. But a 10% production subsidy reduces marginal production costs so that

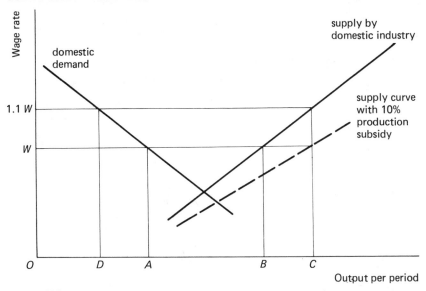

Figure 7.3

when output is *OC* they equal *W*. Thus the two policies will have the same effect on output. However, it is to be noted that the export subsidy raises domestic price to 1.1*W* whilst the production subsidy leaves it at *W*.

A7.6 **FALSE.** Both T-bone steak and sirloin are yielded in fixed proportion by cows (they are in joint supply). The output of each cut must therefore change in the same direction. If a tax is placed on T-bone steak, the net revenue yielded by given quantities of the two cuts must fall (since outputs are the same so must be market clearing prices, but producers will receive less by the amount of the tax on steak). Thus the return from raising cows will fall and less sirloin will be produced and marketed.

A7.7 **FALSE.** If the cost of raising sheep increases then a new equilibrium will be established with fewer sheep being reared. This is shown by the usual demand and supply analysis. Since mutton and wool are joint products of sheep a lower output of each means that with a given demand schedule for these two products both their market clearing prices will rise. However, should the initial change not be a rise in costs but an increase in the demand for mutton, once again more sheep will be raised. If mutton and wool are produced in absolutely fixed proportions it follows that the output of wool will

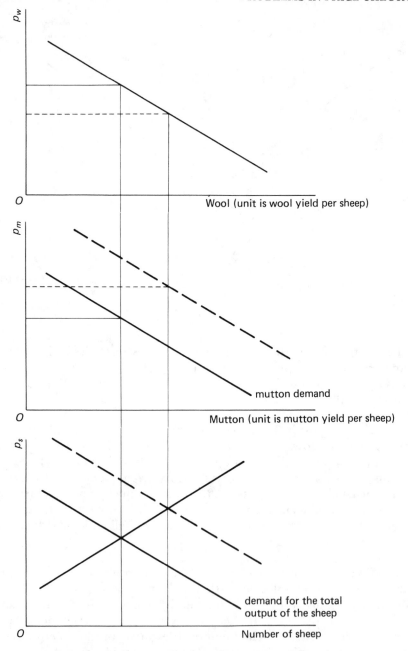

p_w

O Wool (unit is wool yield per sheep)

p_m

mutton demand

O Mutton (unit is mutton yield per sheep)

p_s

demand for the total
output of the sheep

O Number of sheep

The demand price for sheep is found by vertically
adding the demand price of the two products to give $p_s = p_m + p_w$

Figure 7.4

rise and, since the demand curve for this good has not changed, its price must fall. This is shown in figure 7.4 where the dotted curves show the situation after the increase in demand for mutton.

Even if in practice it is possible to vary the proportion in which wool and mutton are produced (perhaps adopting different breeds and different farming procedures) the same result will emerge.

A7.8 FALSE. An effective maximum price will reduce supply of A. With less A available output of B must fall. Consequently its price will rise.

A7.9 FALSE. If an individual firm can reap economies of scale it cannot be in equilibrium since additional output will reduce average cost leaving average revenue unchanged and so necessarily raising profits [profit $= (AR - AC)q$]. But it is possible that as the industry as a whole expands economies of scale are reaped although they are not available when an individual firm grows. That is to say there are economies of scale internal to the industry but external to the firm. This is quite consistent with equilibrium (see Laidler p. 147; Friedman pp. 91–94). Given the level of industry output the marginal cost curve of each firm is determined and is upward sloping. Each firm's output at the ruling market price then follows. As long as the total output of the individual firms is that which when put on the market sustains the ruling market price, an equilibrium exists.

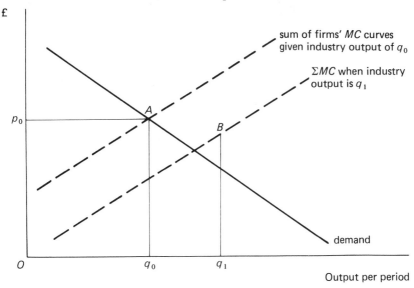

Figure 7.5

In figure 7.5 p_0, q_0 is an equilibrium since the industry, once established at this output and price, has no tendency to move from it. Note that B is also a point on the industry supply curve which is therefore downward sloping. You may care to consider whether A is a stable equilibrium.

A7.10 **FALSE.** An external pecuniary diseconomy is present when an expansion of industry output raises the market input prices each firm must pay. This has not occurred here. Rather, the output each firm obtains from given quantities of inputs (trawlers and crew) falls as industry output rises. This is the definition of an external technological diseconomy. Another example is where pollution by one firm reduces the efficiency of other firms.

A7.11 **TRUE.** Total catch may rise but this is not certain. In figure 7.6 the long-run supply curve (average cost curve) of fish landings is drawn backward bending, illustrating that for each rate of fish landings there are two possible levels of average cost. This reflects the fact that the biological growth rate of a fish population at first increases as the population size rises and then falls, eventually to zero, which defines the equilibrium population size in a state of nature. It follows that there are two population sizes which yield each possible per period change in fish population and therefore sustainable catch. With a larger fish population fish are easier to find and so fewer trawlers are required to maintain the total catch and average cost is lower.

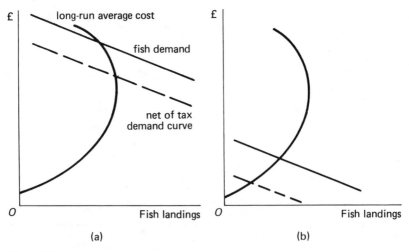

Figure 7.6

A competitive equilibrium occurs where the demand curve intersects long-run average costs (why not marginal costs?). A consumption tax on fish shifts the net-of-tax demand curve downwards and it is this schedule to which producers react. In figure (a) this causes landings to rise and the tax inclusive price to fall, but in figure (b) landings fall and the tax inclusive price rises.

A.7.12 FALSE. This may be proved by contradiction. Suppose the supply curve were backward bending. A rise in output price would then cause industry output to fall. Consequently input prices would fall and the cost curves of the individual firms shift down. Combined with the rise in output prices this means all the individual firms would expand production which is in contradiction to the initial assumption that industry output falls. (Note why this argument fails in the case of technological diseconomies. In that case when large numbers of firms are present they may cause each other to become so inefficient that a high price is required to bring forth the same total output that would be offered if there were fewer firms and a lower price.)

A7.13 TRUE. Since X per cent fewer factors are required per unit of output the minimum average costs of each firm will fall by X per cent, but this minimum occurs at the same level of output as before. In long-run equilibrium, output of each of these firms will therefore be unchanged and so their labour demand fall by X per cent. However, industry price must also fall by X per cent. If demand elasticity exceeds one, then to supply the increased demand the number of firms must rise by more than X per cent. So total labour demand will rise. It would not if market demand were less elastic than unity.

A7.14 FALSE. The supply curve shifts to the left and price falls. However, a fall in price increases total revenue only if demand elasticity is greater than unity. For a competitive industry there is no reason why elasticity should not be less than this and if it is, tax revenue, which is a constant percentage of total revenue, will fall.

A7.15 TRUE. In figure 7.7, if farmers receive P^* per pound of butter the supply is q^*. If this is all put on the market, price will be P. The cost of the deficiency payment scheme is therefore P^*ABP. On the other hand, direct intervention to force market price up to P^* involves the government buying $q^* - q$ pounds of butter (since at this price private demand is only q). The cost of this scheme is therefore $qCAq^*$. To demonstrate the proposition in the question note that if the second scheme is more expensive than the first then

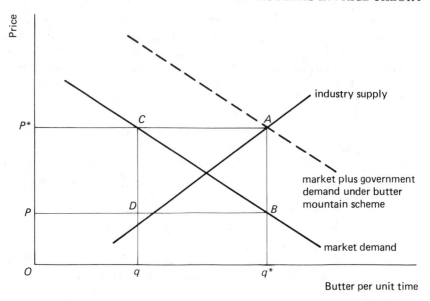

Figure 7.7

$$qCAq* > P*ABP$$

but this can be written

$$CABD + DBq*q > CABD + P*CDP$$

or

$$DBq*q > P*CDP$$

Adding $OPDq$ to both sides this last inequality becomes

$$OPBq* > OP*Cq$$

The left hand side of this inequality is total revenue from market sales when price is P and the right hand side is total revenue when price is the higher $P*$. By definition, the condition holds if and only if demand elasticity exceeds unity over this interval.

A7.16 (a) $X = Y = 400/3$. The firm faces two input constraints. Take the space limitations first. Each unit of X uses 5 sq. ft of floor space and each unit of Y 2.5 sq.ft. As there are only 1000 sq. ft available any production plan must satisfy

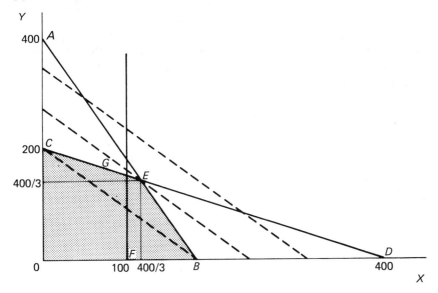

Figure 7.8

$$5X + 2.5Y \leqslant 1000 \tag{1}$$

where X and Y are output levels of the two goods. In figure 7.8 any point inside or on the frontier of the triangle OAB satisfies weak inequality (1). Similarly, the labour constraint is

$$2.5X + 5Y \leqslant 1000 \tag{2}$$

and is plotted as triangle OCD. Only points lying inside or on the frontier of $OCEB$ satisfy both input constraints and so this represents the firm's production possibility frontier. Where on this frontier should the firm operate? Consider its short-run profit function

$$\pi = [20 - 10 - 2.5]\ X + [30 - 17.5 - 5]\ Y$$
$$= 7.5X + 7.5Y \tag{3}$$

The square-bracketed terms show the net revenue yielded by each unit of the good produced (selling price less machine cost, less labour cost). Combinations of X and Y production which earn a given level of total profits may be computed from (3) and are shown in the diagram as straight lines with a 45° slope. An example is the line CB. To maximise profits the enterprise will seek the production program which lies on the iso-profit contour furthest from the origin and which also satisfies the labour and capital constraints. From the diagram it is clear that this requires production at E. Both the labour and the capital constraints hold with equality and hence the firm uses its full allocation of factors. Thus

$$0.5X + 0.25Y = 100$$

$$0.25X + 0.5Y = 100$$

Solving these two linear equations in the two unknowns X and Y yields the optimal production program

$$X = \frac{400}{3} = Y$$

Profits are

$$7.5 \frac{400}{3} + 7.5 \frac{400}{3} = £2000$$

(b) **Do not buy.** If the extra floor area is bought the space constraint now becomes

$$5X + 2.5Y \leqslant 1600 \tag{4}$$

and OAB moves out from the origin. But redrawing the diagram confirms that maximum profits are still earned by producing both goods and leaving no input unused. Thus

$$5X + 2.5Y = 1600 \tag{5}$$

$$2.5X + 5Y = 1000 \tag{6}$$

which solve to give $X = 1760/6$, $Y = 320/6$ (output of the space intensive good rises and that of the labour intensive falls). Before deducting the cost of space, profits rise by £600 to $(1760 \times 7.5/6 + (320 \times 7.5/6) = £2600$. Since the cost of the space is £700 it is not worth buying.

(c) **Profits fall by £125.** An additional constraint has been imposed which requires that

$$10X \leqslant 1000 \tag{6}$$

and therefore X cannot exceed 100. The new feasible output set is shown in the diagram as $OFGC$. Maximum profits are earned at G and $X = 100$. All the labour is still used but not all the floor area. Labour usage in producing X is $2.5 \times 100 = 250$ hours and hence the remaining 750 hours must be used in Y. Since each unit of Y output requires 5 units of labour it follows that $Y = 750/5 = 150$. Profits are $(100 \times 7.5) + (150 \times 7.5) = £1875$ and so fall by £125.

A7.17 (a) **Home price is 30 and foreign price 25.** It must first be determined whether the good is imported into the country, exported, or neither. Excess supply in the rest of the world is

$$q_s^f - q_d^f = 10P_b - 40 - 200 + 2P_f = 12P_f - 240 \qquad (1)$$

Excess demand in the home country is

$$q_d^h - q_s^h = 100 - P_h + 50 - 2P_h = 150 - 3P_h \qquad (2)$$

Suppose the good is imported into the home country. As competition prevails it must follow that the foreign price plus transport costs equal the home price

$$P_h = P_f + 5 \qquad (3)$$

and that excess supply in the rest of the world equals home excess demand. Thus

$$12P_f - 240 = 150 - 3P_f - 15$$

and so $P_f = 25, P_h = 30$. However, before this can be accepted as the answer it must be checked that at these prices the good really is imported. Substituting $P_h = 30$ in equation (2) excess demand is 60. Thus the good is indeed imported.

(b) **Transport costs of 30 eliminate trade, elasticity is 0.5 when transport costs are 10.** Since each unit of the good imported requires a unit of transport the problem is to find import demand as a function of transport cost (t). As a first step $P_f = P_h - t$ can be substituted in (1) and then (1) set equal to (2). Thus

$$12P_h - 12t - 240 = 150 - 3P_h$$

or

$$P_h = 26 + 0 \cdot 8t.$$

Substituting this expression for P_h in (2), the level of imports and hence transport demand, T, is given by

$$T = 72 - 2.4t \qquad\qquad (3)$$

If $T = 0$, and hence imports are zero, it follows that $t = 30$. (Of course, if T is negative this does not mean that the good will be exported from the home country. When $t = 35$ and $T = 0$ the rest of the world is self sufficient and the price in the home economy is 35 higher than abroad. Exports are quite out of the question, as they are if transport costs become even higher still.) Elasticity of transport demand is, from (3)

$$-\frac{dT}{dt}\frac{t}{T} = -\frac{2.4t}{72 - 2.4t} = 0.5 \text{ when } t = 10.$$

8

Monopoly

References

Becker Chapter 6 (lectures 20 and 22). Ferguson Chapters 9 and 10. Friedman
Chapter 5. Hirshleifer Chapter 11. Laidler Chapter 15. Lancaster Chapter 6.
Layard Chapter 8-1. Mansfield Chapter 9. Stigler Chapter 11.

Questions

Q8.1 A profit maximising monopoly will always produce an output
lower than that which would maximise its sales revenue.

Q8.2 A profit maximising monopoly will never operate along the
portion of its demand curve for which price elasticity is greater than
unity.

Q8.3 If there is a fall in the marginal cost of producing a monopolised
good on which is levied a tax at the rate of 10% of total sales revenue,
then total tax revenue will rise.

Q8.4 If a firm faces a declining average revenue schedule its marginal
revenue curve must also be falling.

Q8.5 A monopoly enjoys an increase in demand such that at each
price it can sell 10% more than previously. If it is subject to constant
marginal costs the price it charges will rise.

Q8.6 Imposition of an effective maximum price will cause a monopoly either to raise its output or else to go out of business.

Q8.7 If the supplier stays in business when a maximum price is
introduced there will be unfulfilled demand as a result of the price
control.

Q8.8 A monopolist considers introducing a product improvement which increases the price each consumer is prepared to pay for the good by 10%. Constant marginal costs also rise by 10%, but fixed costs are unaffected. If the improvement is made profits will rise by less than 10%.

Q8.9 If advertising is banned then unless a monopoly reaps economies of scale the price it charges will fall.

Q8.10 If a monopoly is able to practise perfect price discrimination its output will be higher than if it must adopt a conventional uniform pricing policy.

Q8.11 Suppose a monopoly sells in its home market and also exports part of its output. The foreign elasticity of demand for its product is below that in the domestic market. If customer arbitrage between the two markets is impossible it will charge more in the foreign market than in the home market.

Q8.12 If a tax is levied on every unit of the good sold in the home market of the monopolist in the previous question, the volume and value of its exports will rise if its marginal costs are rising.

Q8.13 The volume and value of the monopolists' exports fall if marginal costs are falling.

Q8.14 If a maximum price is imposed on home market sales the volume and value of the monopolists' exports must rise if marginal costs are rising.

Q8.15 Suppose initially the monopolist is not allowed to charge a different price abroad than at home. Price discrimination is then permitted. If marginal costs are constant the volume and total value of exports will rise.

Q8.16 An author receives 10% of the total sales revenue of a book. If he wishes to set a price below that which his publisher favours, it follows that his motive is vanity rather than maximising his income. (Assume both publisher and author share the same beliefs about demand conditions.)

Further Questions

Q8.17 A monopoly operates subject to a constant elasticity demand curve (with elasticity greater than unity) and constant average costs. If a per unit production tax is levied on the monopoly the price it charges will rise by more than the per unit tax revenue.

Q8.18 A monopolist produces subject to constant average production costs. Initially a fixed rate profit tax is imposed. This is then changed to a system under which the rate of profit tax is lower the lower is the mark-up (the difference between price and average cost). What will be the effect on his output?

Q8.19 A firm can price discriminate between two markets. In each market the demand curve is linear, the demand functions being

$$q_1 = a_1 + b_1 P_1 \text{ and } q_2 = a_2 + b_2 P_2$$

Assuming the firm has constant marginal and average costs of c its output will be the same as when discrimination is impossible.

Q8.20 The opportunity to sell in two markets at different prices may reduce output as compared to no discrimination.

Q8.21 If a firm practises price discrimination between two groups of customers, ruling this practice illegal must result in a potential Pareto loss.

Q8.22 Suppose in market A a firm faces demand curve $q_A = P_A^{-2}$ (constant price elasticity of 2) and in market B demand curve $q_B = P_B^{-3}$ (constant price elasticity of 3). The firm has constant marginal costs of 1 and also fixed costs of $43/108$.

(a) If the firm is able to price discriminate between the two markets what prices will it set?
(b) Suppose price discrimination is ruled illegal. What will happen?

Q8.23 There are two types of customer in a market. Type A, of which there are 100, are prepared to pay $10 for a good and the 50 customers of type B will pay $8. No customer wants to buy more than a single unit of good. Marginal and average production costs are constant at $6.

   (i)   A magazine is launched in which the good can be advertised at a cost of $80. The effect of an advertisement is to attract another 100 type B customers. Will the advertisement be placed and what will happen to the selling price of the good?

  (ii)   Suppose the advertising attracts no new customers but raises the price all existing customers will pay by $1. What effect will it have on selling price?

Q8.24 Other things equal, the less elastic a firm's demand curve the more advertising it will undertake.

Q8.25 A multinational monopoly supplies a good to a host country. It can either manufacture the good in the host country or import it from a plant located in its own home market. In the latter case, to the constant marginal production cost in the home market must be added a constant per unit transport cost in order to obtain the marginal cost of supplying the good to the country. If, instead, a new plant is built in the host country marginal production costs will be lower but a fixed cost of setting up the plant must be met. Is it more or less likely that a host country plant will be built:

  (a)   if the government of the host country imposes a tax on the final selling price of the good?

  (b)   if it imposes an effective maximum price (but one which still allows positive profits)?

Q8.26 If a competitive industry facing a linear demand curve and subject to constant returns to scale in production is monopolised the elasticity of its demand for inputs is unchanged.

Answers

A8.1 **TRUE.** Maximum profits occur when marginal revenue equals marginal cost. As marginal costs are positive so must be marginal revenue. Hence by definition additional output adds to total sales revenue. Therefore profit maximisation does imply that output is below that which would maximise sales revenue.

A8.2 **FALSE.** As noted above, if marginal costs are positive so is marginal revenue. But positive marginal revenue implies that demand elasticity exceeds unity. This is because if demand elasticity is unity, then when price falls by x per cent quantity demanded rises by x per cent and so total revenue stays the same. Thus marginal revenue is zero. So if marginal revenue (MR) is to be positive, quantity must rise by more than x per cent and so demand elasticity be greater than unity. To show this formally,

$$MR = \frac{d(PQ)}{dQ} = P + \frac{QdP}{dQ} = P\left(1 + \frac{Q}{P}\frac{dP}{dQ}\right) = P\left(1 - \frac{1}{\eta}\right)$$

where $\eta = -\frac{dQ}{dP}\frac{P}{Q}$. Thus $MR > 0$ only if $\eta > 1$ and the monopolist necessarily operates where the elasticity of demand exceeds unity.

A8.3 TRUE. In figure 8.1, AB is the demand curve and AC the marginal revenue curve. But with the 10% tax the net revenue obtained from selling any given quantity of the good falls by 10% and so therefore does the net-of-tax marginal revenue schedule which is drawn as DC.[1] The monopolist will initially set price P at which marginal revenue both gross and net of tax is positive (i.e. elasticity is greater than unity). If marginal costs fall then output rises. So does total revenue (we have already noted that marginal revenue must be positive). Tax revenue therefore necessarily increases since it now equals 10% of a larger base.

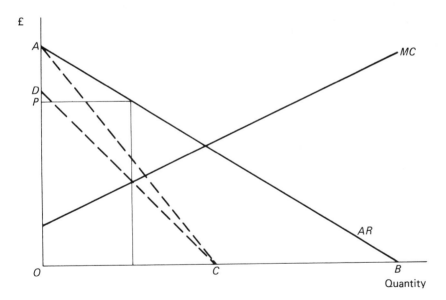

Figure 8.1

1. Without the tax, revenue is PQ and so marginal revenue is $d(PQ)/dQ$. With the tax, net-of-tax total revenue is $(1-t)PQ$ and so marginal revenue is $(1-t)dPQ/dQ$.

A8.4 FALSE. We know from the standard U-shaped cost curve that marginal costs may be rising whilst average costs are falling (this occurs to the left of the point of minimum average costs). The same relationship is possible between average and marginal revenue. To be explicit, since marginal revenue is less than average revenue even if the nth unit sold adds more to total revenue than does the $(n-1)$th, average revenue may still be falling. This can be confirmed by the following numerical example:

Price (average revenue)	Quantity	Total revenue	Marginal revenue
10	10	100	
9	12	108	4
8	16	128	5

A8.5 FALSE – **price remains the same.** The profit maximising price of the monopolist is determined by $P(1 - \frac{1}{\eta}) = C$. If it can be shown that the change specified in the question leaves price elasticity (η) unchanged at any given price then it will not cause any alteration in price. To see that elasticity is unaffected, write the demand function as $q = Af(P)$. Shifts in A change demand by the same percentage at all prices. Elasticity is given by

$$\eta = \frac{dq}{dp}\frac{P}{q} = \frac{Af'(P)P}{Af(P)} = \frac{f'(P)P}{f(P)}$$

which is independent of the value of A, as required.

A8.6 FALSE. The analysis behind this question is the product market analogue of the monopsony case considered in Q6.6 of Chapter 6. Initially the monopolist sets price p_0 and quantity q_0 (figure 8.2). A maximum price of $\bar{p}$ is then imposed. At this price the monopolist can sell as much as q_1 with the result that marginal revenue becomes horizontal at $\bar{p}$ and equals average revenue. Profit maximisation ($MR = MC$) now occurs at output $\bar{q}$ which is less than q_0. However, profits equal the shaded area and so the firm stays in business.

Note that if $\bar{p}$ was set at a point above the intersection of MR and MC, but below p_0, output of the monopolist would expand.

A8.7 FALSE. In the previous diagram if the maximum price is set at $\bar{p}$ the monopolist will supply $\bar{q}$ but demand will be q_1 thus leaving $q_1 - \bar{q}$ unsatisfied demand. However, if the maximum price is set at

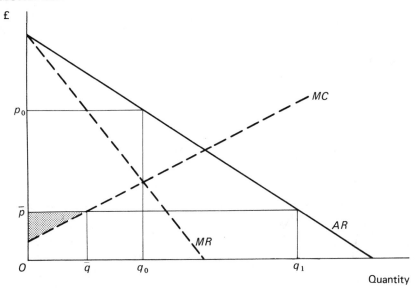

Figure 8.2

a point above the intersection of MC with AR, then there will be no unsatisfied demand.

A8.8 FALSE. Since price increases by 10% at all outputs so must marginal revenue. But as initially marginal revenue equalled marginal cost, which has also risen by 10%, profit maximising output after the improvement must be the same. Price is therefore 10% higher and so is total revenue (TR). Total variable production costs (TVC) rise by 10% since the constant cost of producing each unit is 10% higher. Profit equals $TR - TVC -$ fixed costs (F). The first two terms rise by 10% so total profits rise by the proportion

$$1.1 \, (TR - TVC) - F/(TR - TVC - F) > 1.1$$

A8.9 FALSE. Advertising may be regarded as shifting the demand curve to the right. In figure 8.3 the solid lines show the original average and marginal revenue curves, given the optimal amount of advertising. A price of p_0 will be set. Without advertising the curves may shift in all sorts of ways, perhaps becoming the dotted ones which are more inelastic at any given price. This will tend to happen if advertising has more effect on those who place the lowest values on the good. Price will then be raised to p_1 if advertising is banned.

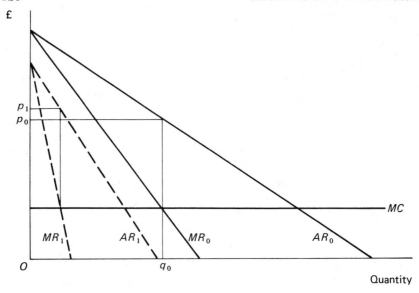

Figure 8.3

A8.10 FALSE. Perfect price discrimination means that the monopolist is able to charge every consumer the maximum he is prepared to pay for a given amount of the good. (This may be achieved by the use of a fixed charge, all-or-nothing offer, or other multi-part tariff schedule.) Under perfect price discrimination the monopolist's marginal revenue curve is therefore the real income constant demand curve for the level of utility achieved when the good is unavailable. If income effects are very strong this could lie to the left of the money income constant marginal revenue curve and if so output will fall. But normally output will increase under perfect discrimination.

A8.11 TRUE. Profit maximisation requires that the marginal revenue to be earned from selling a good in the export market equals that to be earned in the home market. If it does not, revenue can be increased without changing production costs by transferring sales from the market in which marginal revenue is higher to that in which it is lower. Marginal revenue in a market equals price times one minus the reciprocal of elasticity of demand. Thus the required condition is

$$P_h \left(1 - \frac{1}{\eta_h}\right) = P_e \left(1 - \frac{1}{\eta_e}\right) \tag{1}$$

where the subscripts h and e refer to the home and export markets respectively. If $\eta_h > \eta_e$ it follows from (1) that $P_e > P_h$.

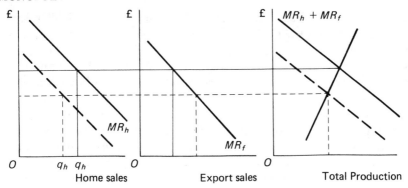

Home sales fall since export sales rise and total output falls

Figure 8.4

A8.12 TRUE. The solid lines in figure 8.4 show the initial equilibrium. When the tax is imposed on home sales this shifts the net of tax schedule of the marginal revenue received by the monopolist for home sales vertically downward by the amount of the tax. The horizontal sum of marginal revenue curves therefore also shifts down. With rising marginal costs it follows, as shown in the diagram, that the new equilibrium at which marginal cost equals marginal revenue in the two markets occurs at a lower marginal revenue. For marginal revenue to be lower in the export market, quantity sold must rise and price fall. However, since marginal revenue in the export market is positive, the additional sales there must add to total revenue.

A8.13 TRUE.

A8.14 FALSE. The initial home price is P_1 (figure 8.5). Suppose a maximum price of $\bar{P}$ is imposed. Marginal revenue in the home

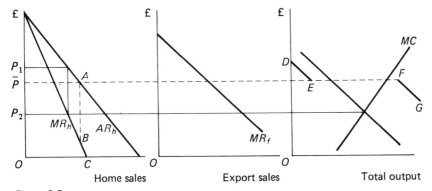

Figure 8.5

market is then given by $\bar{P}ABC$. The summed marginal revenue schedule is then $DEFG$. In the export market marginal revenue must rise, and the volume of exports therefore fall. Since marginal revenue is positive the total value of exports must fall. Note that if the maximum price were set below P_2 these conclusions would be reversed.

A8.15 **FALSE.** By assumption, at any given price, elasticity of demand is higher in the export market than in the home market. It follows that initially marginal revenue from foreign sales is less than that from home sales, although a weighted average of the two marginal revenues must equal marginal cost. When price discrimination is permitted the monopolist will reduce foreign sales until marginal revenue in that market is brought into equality with the constant marginal costs and will increase home sales so as to bring domestic marginal revenue into line with marginal cost. The reduction in export sales will raise the foreign price and, since marginal revenue abroad must be positive, reduce total export revenue.

A8.16 **FALSE.** Suppose the author seeks to maximise his monetary income. Since he receives 10% of total revenue the author would choose a price a which total revenue is maximised, i.e. at which marginal revenue is zero. The publisher will wish to charge a price at which his share of marginal revenue is equal to the marginal cost of book production. As marginal cost (paper and printing costs) is positive he will want to charge a higher price than the author.

It seems natural to enquire why publishing contracts typically take the form of paying authors a percentage of sales revenue. You may find some clues in 'Transaction Costs, Risk Aversion, and the Choice of Contractual Arrangements' by S. Cheung (*Journal of Law and Economics*, April 1969.)

A8.17 **TRUE.** Profit maximisation requires that marginal revenue equals marginal cost. Thus before the tax and using obvious notation,

$$MR = P_0 \left(1 - \frac{1}{\eta}\right) = C \qquad (1)$$

The tax adds to the marginal cost of producing and selling the good, so if its per unit amount is t, then after its introduction

$$P_1 \left(1 - \frac{1}{\eta}\right) = C + t \qquad (2)$$

Subtracting (1) from (2)

$$(P_1 - P_0) \left(1 - \frac{1}{\eta}\right) = t.$$

Since $\eta > 1$ it follows $1 > 1 - \frac{1}{\eta} > 0$ and thus $P_1 - P_0 > t$.

A8.18 Output rises. It is well known that a fixed rate profits tax (as long as it does not exceed 100%) leaves monopoly output unchanged. Even though the government now takes a share, the owner of the monopoly still does best by maximising pre-tax profits. If t is the rate of profit tax and π are profits, which of course depend on ouput, then the owner of the monopoly seeks to maximise $(1 - t)\,\pi$. To do this requires choosing output such that $(1 - t)\,\partial\pi/\partial q = 0$ which in turn means $\partial\pi/\partial q = 0$, i.e. pre-tax profits are at a maximum and marginal cost equals marginal revenue.

Under the second scheme the rate of profits tax $\bar{t}$ is a variable. The higher is output the lower is selling price and so the lower the mark-up. It follows that $\partial\bar{t}/\partial q < 0$. To maximise net return, $(1 - \bar{t})\,\pi$, now requires $-\pi\,\partial\bar{t}/\partial q + (1 - \bar{t})\,\partial\pi/\partial q = 0$. Since the first term of this equation is positive and $1 - \bar{t} > 0$ it follows that $\partial\pi/\partial q$ must be negative. This is to say that the last unit of output has added more to costs than revenue. As marginal cost now exceeds marginal revenue, output must be higher than in the previous instance in which they were equal.

A8.19 TRUE. With price discrimination, profits are

$$\pi = P_1 q_1 + P_2 q_2 - c(q_1 + q_2) \tag{1}$$

Substituting for q_1 and q_2

$$\pi = (P_1 - c)(a_1 + b_1 P_1) + (P_2 - c)(a_2 + b_2 P_2) \tag{2}$$

Maximising with respect to P_1 requires

$$\partial\pi/\partial P_1 = a_1 + 2b_1 P_1 - cb_1 = 0 \tag{3}$$

Hence $P_1 = (cb_1 - a_1)/2b_1$ and from the demand curve $q_1 = (a_1 + cb_1)/2$. In similar fashion $q_2 = (a_2 + cb_2)/2$ and so total output is $q_1 + q_2 = [a_1 + a_2 + c(b_1 + b_2)]/2$.

In the absence of discrimination, $P_1 = P_2 = P$ and therefore profits are

$$\pi = (P - c)(q_1 + q_2) = (P - c)(a_1 + b_1 P + a_2 + b_2 P) \tag{4}$$

$$\partial \pi / \partial P = a_1 + a_2 + 2(b_1 + b_2)P - c(b_1 + b_2) = 0 \qquad (5)$$

giving

$$P = [c(b_1 + b_2) - a_1 - a_2]/2(b_1 + b_2)$$

Therefore

$$q_1 = a_1 + b_1 [c(b_1 + b_2) - a_1 - a_2]/2(b_1 + b_2)$$

and

$$q_2 = a_2 + b_2 [c(b_1 + b_2) - a_1 - a_2]/2(b_1 + b_2)$$

yielding $q_1 + q_2 = [a_1 + a_2 + c(b_1 + b_2)]/2$, as before. Whether or not discrimination is possible total output is the same.

A8.20 **TRUE.** The problem is to find a simple example. We shall use step demand functions (figure 8.6). Suppose in market 1 the demand curve is $ABCDEF$. In market 2 customers are prepared to buy the amount EG at price P_3, nothing at any higher price and no more than EG at lower prices. The total market demand curve is therefore $P_1 BCDEGH$. If no discrimination is possible should a price of P_1, P_2 or P_3 be chosen? At price P_1 profits are $P_1 BKJ$, at price P_2 they are $P_2 DLJ$ and at price P_3 profits are $P_3 GMJ$. By inspection, P_3 is optimal and total sales are OH. Now suppose discrimination is possible. In

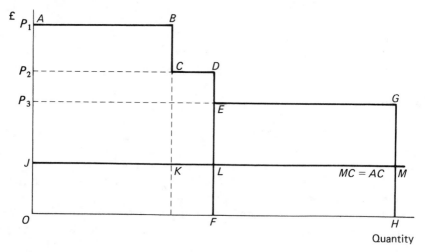

Figure 8.6

market 2, price P_3 will clearly be set and so FH be sold. In market 1 if price P_1 is set profits there $(P_1 BKJ)$ are higher than if price P_2 is set $(P_2 DCJ)$. So in market 1 price is P_1 and sales are JK. Price discrimination therefore reduces total output by LK.

A8.21 **FALSE.** Question 8.19 showed that with linear demand curves banning discrimination leaves total output the same. However, it does lead to the equalisation of price in the two markets. One condition for Pareto optimality is that all consumers should face the same price. Hence we should expect a potential Pareto improvement. This may be shown more directly. In figure 8.7, OO' is total output, AB the demand curve in one market, measured from origin O and CD the demand curve in the other market measured with respect to origin O'. With discrimination, price in market 1 is P_1 and in market 2 is P_2. With no discrimination price in both markets becomes $P = P'$. Consumers in market 2 gain $P_2 EFP'$ and the firm loses $P_2 EGP'$ on its original market 2 sales. In market 1 consumers lose $PFHP_1$ and the firm gains $PGHP_1$ on the original level of sales there. A net potential Pareto gain of EFH results from banning discrimination.

A8.22 (a) $P_A = 2$, $P_B = 1\frac{1}{2}$. For profit maximisation revenue in each market must equal the constant marginal cost. In market A this requires $P_A (1 - \frac{1}{2}) = 1$ and hence $P_A = 2$. Correspondingly, in

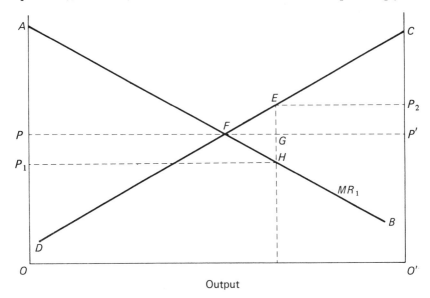

Figure 8.7

market B, $P_B (1 - \frac{1}{3}) = 1$ yielding $P_B = 1\frac{1}{2}$. As expected, price is higher in the more inelastic market. However, before it can be concluded that the answer has been found it must be checked that the firm is making positive profits. At $P_A = 2$, $q_A = (\frac{1}{2})^2 = \frac{1}{4}$. Given $P_B = \frac{3}{2}$, $q_B = (\frac{2}{3})^3 = \frac{8}{27}$. Thus total revenue is $2 \times \frac{1}{4} + 1\frac{1}{2} \times \frac{8}{27} = \frac{102}{108}$. Total cost (remembering marginal cost is constant at 1 so variable cost simply equals total output) is $\frac{1}{4} + \frac{8}{27} + \frac{43}{108} = \frac{102}{108}$. The firm is just able to cover its cost and so stays in business setting $P_A = 2$ and $P_B = 1\frac{1}{2}$.

(b) **Bankruptcy.** With price discrimination the firm just covers cost. Price discrimination is practised because it increases profits. When it is banned the firm will therefore be unable to cover its cost and go out of business.

A8.23 (i) **Advertise.** In the absence of advertising if the monopolist charges a price of $10, total revenue is $100 \times 10 = \$1000$ and costs are $100 \times 6 = \$600$ yielding profits of $400. If a price of $8 is charged, total revenue is $150 \times 8 = \$1200$ and costs $150 \times 6 = \$900$. Thus profits are $300. Without advertising the profit maximising price is therefore $10. With advertising a selling price of $8 yields total revenue of $250 \times 8 = \$2000$ whilst production costs are $250 \times 6 = \$1500$. Since the advertisement only costs $80, placing it increases profits by $20 as compared to the original profit maximising solution but causes selling price to fall to $8.

(ii) Selling price now rises from $10 to $11 when the advertisement is placed.

A8.24 **TRUE.** The less elastic is demand the greater will be the excess of price over marginal production cost.[1] Advertising increases demand at any given price. The extra profit earned by an additional unit demanded is the difference between what it sells for and the rise in production costs it entails. Hence, other things equal, advertising is more attractive to the firm the more inelastic the demand for its products. This analysis is based on Dorfman and Steiner,('Optimal advertising and optimal quality', *American Economic Review*, December 1954).

A8.25 (a) **Less likely.** In figure 8.8 OC is the marginal cost of imported supplies and OC' is marginal cost if a local plant is built. Profits can be measured as the area between the marginal revenue schedule and the marginal cost curve (the difference between the two shows the

1. $P(1 - 1/\eta) = MC$, hence $(P - MC)/P = 1/\eta$

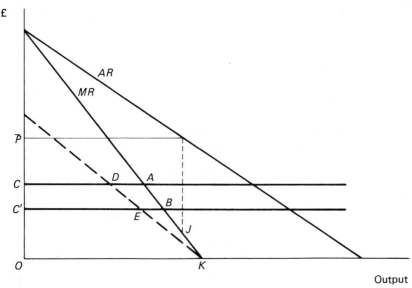

Figure 8.8

contribution to net revenue made by an additional sale and so this measure summed over all units sold yields total revenue less total variable costs) less any fixed cost. Thus a host plant will be established if $CABC'$ exceeds fixed costs.

A tax of t per cent on final selling price reduces the net revenue received by the monopoly for each level of its output by t per cent. Hence the marginal revenue curve it faces pivots down around the horizontal axis by t per cent. The dotted line in the diagram is an example. A host country plant now becomes worthwhile only if $CDEC'$ exceeds fixed costs which is a tougher condition than in the absence of the consumption tax.

(b) **More likely.** Suppose a maximum price of $\bar{P}$ is imposed. The marginal revenue curve in the host country now becomes $\bar{P}FJK$. The gain from a local plant becomes $CGHC'$ which exceeds $CABC'$.

A8.26 **FALSE.** First, without giving a complete proof, let us indicate the broad lines of an answer. A monopolist equates marginal cost to marginal revenue and a competitive industry marginal cost to price. Thus the marginal revenue curve plays the same role for the monopolist as does the demand curve for the competitive industry. Now the elasticity of derived demand under competition depends amongst other things on the elasticity of substitution and the share of the

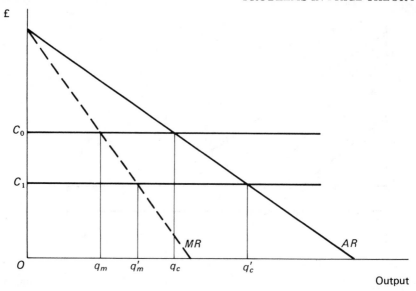

Figure 8.9

factor in total cost. Given constant returns these two parameters are independent of output, and thus the fact that monopolisation contracts industry output will not affect the elasticity of derived demand. The only way a difference can emerge is if under the two market structures the elasticity of the marginal revenue curve differs from that of the demand curve. However, with a linear demand curve it does not do so and hence the elasticity of factor demand is independent of market structure.

Let us illustrate what is happening (figure 8.9). At wage rate W_0, marginal and average costs are C_0, and output under competition is q_c and under monopoly is q_m. Wages then fall to W_1 and thereby reduce costs to C_1. Under monopoly, output would in response expand to q'_m and under competition to q'_c. In percentage terms the expansion in output is the same and therefore the percentage change in labour required will be the same under either market structure.

We shall now justify the statement that for linear demand curves the elasticities of the MR curve and of the demand curve itself are the same when measured at the points where the two curves intersect a horizontal line, i.e. that given falls in MC do cause equal percentage expansions in output.

If the equation of the demand curve is $p = a - bq$ then $dP/dq = -b$ and thus the price elasticity of demand is

$$-\frac{dq}{dP}\frac{P}{q} = \frac{P}{a-P} \ .$$

Hence when $P = C_0$, the elasticity of demand $= C_0/(a - C_0)$. Marginal revenue (MR) is $dPq/dq = a - 2bq = MR$. Consequently $dMR/dq = -2b$ and thus

$$-\frac{dq}{dMR}\frac{MR}{q} = \frac{MR}{a - MR}$$

When $MR = C_0$ it follows that the elasticity of the MR curve $= C_0/(a - C_0)$ equals the elasticity of the demand curve.

9

Imperfect Competition

References

Becker Chapter 6, lecture 21. Ferguson Chapters 11 and 12. Hirshleifer Chapters 12 and 13. Laidler Chapter 16. Lancaster Chapter 6. Layard Chapter 8–2 to 8–4. Mansfield Chapters 10 and 11. Stigler Chapter 12 and 13.

The analysis of markets which are neither perfectly competitive nor completely monopolised has always been a problem for economists. Some, particularly those with Chicago connections, have taken the view that there is no need to go beyond the analysis of the polar cases of pure monopoly and perfect competition. Nevertheless the prevailing view is that imperfect competition is the most common form of market structure and that there is value in attempting to introduce more realistic assumptions which reflect this.

I OLIGOPOLY

Oligopolistic markets are characterised by the presence of few sellers each recognising that its profits depend on how its competitors react to its own market strategy. As usual the firm can be regarded as equating marginal cost to marginal revenue. The problem is correctly to determine marginal revenue in this setting. A general framework may be set out as follows, taking the case of duopoly (two sellers) for simplicity.

1. A particular market state is described by the outputs of the two firms.
2. Given the current market state each firm computes the marginal revenue to be earned from extra output. This will depend on how much the other firm is selling and on how the firm conjectures

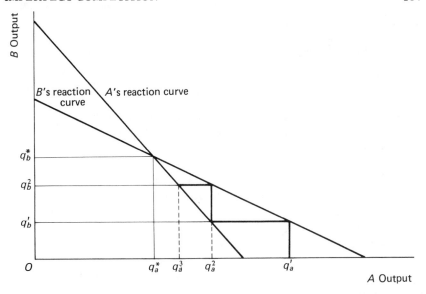

Figure 9.1

its competitor will respond to its own increased output. In general, the higher its competitors' sales the lower will market price be and the smaller the revenue the firm can expect from selling another unit of output. The same conclusion follows to the extent the firm expects its competitor to react to its own expansion by retaliating in like manner for this will depress price yet further.

To see whether an equilibrium will emerge the device of reaction curves may be used. In figure 9.1 curve A shows how much output firm A will produce given the current output of firm B. Curve B shows the output of firm B given that of firm A. Where they cross is an equilibrium. Firm A produces output q_a^* which is optimal for it, given that firm B produces q_b^*, and firm B actually does produce q_b^* because it is optimal for it to do so granted firm A produces q_a^*.

Stability

Suppose the market is displaced from its equilibrium to q_a', q_b'. Next period A output contracts to q_a^2. In response B expands to q_b^2. A then contracts further to q_a^3. Both firms converge towards equilibrium.

It is clearly of some importance to check the shape and relative slopes of the reaction curves and you will be asked to do this in the following questions.

Questions

Q9.1 In 1838 Cournot made the following assumptions:

(a) Both sellers produce the same good subject to the same constant costs.
(b) Each seller fixes his output on the assumption that his competitor does not change his output in response (known as zero conjectural variation).

As a particular case, let the inverse market demand curve be $p = 70-q$. Suppose there are two firms each with constant marginal costs of 10. Assuming they behave as Cournot duopolists, what will be the price and total industry output? Compare with the outcome under pure monopoly and perfect competition.

Q9.2 (i) Show that in general the Cournot assumptions yield a stable equilibrium.
(ii) What criticisms can be made of Cournot's assumptions?

Q9.3 Consider an alternative model to that of Cournot. Two firms sell a homogeneous product and are subject to the same constant costs. Consumers are perfectly informed of the selling prices charged by the two firms. Assume that there is no direct collusion but that both sellers act in a rational fashion, each correctly anticipating how the other will react to the price it charges.

(a) What price will be established?
(b) If one of the firms makes a cost-saving technological discovery whilst the other does not, what will happen to price and output? Once the first firm has made the discovery, is the incentive of the second firm to make a similar discovery increased?

Limit Pricing

The basic assumption is that all the existing firms in the industry produce a homogeneous output and collude to choose an output such that, if this output is maintained when an additional firm enters, the new entrant cannot earn positive profits. In figure 9.2 let AD be industry demand. Suppose the firms in the industry produce a total output of q^* and would maintain it if a new firm entered. The demand curve the entrant would face is BD measured with respect to origin q^*. If CC' is its average cost curve, it could not make a profit. As long as no entry occurs the existing firms charge p^* for their sales of q^*. If

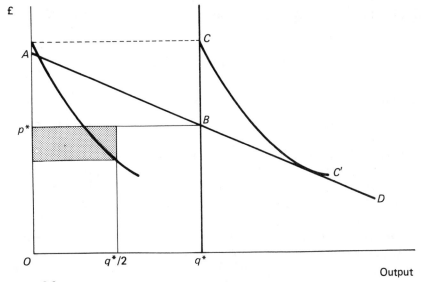

Figure 9.2

there are two firms in the industry and they share output they will each make profits equal to the shaded area. See F. Modigliani, 'New developments on the oligopoly front', *Journal of Political Economy*, LXVI, 1958, for further exposition.

Questions

Q9.4 Suppose the average cost of all firms are equal and constant. What will be the limit price and oligopoly profits?

Q9.5 Let there be two firms in an industry, both subject to constant and equal production costs. Each firm can engage in advertising expenditures. These do not generate new industry demand, merely switch expenditure from one firm to another. If both firms spend the same amount on advertising and sell at the same price, then industry demand is split equally between them. Consumers are highly price sensitive which means that both firms must sell at the same price, for otherwise the higher priced firm will make no sales. When both firms charge the same price, all consumers buy the most heavily advertised product and so, if one firm initiates an advertising programme it knows the other must at least match it or go out of business.

(i) Is it rational for either firm to advertise?
(ii) Would a ban on advertising represent a social gain?

Q9.6 What criticisms may be made of the limit pricing model?

II MONOPOLISTIC COMPETITION

Assumptions

1. Each of the many firms in the industry makes a different but related product.
2. There is freedom of entry into the industry.
3. The firms do not collude to establish the joint profit maximising outcome. Instead each firm maximises profits on the assumption that all other firms in the industry keep their prices fixed. Since the goods are heterogeneous each firm's marginal revenue schedule drawn up on the assumption of no retaliation is downward sloping.

An industry equilibrium must be characterised by all firms in the industry at least covering their costs and the requirement that any potential entrant would make a loss.

A further *symmetry assumption* makes it possible to represent the monopolistic competition equilibrium diagrammatically and is simply that, although goods are heterogeneous, all firms face identical cost and demand functions. Granted the symmetry assumption all firms will set the same price and output.

A full monopolistic equilibrium is shown in figure 9.3. AC is the average cost curve of a representative firm, AR is the industry demand curve divided by the number of firms in the industry and dd is the demand curve each firm faces if it alone varies its price, dm is the associated marginal revenue curve. At the full monopolistic competition equilibrium p_C, q_C, it may be seen that $dm = MC$ and so each firm maximises its profits. But as AC is equal to p_C normal profits are made and there is no incentive for entry into or exit from the industry (if $MC = dm$ and $AC = dd$ then AC must be tangential to dd. Can you prove this? See the analytically related answer to Q5.7 of Chapter 5). Finally, as dd crosses AR at p_C the industry is on its demand curve and so the expectation of each firm that it will be able to sell q_C at price p_C is fulfilled.

Under monopolistic competition each firm will produce an output below that which would minimise its average costs. It is therefore sometimes said that the firms operate with excess capacity. But note that the fact that average costs are not at a minimum has no direct welfare significance. (See Dixit and Stiglitz 'Monopolistic competition and optimum product diversity', *American Economic Review*, June 1977.)

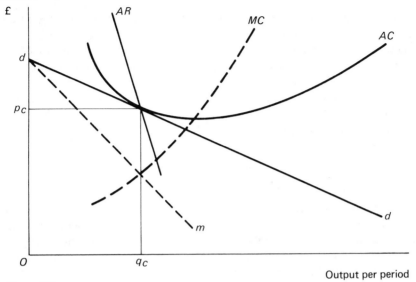

Figure 9.3

Question

Q9.7 Suppose all the firms in a monopolistically competitive industry were merged and a pure monopoly created. Would the monopoly produce as many types of good as existed under monopolistic competition?

III CARTELS

Where there are many firms in an industry they may nevertheless attempt to organise themselves so as to reap monopoly profits. In doing so, they face a number of problems. To the extent they success-fully raise price and profits they will attract new entrants. A successful cartel must therefore establish barriers to entry. Once this is done there is still the problem that each individual firm has an incentive to cheat on the cartel by cutting price (known as chiselling). Every seller is better off if price is raised above the competitive level. But as long as the other firms continue to keep their price high, each firm has an incentive to make a small price cut and increase its share of the market. As each firm tries to do this, the cartel will break up. (Stigler, ' theory of oligopoly', *Journal of Political Economy*, February 1964 discusses the conditions which favour price cuts which can be kept secret from other cartel members.)

If the cartel is able effectively to enforce the prices its members charge, this will tend to divert their attempts to 'cheat' into different channels. Each firm will try to offer extra services and attractions (e.g. free films on air journeys). This is known as non-price competition. It plays a similar role to price cuts. However, non-price competition of this kind tends to be socially inefficient since it is an imperfect substitute for what customers really want, price cuts. Like price cutting it also tends to destroy the effectiveness of the cartel.

Question

Q9.8 Annual demand for round trips on a particular airline route is given by $q = 1{,}000{,}000 - 1760p$, where p is the fare charged. Demand is spread uniformly throughout the year. Each plane on the route can carry a maximum of 100 passengers and is able to make 300 round trips per year. Fuel and other running costs are £10,000 per round trip. Fixed costs of owning a plane are £600,000. A cartel operates and sets a fare of £200 per round trip; however airlines can operate as many planes on the route as they wish.

(a) What will be the load factor on planes (i.e. the percentage of seats that are occupied) and how many planes will be operated?
(b) If the cartel lowers the price to £171.4 per round trip what will be the effect on the load factor and on the number of planes operating?
(c) Suppose when the fare is set at £200 the cartel is able to limit the number of planes to 30. Would you expect this to result, in practice, in the airlines making positive profits?

Answers

A9.1 **Under Cournot:** output is 40 and price 30; **under monopoly:** output is 30, price is 40; **under competition:** output is 60 and price is 10

Total output is $q = q_1 + q_2$. The profit of firm 1 is

$$\Pi_1 = pq_1 - 10q_1 = (70 - q_1 - q_2) q_1 - 10q_1 \tag{1}$$

By the Cournot assumptions, each firm takes the output of the other as fixed. Thus the maximising conditions for the two firms are

$$\partial\Pi_1/\partial q_1 = 60 - 2q_1 - q_2 = 0 \tag{2}$$

$$\partial\Pi_2/\partial q_2 = 60 - q_1 - 2q_2 = 0 \tag{3}$$

These two linear equations solve to give $q_1 = q_2 = 20$ and thus $q = 40$ and $p = 30$.

Under monopoly the firm maximises

$$\Pi = pq - 10q = 70q - q^2 - 10q \tag{4}$$

The first-order condition is

$$\partial\Pi/\partial q = 60 - 2q = 0 \tag{5}$$

Hence $q = 30$ and $p = 40$, price being higher and total output lower than under Cournot oligopoly.

Perfect competition results in price equal to marginal cost and hence $p = 10$, $q = 60$.

A9.2. (i) Making use of the reaction curve diagram (figure 9.1), first consider the point at which B's reaction curve crosses the vertical axis. This intersection occurs when A sells nothing. Under these circumstances, B is a monopolist and will set the monopoly output. On the other hand, firm A's reaction curve intersects the vertical axis at the level of B output at which A finds it unprofitable to produce anything at all. This intersection is at the competitive level of total output, for if B were to produce the industry competitive level of output (i.e. where price equals average cost), then if A were to produce a positive quantity of the good, price would fall below average cost and so A would make losses. Thus A's reaction curve must cut the vertical axis above B's reaction curve (as shown).

Similar reasoning reveals that B's reaction curve intersects the horizontal axis to the right of A's. This is sufficient to demonstrate that A's reaction curve must somewhere intersect B's from above. Hence a stable equilibrium must exist.

It can be shown that under very weak assumptions a stable unique equilibrium exists for Cournot duopolies even if both firms have positive and different costs (F. Hahn, 'The stability of the Cournot oligopoly solution', *Review of Economic Studies,* 1961).

(ii) No explanation is offered why each firm should assume the other will not change its output in response to its own output changes, despite the fact that every time a firm alters output its competitor does react. There is therefore no learning from experience. Further more, no explanation is offered why the firms do not choose to set prices rather than quantities, assuming that the other firm keeps its price fixed. This model would lead to the competitive outcome.

A9.3 (a) **The monopoly price will emerge.** Each firm, if it is rational, will adopt the following (personified) reasoning. If I set the monopoly price and my competitor matches me we shall share monopoly profits equally. But if he undercuts me and I fail to respond I shall lose all my market. Therefore I shall have no option but to speedily follow his price cut. Both our profits will fall since we will then end in charging a price below that which maximises monopoly profits. A sensible competitor would not provoke such a result. Nor will my competitor set a price in excess of the monopoly level. If I do not follow him I shall enjoy all monopoly profits and he will go out of business. Thus if I set the monopoly price I can expect half monopoly profits. Should I set a higher price I shall go out of business and if I choose a lower price the market will be shared at a less profitable output. As long as both firms think in like manner the monopoly price will be established without any explicit collusion being necessary. In effect, this is the kinked demand curve model with the kink now identified as occurring at the monopoly price. (For an exposition of the kinked demand curve model in its usual form see Laidler p. 168–170.)

(b) **Price falls, output rises, the incentive of the second firm is increased.** In figure 9.4 AB is the industry demand curve and AC its marginal revenue curve. OD is the original level of marginal cost and hence price is initially p_0 and total output q_0. Now one of the firms experiences a fall in marginal costs to OE. Suppose it sets a price of p_1 which maximises monopoly profits, given costs of OE. The other firm will have no option but to follow price down to p_1 if it is to stay in business. The profits of the first firm rise by $\frac{1}{2}DGFE$ (the increase in the area between marginal revenue and marginal cost, but divided by 2 since each firm supplies only half the market), whilst the profits of the second firm fall by $\frac{1}{2}GHF$ (through having to sell at a lower price than is optimal given its costs of OD). It follows that after the first firm has made the discovery the incentive of the second to do the same rises by $\frac{1}{2}GHF$.

A couple of additional points may be noted. The first firm may find it worthwhile to drive the second out of business. It certainly will if $DJKE > \frac{1}{2}AGD$ for then by setting a price marginally below OD and driving the other firm out of business, the total market profits are increased. Also, the firm with the lower costs has an incentive to

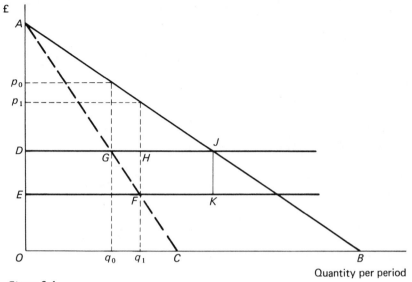

Figure 9.4

take over the second since it can increase its profits. However, both these responses depend on how long it is before the second firm may be expected to make a similar discovery. The attractiveness of the take-over strategy also depends on whether other firms may enter the industry to take the place of the firm which has vanished.

A9.4 Zero profit. If industry price exceeds average cost, a new firm can always enter and make positive profits, since even at low outputs the entrant enjoys the same average cost as the established firm. Hence the entrant will only be deterred when price equals average cost and thus profits are zero.

A9.5 (i) YES. In figure 9.5 AB is industry demand and ON the level of average costs. In the absence of advertising and with the freedom of entry ON would be the only sustainable industry price. However, consider the following possibility. Suppose the two existing firms produce total output of q^* and will maintain this output if a new firm enters. The demand curve of such a new entrant will therefore be DB measured with respect to origin q^* and its marginal revenue curve be DE. It could therefore earn profits of $FGHJ$. But suppose that each of the existing firms spend on advertising and promotion an amount just exceeding $FGHJ$. The new entrant would have to match this expenditure and thus be unable to make positive profits. Thus each of the existing firms, by charging a price of OJ and producing $q^*/2$, makes profits of $KLMN - FGHJ$, which is evidently

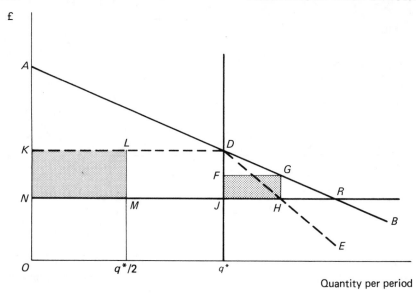

Figure 9.5

positive. Advertising is here profitable, even though each firm knows its competitors will match it. This is because the advertising expenditure acts as an effective barrier to entry. It is possible that this also provides an explanation why a firm (e.g. a detergent manufacturer) may find it profitable to engage in apparently competitive advertising between its own brands.

(ii) There would be a potential Pareto gain. Consumers would have an increased surplus of *KDRN* and existing firms lose *KDJN* − 2*FGHJ*. Hence the net gain is *DJR* + 2*FGHJ*.

A9.6 The existing firms in the industry must collude to maintain the limit price. However, there is the usual problem of the cartel preventing the firms undercutting each other to capture more of the market. This kind of 'chiselling' is more likely the greater the number of firms in the industry. The second problem is that if an interloper actually does enter the industry, the existing firms instead of maintaining their output, have an incentive to take the new entrant into the cartel and maintain price so as to preserve an optimal barrier; but if additional entrants believe this will happen, the limit price policy fails.

A9.7 The monopoly may produce either more or fewer varieties than under monopolistic competition. In the exposition below, it is

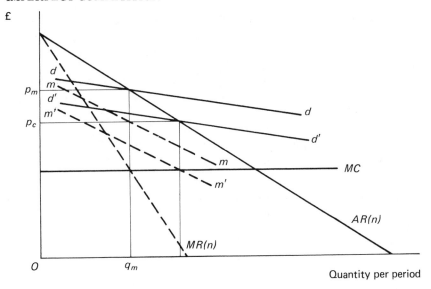

Figure 9.6

assumed for convenience the industry is monopolised and then a monopolistically competitive equilibrium is established.

Suppose each product is produced to constant marginal costs (MC) but also requires a fixed cost. $AR(n)$ in figure 9.6 is the industry demand curve when n goods are produced. If a monopolist produces n types of good its total output will be q_m and it will charge p_m for each good. If it were to produce $n + 1$ goods the demand curve would shift to the right (having more varieties can only increase total demand) and the surplus over variable costs would increase. But if n is an optimum the fixed costs of the $n + 1$ variety would exceed this extra surplus.

Now suppose each good is produced by a separate firm. At price p_m, dd is n times the demand curve each firm faces if it varies its own price, but the other firms still charge p_m. Starting from p_m each firm will therefore cut price. But as they all do so, dd will slide down $AR(n)$. At price p_c each firm maximises its profits given the prices set by the other firms. However, it does not follow that firms are covering their fixed costs or conversely that they are not making supra-normal profits. In the former case, firms will be leaving the industry and in the second case new firms will be entering. Thus the number of types of good under monopolistic competition may either be greater or less than under monopoly.

A9.8 (a) Load factor is 60% and 36 planes will be operated. Airlines will find it worthwhile to run additional planes if they earn positive profits. In equilibrium, the total cost of operating a plane must equal the revenue it earns. If the number of passengers per plane is x and the fare is £200, zero profit per plane requires that $(200 \times 300x) - (300 \times 10,000) - 600,000 = 0$ and therefore $x = 60$. During the year each plane consequently carries $60 \times 300 = 18,000$ round trip passengers. At a fare of £200 the total number of journeys that will be made is $1,000,000 - 1760 \times 200 = 648,000$ and hence $648,000/18,000 = 36$ planes will be operated.

(b) **Load factor increases, 33 planes will be operated.** When the fare is £171.40 the calculations are

$$(171.4 \times 300x) - (300 \times 10,000) - (600,000) = 0$$

$$x = 70$$

$$q = 1,000,000 - (176 \times 171.4) = 698,336$$

Therefore the number of planes $= 698,336/300 \times 70 = 33.25$ which will in practice be 33, since if 34 are operated each will make a loss. It is interesting that cutting the cartel price increases the number of passengers carried but reduces the number of planes operated (but note that for other demand and cost functions this may not be so).

(c) **NO.** If another passenger can be attracted to a plane the revenue it earns will rise by £200 and its costs raised not at all. It is therefore worth spending up to £200 on advertising and improved service (in-flight movies, pretty hostesses and so on) to capture an extra traveller. However, these expenditures will tend to attract passengers from other airlines rather than expand the overall market. So as all airlines undertake similar expenditures each of them will find no change in their number of passengers. But if they cut out these services and their competitors do not, they will lose passengers. In this way, non-price competition will tend to eliminate positive profits.

10

Welfare Economics

References

Ferguson Chapter 16. Laidler Chapters 21 and 22. Lancaster Chapter 10. Layard Chapter 1. Mansfield Chapters 15 and 17. *Social Efficiency* (Macmillan 1974) is a lucid text solely on this topic. Two comprehensive, though rather taxonomic surveys by F.M. Bator are 'The simple analytics of welfare maximisation' (*American Economic Review*, March 1957) and 'The anatomy of market failure' (*Quarterly Journal of Economics*, August 1958).

Questions

Q10.1 A cake is to be divided between two individuals. Pareto optimality requires that they receive equal shares.

Q10.2 Jack Sprat could eat no fat,
His wife could eat no lean,
And so between them both you see,
They licked the platter clean.

There is only one Pareto optimal allocation for this economy.

Q10.3 The utility possibility frontier of an economy must be downward sloping and concave to the origin with society being indifferent to any point on the frontier.

Q10.4 An actual Pareto improvement occurs if the economy moves from a point inside its utility possibility frontier to one on it.

Q10.5 Economists usually accept the proposition that an actual Pareto improvement represents a rise in social welfare since it seems to be based on the weakest possible ethical judgement. But suppose a certain policy raises the income of A whilst leaving that of B unchanged. B may be so jealous of A that it would be quite wrong to conclude that social welfare had risen. Hence economists are much too gullible in concluding that an actual Pareto improvement must lead to a rise in social welfare.

Q10.6 A policy change will yield a rise in social welfare if, and only if, it represents an actual Pareto improvement.

Q10.7 A potential Pareto improvement occurs if the economy moves from a point inside its utility possibility frontier to one on it.

Q10.8 A utilitarian has the ethical objective of seeking to maximise the sum of individual utilities (i.e. has a linear social welfare function) and so if a fixed sum of money is to be distributed between two individuals he would favour complete equality.

Q10.9 In contrast to utilitarians, Harvard philosopher John Rawls believes the correct ethical objective is to maximise the welfare of the least well off person in a society. This implies under all circumstances complete equality of welfare distribution.

Q10.10 Suppose the government is considering building a power station which will destroy the local environment. The government wishes to implement every policy that represents a potential Pareto improvement. If it discovers that building the station represents a potential Pareto improvement then, according to the government's criterion, it should be built.

Q10.11 If all markets but one are competitive, a removal of the imperfection would represent an actual Pareto improvement.

Q10.12 An economy produces two goods, both of which are monopolised. If one of the monopolies can be broken up and made to operate competitively, a potential Pareto improvement will result.

Q10.13 In the presence of pollution externalities an economy can never achieve Pareto optimality without government intervention.

Q10.14 A labour market dominated by a single buyer achieves Pareto efficiency if the buyer operates as a perfectly discriminating monopsonist.

Q10.15 If there is a tax on investment income the social value of investment must exceed that of current consumption. Thus, $1 of investment forgone represents a greater loss to society than $1 of consumption forgone.

Q10.16 Setting the prices of public utilities equal to marginal costs and covering any consequent losses by imposing taxes in other parts of the economy must be superior to setting price equal to average cost.

Q10.17 If the Ministry of Transport adopted the continental system of toll motorways this would ensure that only those individuals who valued the roads at the cost to society would use them and hence must result in a potential Pareto improvement.

Q10.18 The government is correct in arguing that, for efficiency, prices in public sector enterprises should always be set equal to long run marginal cost. (Assume for this question that lump sum non-distortionary taxes are available.)

Q10.19 A rise in the price of imported oil is no excuse for a nationalised gas industry to increase its price. On the contrary, the price of gas should be kept low to encourage substitution away from the more expensive fuel.

Q10.20 Although Britain is a net importer of oil she is also a producer. A fall in the world price of oil may therefore not be in Britain's interest if it means her expensive investments in North Sea production become uneconomic.

Further Questions

Q10.21 The local university owns flats in the centre of town. It lets them to students at a rent well below that which they would fetch on the open market. At this price there is excess student demand for the flats which are therefore allocated by administratively set quotas.

    (a) If the rent were raised to a level at which excess student demand is eliminated, the extra revenue raised could be used to ensure that every student could be made better off.

    (b) If the rent were raised still further, to the open market level, and lets not restricted to students, another potential Pareto gain would be made.

    (c) A policy of charging the market rent should be adopted.

Q10.22 One problem in deciding on social policy is that those who benefit from a particular policy are biased in favour of it and those who are harmed are biased against it. A rather appealing suggestion for avoiding this subjectivity is that individuals should (as an ethical principle) assume they have an equal chance of being each of the people affected by the decision. They will then be in a position objectively to decide whether a policy is in the social interest. To fix these ideas, suppose society consists of two individuals, one with utility of income function $U_A = f(Y_A)$ and the other with utility of income function $U_B = g(Y_B)$. There is a fixed income of $\bar{Y}$ to be distributed between the individuals. If you have an equal chance of being either A or B how would you want income to be distributed?

Q10.23 In a constant returns competitive economy an inflow of immigrants will lead to a potential Pareto improvement for the original residents. (Assume no externalities, no taxation, a fixed capital stock in the host country and that immigrants bring no capital with them.)

Q10.24 An economy enjoys a potential Pareto gain between two periods if the value of its net national product (net means capital depreciation has been deducted) grows when measured at final period prices. However, the information that net national product is higher when measured at base period prices yields no welfare conclusion.

Q10.25 A monopoly faces demand curve $q = 400p^{-2}$ (constant elasticity equal to 2). Its production is subject to constant average and marginal costs of 1. The government sponsors research costing the annual equivalent of 11 and which reduces the monopolists average costs to 0.5. No charge is made for the knowledge discovered. Monopoly profits are taxed at the rate of 60%.

  (i) Would the monopolist undertake the research if the government did not?
 (ii) Does the government spending lead to a potential Pareto gain?
(iii) Does it lead to an actual Pareto gain?

Q10.26 If a car breaks down it costs £100 to repair. A manufacturer can produce either an unreliable car or, at an extra cost of £28, a reliable model. When customers take proper care of the car the probability that the reliable model will break down is 0.1 and the probability that the unreliable model will break down is 0.2. However, the cost to a customer of taking care is £20 (this cost may represent the time and effort required). If no precautions are taken the probability of breakdown of the reliable model is 0.2 and the unreliable model is 0.5. Both the manufacturer and the customer are risk neutral.

(a) If the customer must pay repair costs, which type of car will be manufactured?

(b) If a law is passed making the manufacturer liable for repair costs which model will be produced?

(c) Does the move from customer to producer liability represent a potential Pareto improvement?

(d) If the manufacturer is free to decide whether or not to be responsible for repair costs, will he choose to be so and which model will be produced?

(e) Suppose repair costs are £250, answer questions (a) to (d) again.

(f) If repair costs are really £250 but customers believe they are only £100, will a move from consumer to producer liability represent a potential Pareto improvement?

Q10.27 A profit maximising automobile manufacturer must choose whether to produce either or both of two versions of a new car which differ from each other only in the respect that model A incorporates safety features not possessed by model B. Fixed production costs for model A are $10,500,000 and marginal costs per car are $4000 whilst for model B fixed costs are $10,000,000 and marginal costs $3000. There are three groups of potential consumers numbering 1000 in category I and 2000 in each of categories II and III. The maximum prices each member of these groups is prepared to pay for the two types of car are as shown below.

Model	Max. price Group I	Max. price Group II	Max. price Group III
	$'000	$'000	$'000
A	15	8	6
B	10	7	5.5

No consumer will buy both an A model and a B model.

(a) Assuming that the manufacturer must charge the same price to all purchasers what marketing strategy will he adopt?

(b) If a full Pareto optimum is to be established which type of car will be produced?

(c) If legislation is passed banning the sale of 'unsafe' cars of type B who will gain and who will lose? Will such legislation bring about a potential Pareto improvement?

(d) Suppose only group I consumers recognise the 'true' value of the safety features of model A. As for groups II and III if they really knew what was in their own best interest they would be prepared to pay $10,500 and $9000 respectively for model A. In this light re-answer questions (a), (b) and (c).

Note that questions on public goods are to be found in Chapter 13.

Answers

A10.1 **FALSE.** Pareto optimality is defined as a state in which it is impossible to make one person better off without making anybody else worse off. Suppose the cake is divided ¼, ¾. To make the individual with ¼ better off some cake *must* be taken from the other person who is therefore worse off. All divisions of the cake are Pareto optimal (assuming both individuals like cake).

A10.2 **TRUE.** It is Pareto optimal for Jack to have all the lean and no fat. If he had an allocation with some fat he could give it to his wife at no cost to himself but at some benefit to her. Thus one person could be made better off without anyone else being worse off. This kind of change is impossible only with the allocation specified in the rhyme.

A10.3 **FALSE.** The first part of the statement is true but the other two parts are false. By definition, points on the utility possibility frontier maximise the welfare of one individual given the welfare of others. It follows that if individual A is to enjoy an increase in welfare along the frontier, B must be worse off. If B were not worse off then the original point could not have been on the frontier since it would have been possible to make A better off without making B worse off. Hence, as shown by the solid curve in figure 10.1, the utility possibility frontier must be downward sloping. However, there is no argument to prove that it is smoothly concave to the origin or, indeed, any other particular shape. It all depends on the nature of the individual's utility functions about which we do not have sufficient information. The marginal utility of income may be rising, falling or constant and this will influence the shape of the frontier.

The frontier does, however, give a menu of choices of welfare distributions open to the society. How should it choose where on the frontier to operate? Conventionally this is determined by a social welfare function which ranks the various possible distributions of welfare in terms of social desirability. Where do such judgements come from? They may be those of an individual or, in some sense, those of society as a whole. However, it is important to note that they are ethical in nature, are not observable and are not a part of

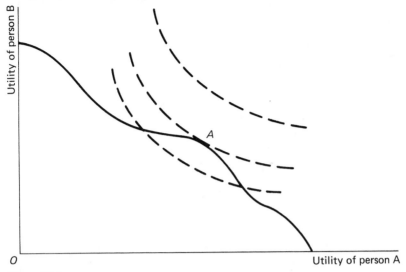

Figure 10.1

positive economics. Nevertheless it is usually assumed that the social welfare function possesses the well-ordered consistency properties of the utility functions of individuals. In figure 10.1 the social indifference curves are shown by the broken lines and a social optimum occurs at A.

Let us recapitulate the steps necessary to arrive at A and to describe it as a social optimum. Interpersonal welfare judgements have to be made, and once made it must be decided how welfare should be distributed. There is no obvious method of scientifically undertaking either step (indeed the second step is pure ethics), yet whenever a policy decision is made such judgements must either implicitly or explicitly be made.

A10.4 **FALSE.** An actual Pareto improvement is defined as a change which makes at least one person better off and nobody any worse off. In figure 10.2 the move from X to Z satisfies the conditions specified in the question but individual A is made worse off. Thus the change is not an actual Pareto improvement.

A10.5 **FALSE.** As a result of the policy change specified in the question, A is better off but B's jealousy makes him worse off. An actual Pareto improvement is defined as occurring when at least one person is better off and nobody is worse off. This definition is in terms of utilities, not income and so the change specified in the question clearly does not represent an actual Pareto improvement. The conclusion we are left with is that although the interpretation of

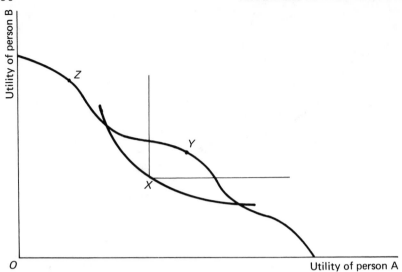

Figure 10.2

an actual Pareto improvement leading to a rise in social welfare is secure, hardly ever is an actual Pareto improvement to be encountered in reality, particularly when jealousy, altruism and associated externalities are involved.

A10.6 FALSE. The first part of the statement is correct. If one person is better off and no one else any worse off, then according to virtually any ethical judgement society is better off. However, changes which are not Pareto improvements may also increase social welfare. For example, point Z in figure 10.2 may lie on a lower social indifference curve than point X. Thus although the move from Z to X is not a Pareto improvement it does raise social welfare.

A10.7 TRUE. A potential Pareto improvement occurs if, after some change, the gainers *could* compensate the losers and still be better off. In figure 10.2 after the move from X to Z redistribution *could* take place along the frontier to a point such as Y at which everybody is better off. A potential Pareto improvement therefore occurs, as is the case whenever the economy moves on to its frontier.[1]

1. Note, in this answer we have implicitly assumed that it is possible to move from one point on the frontier to another one on it. This really requires that non-distortionary lump sum taxes can be levied. If they cannot be imposed then attempting to move round the frontier by, for example, imposing income taxes, will involve efficiency costs and take the economy inside the frontier. Taking account of this kind of problem it would be possible to define a

A10.8 FALSE. By familiar reasoning, to maximise the sum of utilities the marginal utility of \$1 to each individual must be the same. But this does not mean that income equality will achieve this result. Suppose individual A is ill but can be cured by expensive medical treatment. Starting from complete equality, if B gives income to A, A may gain more utility than B loses. Utilitarianism does not imply income equality unless all individuals have the same utility function.

A10.9 FALSE. At first sight it may seem true. After all, if A is better off than B it is possible to take some income from A and give it to B and therefore increase the welfare of the least well off person. Only if A and B are equally well off is this impossible. There are two reasons why this is false. Firstly, it may be impossible to compensate some people for their disadvantages (e.g. blindness). Secondly, incentive effects will generally result in redistribution stopping well short of complete equality. For example, as the tax rate on the rich is increased this may lead them to reduce their work effort and thus to there being less revenue to redistribute to the poor whose absolute welfare will consequently fall even though welfare equality has risen. Therefore, there will be some tax rate below 100% which maximises the welfare of the poor. (See A.B. Atkinson, 'How progressive should income tax be?' in *Penguin Readings in Economic Justice,* ed. E. Phelps).

A10.10 FALSE. The potential Pareto improvement criterion is not sufficient to yield a solution to the problem of project selection. Paradoxically (as Scitovsky originally pointed out) it can recommend both accepting and rejecting a particular project. This is because even though undertaking the project represents a potential Pareto gain the loser from the policy may be able to bribe those who gain to return to the initial position. To see how such a situation may arise, let us consider the utility possibility curves in figure 10.3. Accepting the project involves a move from point Z_1 on utility possibility frontier I to point Z_2 on frontier II. Individual A gains from the power station while B, a local resident, loses. Since point X can be achieved by lump sum redistribution after Z_2 is attained, the policy will lead to a potential Pareto improvement.

Let us suppose that planning permission is granted for the con-

utility feasibility frontier which except for the *laissez-faire* outcome lies everywhere inside the utility possibility frontier. By incorporating the institutional constraints on society it shows the true menu of possibilities open to it. Our answer could have been expressed in terms of the utility feasibility frontier with no loss of content.

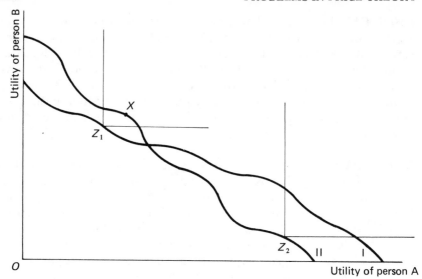

Figure 10.3

struction of the power station so that we are effectively at point Z_2 and compensation has not been paid. The question we now need to answer is, will it be possible for A to bribe B to campaign for the removal of planning permission? A move from Z_2 to Z_1 would make group B better off. Likewise, a move to any point north-east of Z_2 must make group A better off. Therefore, it is possible for group B to compensate A for moving back from Z_2 to Z_1. There is no reason why this cyclical process should terminate, which indicates the uselessness of the potential Pareto criterion for taking a decision in this case.

A10.11 FALSE. A change does not yield an actual Pareto improvement if it makes at least one person worse off. To illustrate how restrictive this criterion can be, let us show that the removal of a monopoly does not fulfil the conditions for a Pareto improvement. Using the familiar diagram (figure 10.4), we have A as the monopoly profit obtained by charging the profit maximising price p_1. AR is the market demand curve, the area under which represents the total value of output to consumers.

If the monopoly is abolished, the monopolist will lose A. Even though consumers gain $A + C$ by expanding output to a point where price $= p_0$, the change in the distribution of income as a consequence of such a move cannot be justified by the criterion that any policy change must represent an actual Pareto improvement.

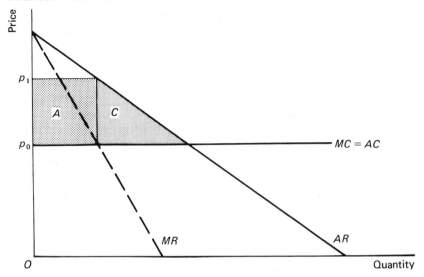

Figure 10.4

A10.12 **FALSE.** A necessary condition for Pareto efficiency is that the ratio of product prices should equal the ratio of marginal costs (i.e. the ratio at which goods can be substituted in production should equal the ratio at which consumers are prepared to substitute them). A monopoly firm equates marginal revenue to marginal cost and thus if both goods are monopolised,

$$p_X \, (1-1/\eta_X)/p_Y \, (1-1/\eta_Y) = MC_X/MC_Y.$$

If the elasticity of demand for X equals that for Y (which by chance it might) the first best condition is established. Making industry X equate price to marginal cost whilst leaving Y as a monopoly equating marginal revenue to marginal cost will therefore lead to a departure from Pareto efficiency. The price in the competitive industry will be below the opportunity cost of its output. There will be a movement to a position inside the utility possibility frontier and so a potential Pareto loss.

One qualification should be mentioned. If both industries are monopolised with the same elasticity of demand, Pareto efficiency will only be established if factors are in fixed supply. (Can you see why?) But even in the presence of elastic factor supplies, the general second best principle still applies and establishing the first best conditions in one sector of the economy only guarantees a potential Pareto improvement if first best conditions already hold in all other sectors.

A10.13 FALSE. Although normally such externalities do result in Pareto inefficiency, at least three cases may be cited where this does not happen.

Suppose an extra unit of output of industry X creates a pollution externality which raises the cost of industry Y by the amount α. If p_X is the price of X it follows that the net social value of the extra unit of X is $(p_X - \alpha)$. However, suppose that an extra unit of output of Y creates a pollution cost to X of β. The social value of the increase in Y output is therefore $(p_Y - \beta)$. If X and Y are the only two industries in the economy the condition for Pareto efficiency is that $(p_X - \alpha)/(p_Y - \beta) = MC_X/MC_Y$. Should both industries be competitive and if, by chance, $p_X/p_Y = \alpha/\beta$ this condition will be achieved since then $p_X/p_Y = (p_X - \alpha)/(p_Y - \beta)$. The case of offsetting imperfections here is analytically analogous to that considered in the previous question.

A second case may be given where an externality does not lead to Pareto inefficiency. Consider a price taking firm with a marginal cost curve which eventually becomes vertical because of a capacity constraint. At the market price p in figure 10.5 the firm produces X_0. Deducting the cost of the pollution it creates from the market price, the social value of its output is $\bar{p}$. But even having done this, marginal social costs and benefits are still equated at output X_0 and hence the presence of an externality has not prevented the market from arriving at a Pareto efficient solution.

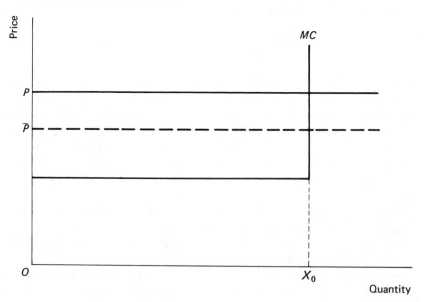

Figure 10.5

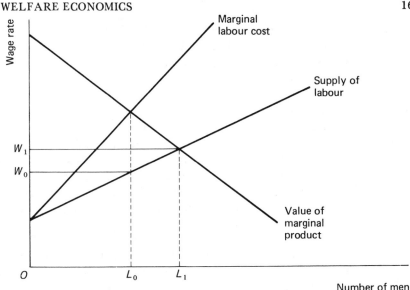

Figure 10.6

Finally, suppose a monopoly produces an external diseconomy. If the industry were competitive its output would be socially excessive since it does not take into account the external costs it imposes. But under monopoly output is restricted to raise price and so it is possible that a Pareto efficient solution emerges.

A10.14 **TRUE.** In the case of ordinary monopsony we know that the marginal private cost of hiring an additional worker exceeds the marginal social cost. This is because of the institutional practice that all men of a given skill must be paid the same wage. In the case in figure 10.6 this results in a wage rate of W_0 and employment level L_0. If the employer can pay each worker the minimum wage he will accept to enter employment, the level of employment would rise to L_1 and the marginal private cost of employment would equal the marginal social cost. Given that output is produced under competitive conditions the ability to discriminate perfectly allows the employer to fulfil the conditions for Pareto efficiency.

A10.15 **UNCERTAIN.** In general, where markets other than savings markets are imperfect the statement is false. However, let us assume that no other imperfections exist and also ignore distributional issues.

As investors are only interested in the net return, they will equate this to their subjective rate of time preference. Thus, because of the tax, investment stops short at a point at which the 'social' return is in

excess of the 'social' cost. In such a situation any policy which reduces investment and raises consumption by \$1 would produce a
net loss in potential Pareto terms equal to the difference between the
social and private returns.

A10.16 FALSE. Take the case of a public corporation subject to
decreasing average costs. In figure 10.7, setting price equal to marginal cost instead of equal to average costs yields a gain in consumer
surplus of P_1ABP_2 and an operating loss of $EDBP_2$. There is a direct
potential Pareto improvement of ABF which can be measured as the
value of the additional output (area under the demand curve) less the
cost of providing the output (area below the marginal cost curve).
But how is the operating loss to be covered? Suppose a production
tax of t is imposed on the competitive industry of figure 10.8. The
revenue raised is $P(1 + t)GHP$, equal to losses in X. Consumer surplus
in Y falls by $P(1 + t)GJP$. The direct potential Pareto loss in market
Y is GHJ. There is no reason why GHJ should not exceed ABF in
which case average cost pricing in X is superior to marginal cost
pricing on potential Pareto improvement grounds.

A10.17 FALSE. The argument of this question was used by town-
planners as long ago as the seventeenth century. It is based on the
age-old confusion between an accounting cost and the economic
costs of using the public facility. Once a road has been built, if there
is no congestion problem, the social cost of a car using it is zero.

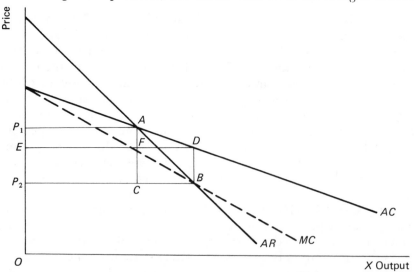

Figure 10.7

That is, no unpriced resources are used up in an additional trip along the motorway and therefore no direct reason for a toll exists. This is not quite correct in practice as we have ignored maintenance costs, but these tend to be related more to the weather than to the volume of traffic.

In the case of a road subject to congestion, the cost of an additional trip is the burden of longer jams imposed on existing users which should, where possible, be charged for.

To charge to recoup the original construction costs would result in a waste of resources in so far as a positive price discourages potential users (and there would also be the administrative cost of collecting tolls). Thus a positive price would lead to an under-utilisation of the road. However, in the absence of tolls, construction and maintenance costs will have to be covered by general taxation, and as we argued in the previous question this will cause efficiency losses elsewhere in the economy. Hence we cannot simply say a zero price is necessarily optimal, though it might be. Finally, we note that a tax on the ownership of cars would not necessarily be an efficient way of raising revenue to cover the loss. This is because the tax will reduce the demand for cars and thus again lead to under use of the roads.

A10.18 **FALSE.** The long-run marginal cost is the cost of producing an additional unit of output per period when both labour and capital plant can be freely varied. This cost bears no relationship to the opportunities forgone in using existing capacity. As a Pareto optimal

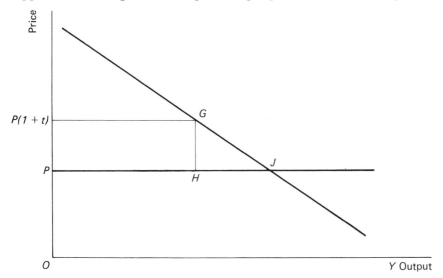

Figure 10.8

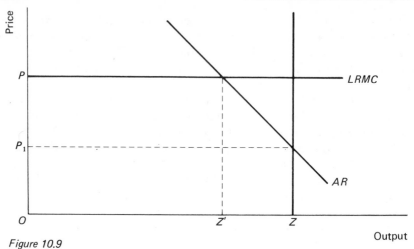

Figure 10.9

allocation of resources is achieved when all activities are priced at their opportunity cost, to price at *LRMC* in the short run runs the risk of misallocating existing capacity.

To illustrate the point let us look at figure 10.9. Up to output Z the cost of using existing capacity is zero. To price at P will clearly lead to a waste of resources as some capacity is left idle. Once output Z has been achieved we are faced with the problem of allocating a fixed output. Given the demand curve, optimality will be obtained by charging a price of P_1, not P. However, it is also the case in this example that capacity is excessive since consumers are willing to pay less for the last unit of the good than the *LRMC* of producing it. In the long run disinvestment should take place until a capacity of Z' is achieved.

A10.19 **FALSE.** At the initial oil price the marginal social opportunity cost of current gas consumption will be an upward sloping curve. Firstly, short-run marginal production costs are likely to be increasing. Secondly, gas is an exhaustible resource and more current consumption means less in the future. The oil price will increase both current and future gas demand as the two fuels are substitutes. With gas more valuable in the future, the marginal social opportunity cost of current gas consumption schedule must shift upwards and intersect the raised current demand curve at a higher price. Pareto efficiency therefore requires a gas price increase with the rise in profits distributed as equity dictates.

A10.20 **FALSE.** If the world price of oil falls then the cost of Britain's present level of imports would fall and the costs of her

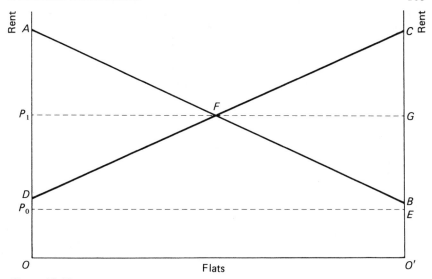

Figure 10.10

domestic production would be unchanged. Thus there is no question but that she would be better off. Of course, if there is a low import price North Sea investments may have proved to be a waste of money, but since they are already there, they represent a 'sunk' cost and therefore their cost is irrelevant to current decision taking or the assessment of the welfare effects of price changes. This is sometimes summarised in the phrase 'bygones are forever bygone'.

A10.21 (a) **TRUE.** In figure 10.10, OO' is the supply of student flats. The demand curve of those students who are allocated flats is AB, measured with respect to origin O and the demand by the rest of the student body is CD measured with respect to origin O'. Initially a price of P_0 is charged. To eliminate excess student demand price must be raised to P_1 at which price everyone who wants a room can get one. This generates an increase in revenue of $P_1 GEP_0$. The new residents gain CFG of consumer surplus and the previous residents lose $P_1 FBEP_0$. Thus the net gain is CFB.

(b) **TRUE.** Let OO' in figure 10.11 again be total supply of student flats and SS' be total student demand when no administrative rationing scheme is operated. P_1 is the market clearing price when only students can rent, but the open market price is the higher P_M. If flats were rented at the market price of P_M the loss in students' consumer surplus would be $P_1 P_M LK$ but extra revenue of $P_M JKP_1$ would be generated. Hence the revenue raised exceeds by LJK that necessary to compensate the students who loose.

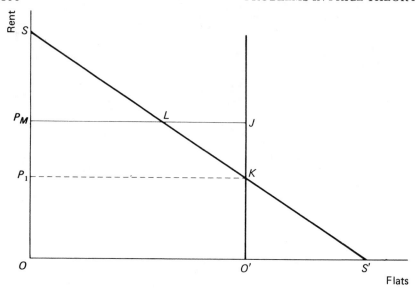

Figure 10.11

(c) **UNCERTAIN.** Economics can never determine what should be done, at best it can demonstrate the consequences of certain courses of action. In the present context we should first note two efficiency considerations that have as yet been ignored. The first is that it has been implicitly assumed that students know what is in their own best interest. Yet it may be argued that for their own good (though they do not realise it at present) some students are better off if supervised at least indirectly by the University. Secondly, externalities have been ignored. However, it is possible that a certain balance of students of different types may lead to a more attractive community for all. The best way this can be achieved may be by administrative rationing. Similar arguments may also suggest that there should be no letting to members of the public.

Now let us introduce equity considerations. As always, the fact that gainers could compensate the losers does not mean that they actually will, and therefore if the particular policy affects income distribution in an undesirable fashion it will not necessarily be worth pursuing. However, in this particular case, there seems no reason why the authorities could not directly compensate the students to whom otherwise they would have allocated a room. This would almost certainly be regarded as unfair and an arbitrary distribution of largesse. More reasonable, perhaps, would be an equal division of the revenue from letting amongst all the students.

A10.22 So as to maximise the sum of utilities. According to the standard economic theory of decision making under uncertainty the objective would be to maximise expected utility. Thus if A receives Y_A and hence B receives $\bar{Y} - Y_A$ expected utility is $E(U) = \frac{1}{2}f(Y_A) + \frac{1}{2}g(\bar{Y} - Y_A)$ since there is an equal chance of being either individual. Maximising $E(U)$ requires that $f(Y_A) + g(\bar{Y} - Y_A)$ be maximised, which in turn requires that $df/dY_A = dg/dY_B$. This is the utilitarian criterion that the sum of utilities be maximised for it specifies that the marginal utility of income be the same for everyone.

The above reasoning seems to present a very persuasive ethical case in favour of utilitarianism. It was first put forward by M. Fleming ('A cardinal concept of welfare', *Quarterly Journal of Economics*, vol. 66, 1952) and developed by J. Harysani ('Cardinal welfare, individualistic ethics and interpersonal comparisons of utility', *Journal of Political Economy*, August 1955), both reprinted in Phelps E.S., *Readings in Economic Justice*, Penguin. Rawls adopts a similar impersonality axiom but assumes that individuals in deciding the kind of society they would like to live in look only at the outcome if the worst comes to the worst. They would therefore always prefer a society in which the worst off individual is better off than another social arrangement in which the worst off individual was just a little worse off but everyone else was much better off. Neither of the present authors feel this is reasonable.

A10.23 TRUE. In figure 10.12 MP_C is the marginal product of labour schedule given the country's capital stock and L_0 is the in-

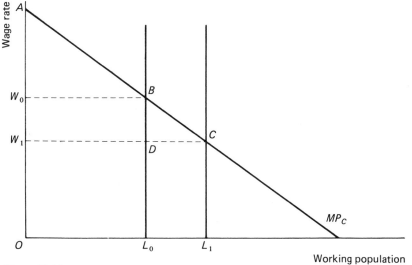

Figure 10.12

digenous population. Hence before the immigration, the wage is W_0 and labour receives OW_0BL_0 and capital ABW_0 (total output is the area under the marginal product of labour schedule and capital receives what labour does not). Now suppose immigration increases the population size to L_1. The wage falls to W_1, indigenous labour loses W_0BDW_1, capital gains W_0BCW_1 and hence the original residents enjoy a potential Pareto gain of BDC. You may wish to consider how realistic this question is and whether changing the assumptions would change the answer significantly.

A10.24 TRUE. From the theory of consumer behaviour we know an individual is better off if the cost of her original consumption bundle is less than the cost of her final bundle when both are measured at final period prices (because this implies that in the final period the original bundle is also available but is rejected). If the economy's total output satisfies this condition it is possible (at least with lump-sum redistribution) to ensure that every individual in the final period is given an income which enables purchase of his or her base period consumption bundle. Thus everyone can be made better off and a potential Pareto improvement has occurred.

   To show this consider figure 10.13. In the final equilibrium suppose one person consumes at A and the other at B. Total output of the economy is at C. In the base period the economy's production mix was at a point inside the final period price line passing through

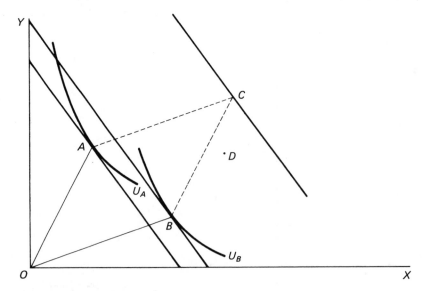

Figure 10.13

C, say point D. Suppose we give consumer B the same utility in the base period as he receives in the current period. To do this must mean that his consumption point either remains at B or else lies on a line parallel to the one through B but further from the origin. However, the horizontal sum of the lines passing through A and B is the line through C. Since in the old equilibrium the sum of the lines through the two consumption points passes through D, if consumer B is to be just as well off, the line along which consumer A's consumption point lies must be closer to the origin than the one through A. Thus if in the old equilibrium B was just as well off, A must have been worse off. Consequently, the change in output mix from the base to the current period must represent a potential Pareto improvement.

Utilising the above form of argument you should find it easy to show that if NNP falls at base prices then a potential Pareto loss must have occurred but if NNP rises then it does not follow that the economy has enjoyed a potential Pareto gain. (To help you see this, consider the threshold case. In figure 10.13 let all lines now represent base prices and the current period economy output mix be along the same price line as the base period mix. Then if B's consumption is the same in the two periods, A's current consumption must be along the same budget line as originally but away from point A. Hence consumer A must have a lower utility. Alternatively, if B's utility is preserved at U_B but his consumption shifts from B, then A's consumption point must lie on a budget line closer to the origin than the one through A so again consumer A is worse off.) On the issues discussed here see P. Samuelson 'The evaluation of real national income', *Oxford Economic Papers*, 1950 and reprinted in Phelps.

A10.25 (i) **NO.** Setting marginal revenue equal to marginal cost in the pre-discovery situation requires $p(1 - \frac{1}{2}) = 1$, i.e. $p = 2$. Hence $q = 400 \times (\frac{1}{2})^2 = 100$. Thus total revenue is 2×100 and costs are 1×100 giving pre-tax profits of 100 and post-tax profits of 40. If marginal costs fall to 0.5 profit maximising price falls to 1 and output rises to 400. Pre-tax production profits rise to 200 and after deducting research costs overall pre-tax profits are 90. It follows that the research is not privately worthwhile to the monopolist and in the absence of government intervention would not be undertaken.

(ii) **YES.** The government spending increases pre-tax profits by 100 and so post-tax profits by 40. The government gains 60 of profits-tax revenue. As the price of the good falls by 1, the 100 original buyers gain 100 and there will also be gains arising from new purchases generated by the fall in price. However, total gains are at least $40 + 60 + 100 = 200$ and so greatly exceed the cost of 110.

(iii) **NO.** The government spends 110 and receives 60 extra tax revenue. Tax payers are worse off by 50.

A10.26 (a) **The unreliable model is produced and consumers do take precautions.** If the manufacturer produces the reliable car and the customer takes no precautions his expected repair costs are 0.2 × 100 = £20. As the time and effort costs of taking precautions are £20 and reduce expected repair costs to 0.1 × 100 = £10, the customer will not find it worthwhile to take precautions. Should the unreliable car be sold, the customer faces expected repair costs of 0.5 × 100 = £50 if no precautions are taken and total expected costs, including time costs are (0.2 × 100) + 20 = £40 if precautions are taken. Thus in this case the customer does find it worthwhile to take full care. If the reliable car is sold instead of the unreliable one customers expected total costs fall by £40 − 20 = £20. The manufacturer can therefore charge this much more for the reliable than the unreliable car. But since it costs £28 more to produce, he will not find it worth his while to do so.

(b) **The reliable model.** Since the manufacturer is liable it is not worth the customer taking any precautions. Thus, with the reliable model the manufacturer faces expected costs of 0.2 × 100 = £20 and the unreliable of 0.5 × 100 = £50. Since the reliable model saves £30 of expected repair costs and only costs an extra £28 to produce, this is the one the manufacturer will select.

(c) **NO.** Under (a) the unreliable car is produced and precautions are taken. Thus total expected repair and precaution costs are £40. With the producer liable in (b) no precautions are taken and the reliable model is produced, so expected repair costs are £20 and production costs are £28 higher. Thus the move from (a) to (b) represents a potential Pareto loss of £8.

(d) **The manufacturer will reject liability and produce the unreliable car.** Under (a) the customer faces expected costs of £40. With producer liability the customer gains £40 and can therefore be charged this much extra for the car. As the manufacturer faces additional costs of £20 + £28 it is profitable for him to reject liability and produce the unreliable car.

(e) (a) The unreliable car is produced and customers take precautions. (b) the reliable car. (c) **NO.** Under (a) expected repair costs are £50 and precaution costs are £20 giving a total of £70. Under (b) the extra production cost of the reliable car is £28 and expected repair costs are £50 so total costs are £78. (d) If the manufacturer accepts liability his costs rise by £78 and the selling price of the car by only £50 and so he will reject liability and produce the unreliable car.

(f) Under customer liability with buyers believing repair costs are £100 then, as in the first part of the question, the unreliable car will be produced and precautions be taken. With producer liability the reliable car is manufactured by the reasoning of (f) and (b). Given the option the producer would rather have consumer liability; but now with consumer liability, true expected repair costs are £125 and with producer liability they are only £50. So even when the extra manufacturing costs of £28 are added, with customer misinformation producer liability can represent a potential Pareto improvement.

A10.27 (a) **Model B priced at 5.5.** Suppose model A is produced:

at price 15 profit (revenue, minus variable costs, less fixed cost) is
$15 \times 1 - 4 - 10.5 = 0.5$
at price 8 profits are $24 - 12 - 10.5 = 1.5$
at price 6 profits are $30 - 20 - 10.5 = -0.5$.

For model B:

at price 10 profit is $10 - 3 - 10 = -3$
at price 7 profit is $21 - 9 - 10 = 2$
at price 5.5 profit is $27.5 - 15 - 10 = 2.5$.

It follows that profits are maximised when the relatively unsafe model, B, is produced and sold at price 5.5. (If model A were sold in addition to B it could be sold for 12 if B is priced at 7, but this leads to a loss of 4.5. Indeed, because of the high fixed costs no price combination yields positive profits if both models are produced.)

(b) **MODEL A.** Suppose model A is produced. Each group I consumer values this model at 11 more than marginal production cost, group II at 4 more and group III at 2 more. Thus the total surplus is $11 + 8 + 4 = 23$ from which must be deducted fixed costs to get the net surplus of $23 - 10.5 = 12.5$. Performing the same exercise for model B, a net surplus of $7 + 8 + 5 - 10 = 10$ is obtained. Thus a full social optimum is achieved by producing model A.

(c) **The manufacturer and group II lose. Group I gains.** A potential Pareto deterioration occurs. From the arithmetic in (a) it can be seen that if model A is produced it will be sold at price 8. The manufacturer's profit therefore falls by 1 from the case when B production is permitted. On the other hand group II consumers who previously enjoyed 1.5 surplus now have none (total loss 3) and group I, who previously enjoyed 4.5 per car now gain 7 (total gain 2.5). The net change is $2.5 - 3 - 1 = -1.5$ loss.

(d) The answer to (a) is clearly unchanged since consumer behaviour is unaltered. But now the true values to groups II and III are different from the price they are prepared to pay, and these are the values which must be used to compute social costs and benefits. Since the true values of model A exceed payable prices, clearly a full social optimum still requires production of model A. As for the answer to (c), if model A is produced and sold at 8 the sum of the actual (not perceived) gains to all participants is $1.5 + 5 + 7 = 13.5$ and for model B sold at 5.5 is $2.5 + 3 + 4.5 = 10$. There is now a net gain from the legislation.

11

General Equilibrium

References

Becker Chapter 8, lectures 30 and 31. Ferguson Chapter 15. Friedman Chapter 8. Hirshleifer Chapters 7 and 8 and Appendix. Laidler Chapter 20. Lancaster Chapter 9. Layard Chapter 2. Mansfield Chapter 14.

General Equilibrium Analysis (Allen and Unwin) by M. Krauss and H.G. Johnson or Johnson's *The Two-Sector Model of General Equilibrium* (Allen and Unwin) are fairly close to the approach taken here.

I AN EXCHANGE ECONOMY

In this chapter the interrelationships between all the markets in an economy are considered. A general equilibrium obtains when demand equals supply in all the markets in the economy. Many of the conceptual issues involved can be illustrated by a simple two-good exchange economy. Suppose there are two types of consumer, A and B. Each consumer is initially endowed with a fixed stock of the two goods, X and Y (there is no production in the economy, the goods just exist like manna from heaven). All consumers of type A have $\bar{X}_A$ of X and $\bar{Y}_A$ of Y and, similarly, type B consumers are endowed with $\bar{X}_B$ and $\bar{Y}_B$ and the goods are potentially tradeable. For simplicity we shall assume that all consumers of type A have the same preferences as each other, that this is also true of type B consumers and that all consumers act as price takers.

Questions

Q11.1 If at a certain price ratio demand equals supply in the market for X it follows that equilibrium is also achieved in the market for Y.

Q11.2 Granted conventionally shaped indifference curves a competitive equilibrium must exist for the exchange economy.

Q11.3 The competitive equilibrium for an exchange economy must be unique.

Q11.4 If both goods are normal for both types of consumer the competitive equilibrium for an exchange economy must be unique.

Q11.5 If X is an inferior good for the sellers and a normal good for the buyers the competitive equilibrium must be unique.

Q11.6 Suppose a competitive exchange economy is in equilibrium. It is then opened up to world trade and can buy and sell as much at world prices as it wishes. If, before trade, the relative price of X in the home economy was below that in the world market, when the economy is opened up to international trade it will export X.

Q11.7 If price is not at a competitive equilibrium, suppose an adjustment process is set in motion such that if there is excess demand for X its relative price rises and if there is excess supply its price falls. An equilibrium is stable if, when price is disturbed from its equilibrium level, it returns back to it (the equilibrium is locally stable if price converges on the equilibrium only when small disturbances occur and is globally stable if it converges on the equilibrium for all disturbances). If the equilibrium is unique it must be globally stable.

Q11.8 If multiple equilibria exist they must be alternately stable and unstable.

II PRODUCTION ECONOMIES

Q11.9 A closed economy consists of 100 farms, 40 of which can produce milk (M) and wheat (W) according to

$$M = 60 - 6W \ (0 \leqslant W \leqslant 10)$$

and the remaining 60 produce according to

$$M = 40 - 2W \ (0 \leqslant W \leqslant 20)$$

In equilibrium one unit of wheat exchanges for four units of milk. The opportunity then arises to buy and sell wheat on the world market at a price of 3 units of milk. A referendum is held to decide whether to allow residents of the country to trade freely in the world market.

(a) If each farm is owned and worked by a single farmer who casts his vote according to his self interest the outcome of the referendum will be a vote in favour of free trade.

(b) If lump sum transfers are possible everyone could be made better off with international trade.

(c) What will be the outcome of the referendum if the world price of wheat is even lower, at say one unit of milk?

Let us now extend the two-good exchange economy into the production sphere in a somewhat different fashion. Suppose that the two final outputs X and Y require as inputs the same two primary factors which we shall call labour and capital which are in fixed supply to the economy. Both X and Y are produced under conditions of constant returns to scale in capital and labour and subject to smooth isoquants convex to the origin.

Q11.10 The production possibility frontier for the economy can have no portions that are convex to the origin.

Q11.11 Given the constant returns technology the production possibility frontier must be linear.

Q11.12 In a competitive equilibrium in which both goods are produced the slope of the production possibility frontier must equal the commodity price ratio.

Q11.13 Suppose industry Y is labour intensive. A change in preferences towards Y which leads to an expansion of Y output will have the following effects:

(a) The wage relative to the rental on capital will rise.

(b) The real wage will rise whether measured in terms of purchasing power over X or Y.

(c) The wage will rise by a higher percentage when measured in terms of purchasing power over Y than in terms of purchasing power over X.

(d) The wage will rise by the highest percentage when measured in terms of the return to capital, the next highest in terms of X and the lowest percentage in terms of Y.

Q11.14 If the recipients of wage income have a higher marginal propensity to consume the labour intensive good than do the recipients of the income from capital, then, if both goods are normal for both consumers, a (statically) unstable competitive equilibrium is impossible.

Q11.15 An import tariff increases the price of the imported good. This tends to expand domestic production of this good and thus raise the income of the factor employed intensively in its production. However, if the factor spends most of its income on the imported good it may be worse off because of the price rise.

Q11.16 A small country producing two goods is engaged in inter-national trade. In the world market relative prices are determined independently of the imports and exports of the domestic economy. Suppose that the country experiences an increase in its supply of labour. If the country continues to produce both goods, the wage rate will fall, and outputs of both goods will rise.

Q11.17 An economy facing fixed terms of trade produces two goods, X and Y. In equilibrium, production of each unit of X requires 6 units of labour and 4 units of capital whilst Y requires 2 units of labour and 2 units of capital. The economy has a factor endowment of 50 units of labour and 40 units of capital.

(a) If equal amounts of X and Y are consumed in the home economy and its factor endowments are fully employed will the economy export X or Y?

(b) Suppose the economy were endowed with 60 units of capital and 50 units of labour what would be the characteristics of the trade equilibrium?

Answers

I An Exchange Economy

A11.1 **TRUE.** This is Walras' Law. Consider the budget constraint of type A individuals.

$$P_X \bar{X}_A + P_Y \bar{Y}_A = P_X X_A + P_Y Y_A \tag{1}$$

The left hand side of this equation shows the value of A's initial endowments. X_A, Y_A are A's desired consumption of X and Y and the cost of this consumption bundle, the right hand side of (1), must equal what is available to spend. Rearranging (1)

$$P(X_A - \bar{X}_A) + (Y_A - \bar{Y}_A) = 0 \tag{2}$$

where $P = P_X/P_Y$ is the price of X in terms of Y (that is Y is chosen as numeraire, as one of the goods must be, for since there is no money as such in this economy, only relative prices exist and the earlier usage of P_X and P_Y was for expositional convenience). A similar equation to (2) can be derived for the B consumers. Adding these two equations gives

$$P(X^d - \bar{X}) + (Y^d - \bar{Y}) = 0 \tag{3}$$

where X^d is total demand for X and $\bar{X}$ total endowments. $X^d - \bar{X}$ is the difference between demand for X and the amount available (supply) and is known as excess demand. Equation (3) states that the value of the excess demand for all goods must add up to zero. If the market for X is in equilibrium $X^d = \bar{X}$ and from (3) it follows that $Y^d - \bar{Y} = 0$, i.e. that the market for Y is also in equilibrium.

A11.2 **TRUE.** A competitive equilibrium exists if there is some price ratio at which both markets are in equilibrium. To illustrate this, the device of an Edgeworth exchange box is useful. In figure 11.1 the length of the box shows the total amount of X in the economy and the height shows the total of Y. The origin for type A consumers is O_A and for type B is O_B. (We assume equal numbers of the two types.) Any point in the box represents a possible allocation of the total of goods between the two groups. Point E shows the initial endowment point.

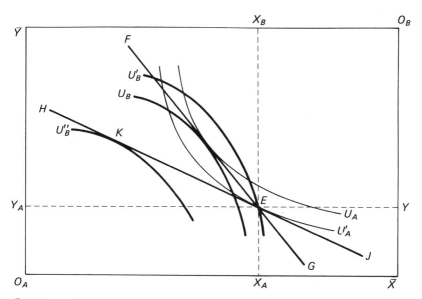

Figure 11.1

Now consider the budget constraint for type A individuals. They can always choose not to trade and so consume their initial endowment. Thus the endowment point, E, must lie on their budget constraint. However, given market prices it is also possible to trade off one good for another, as along FEG which is the budget constraint for type A consumers measured with respect to origin O_A. Given the preferences shown, at the relative prices implicit in the slope of FEG, type A consumers wish to give up some X in exchange for Y. For type B consumers their budget constraint is FEG measured with respect to origin O_B. Given their preferences, type B consumers maximise utility by trading to point C, buying X in exchange for Y. Since U_B and U_A are tangent along FEG at the same point the amount of X offered by type A consumers equals that demanded by type B and the reverse is true for Y. In other words a general equilibrium has been found. But how do we prove that one must always exist?

Consider the budget constraint HEJ which embodies a lower relative price of X than does FEG. HEJ is drawn tangent at E to U'_A, the A indifference curve passing through E. Thus at this relative price A consumers would not wish to trade. If along HEJ the B consumers did not wish to trade either we should immediately have a general equilibrium. But as drawn U'_B, the B indifference curve through E, cuts HEJ and the B consumers maximise utility at K which involves buying X. Since A consumers do not wish to sell any X there must be excess market demand for X. If a budget constraint is now drawn tangent to U'_B at E the B consumers will not wish to trade X, but it

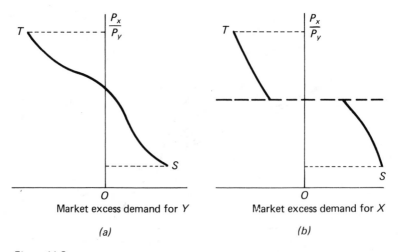

Market excess demand for Y Market excess demand for X

(a)   (b)

Figure 11.2

can be shown in a similar way to previously that A consumers will wish to sell X (you should check this). Thus, at this necessarily higher price of X there will be excess supply of X (negative excess demand). We have therefore found a price ratio at which there must be negative excess demand for X.

The first price ratio at which there was excess demand for X and the second in which there was excess supply are plotted in figure 11.2(a) as S and T. If the excess demand function is continuous, as drawn in figure 11.2(a) then, since T and S lie on different sides of the vertical, the line connecting them must somewhere cross the vertical. At the price ratio at which this happens excess demand for X is zero. By Walras' law so must be that for Y. In other words, a general equilibrium has been found.

To establish that a general equilibrium *must* exist, the possibility of figure 11.2(b) in which the excess demand function has a quantum jump to the right and does not satisfy the continuity requirement must be ruled out.

To show that the standard assumptions imply continuity it is sufficient to show that each consumer's excess demand function is continuous, for then so must be the sum of them. Now, if there is to be a discontinuity in the excess demand function of a consumer then his price consumption curve must have a jump in it as, for example, does $OABHC$ in figure 11.3. The price ratio implicit in the slope of budget constraint DF is the threshold at which fractional changes in

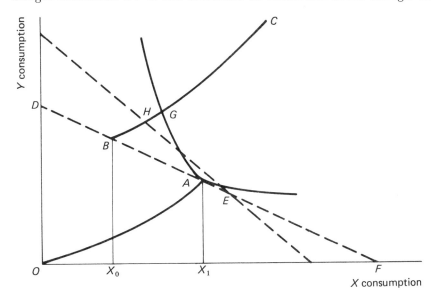

Figure 11.3

the price ratio induce the consumer to switch consumption of X by a discrete amount from X_0 to X_1. However, if indifference curves are strictly convex to the origin the one tangential to DF at A must intersect BC above B, say at G. If E is the endowment point then it is always possible to draw a new budget constraint such as that passing through E and H. Along EH utility is clearly not maximised at H and thus with convex indifference curves it is impossible that the price consumption curve be discontinuous as drawn. Whatever the nature of the discontinuity and endowment point, similar contradictions must arise. Thus discontinuities may be ruled out (this is perhaps more easily seen by noting that, roughly speaking, an indifference curve must be tangent at A and B if both are on the price consumption curve and this is impossible with strict convexity). Hence for the standard case we have continuity and a proof of general equilibrium.

A11.3 **FALSE.** In figure 11.2(a) the excess demand function intersected the vertical only once. However, there is nothing to prevent the situation shown in figure 11.4 in which A, B and C are all competitive equilibria.

A11.4 **FALSE.** We shall show that in figure 11.4 the intersections at A and B are quite consistent with both goods being normal. Start at A then reduce the relative price of X to that at B. The substitution effects of this price fall definitely increase demand for X, tending therefore to create positive excess demand for X. For the buyer of X the fall in the price of X will have made him better off. This rise in real income will further increase his demand for X if X is a normal

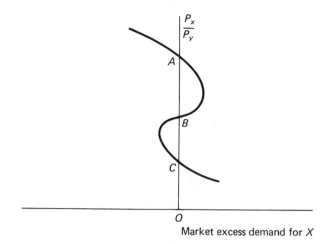

Figure 11.4

good. On the other hand, the seller of X is worse off, and if X is a normal good for him, this will reduce his desired consumption of X and hence increase the net amount he supplies. This may offset the two previously specified effects if X is more strongly normal for the seller than the buyer. It is therefore possible that the fall in price leaves total consumption demand unchanged and thus that multiple equilibria exist.

A11.5 **TRUE.** When the price of X falls both income and substitution effects work to increase the demand for X by the seller. The same is true for the buyer. Hence when price falls excess demand for X must always increase. Multiple equilibria (i.e. two different prices at which excess demand is zero) are therefore impossible.

A11.6 **FALSE.** In figure 11.5 let P_D be the domestic price ratio. The world price ratio is higher at P_W. It follows that this price ratio will be established in the domestic economy since no seller of X would accept less than he can get on the world market or buyer of X pay more than he has to. At price P_W domestic excess demand for X is the negative amount EO. In other words residents are trying to sell EO more X than the total endowment of the economy and in exchange buy an equal value of Y in excess of the economy's endowment of Y (this follows from Walras' law). With international trade they are able to do this by exporting EO of X and importing an equal value of Y.

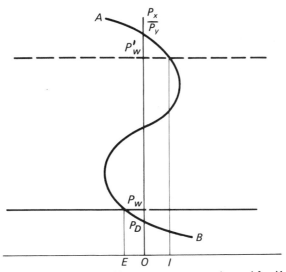

Figure 11.5

However, suppose the world price ratio is P'_W, again higher than the domestic price ratio. Now when the economy is opened up to international trade it will import OI. This possibility arises because of the multiple equilibria.

A11.7 **FALSE.** A unique equilibrium implies that the excess demand function intersects the vertical only once. In figure 11.6, at price P_1 there is excess demand. According to the specified adjustment mechanism price will tend to rise towards the equilibrium P_e. If price is above the equilibrium at P_2 there is excess supply and price tends to fall. Why therefore is the economy not globally stable? Well it is stable in the sense that negative feedback is present and, out of equilibrium, forces are set in motion which move price back towards equilibrium (this is known as static stability). However, this does not necessarily mean that price will converge on equilibrium since the adjustment mechanism may be so powerful that it causes price to overshoot. Starting from too low a price the next move may be to a price that is too high and price may continue to oscillate ever wider, never reaching equilibrium. To know whether price will actually converge to its equilibrium level, more must be specified than that it rises in the presence of excess demand. Something about the speed and strength of the adjustment process must be known. If the economy will actually converge to equilibrium it is known as dynamically stable.

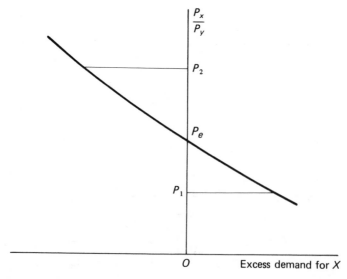

Figure 11.6

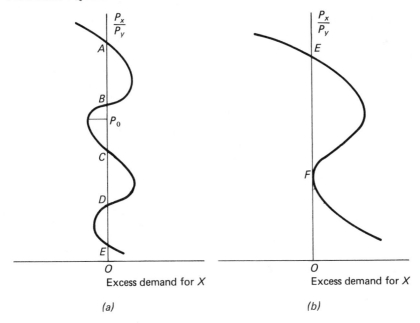

Figure 11.7

A11.8 **FALSE.** Starting at the competitive equilibrium at B in figure 11.7(a) suppose price is deflected to P_0. This results in excess supply of X so the adjustment mechanism causes price to fall even further. Thus B must be an unstable equilibrium. It can easily be checked that A, C and E are locally (statically) stable and B and D are unstable equilibria. This does suggest that the equilibria alternate as stated in the question. But what do you make of figure 11.7(b)?

II Production Economies

A11.9 (a) **FALSE.** If a unit of wheat exchanges for four units of milk each of the farmers with production possibilities $M = 60 - 6W$ (drawn as AB in figure 11.8) maximises his utility by specialising in milk production and consuming along budget constraint AC. Any other production point would lead to a budget constraint lying inside AC. At a world price of wheat equal to three units of milk each farmer will still specialise in milk production but is now able to consume along AD. Consumption possibilities along AD are clearly superior to those along AC and so each of these 40 farmers will vote for free trade.

A similar analysis for the farms with production possibilities $M = 40 - 2W$ shows that at both closed and open economy price

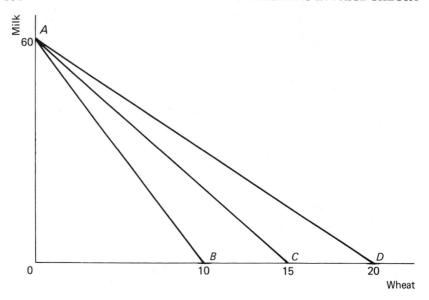

Figure 11.8

ratios these farms will specialise in wheat production. But the lower world price of wheat will make their owners worse off (assuming they consume some milk) and so they will vote against free trade. The outcome of the referendum will consequently be a majority of 20 in favour of isolation from the world market (autarky).

(b) **TRUE.** For example, allocate to each farmer his closed economy consumption bundle (as domestic output is unchanged this is a feasible allocation). Then allow each farmer to trade that bundle at the ruling world prices if he so wishes. This is illustrated in figure 11.9 for a farmer consuming $W_0 M_0$ when wheat costs 4 milk. If he is able to trade this bundle at a world price of wheat equal to 3 milk his utility rises from U_0 to U_1.

(c) **UNCERTAIN.** The 40 original milk producers will benefit even more from the further reduction in the price of wheat. On the other hand the original wheat producers will now also specialise in milk and may be even better off. This is illustrated in figure 11.10 where LK is the production possibility schedule of these farmers, LN their consumption possibilities in the closed economy, and KP consumption possibilities with free trade. As drawn a higher level of welfare can be achieved with free trade and so it is now possible that both types of farmer may favour free trade.

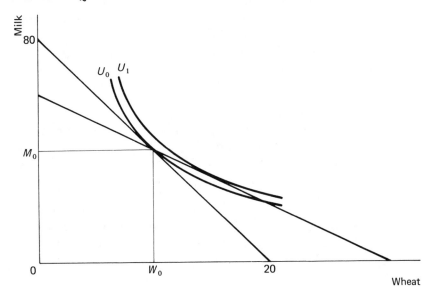

Figure 11.9

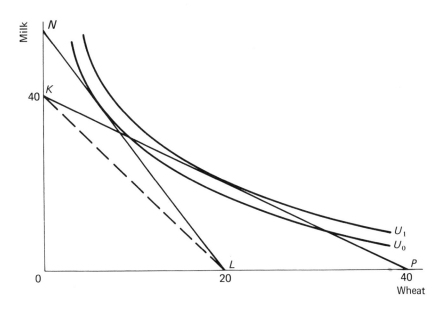

Figure 11.10

A11.10 TRUE. To demonstrate this we show that the contrary is impossible. Suppose the production possibility frontier is as in figure 11.11. It will be demonstrated that if the economy could produce at A or B then it could also produce at points along the straight line connecting A and B. In other words the production possibility frontier cannot in reality lie inside this straight line and therefore cannot be convex to the origin as shown.

Now we demonstrate that points along the straight line AB are feasible. At A the economy produces X_A, Y_A and at B the output mix is X_B, Y_B. Suppose instead of using all its factors in the techniques chosen at point A, the economy used only λ per cent of them, in this way. With constant returns, production of X would be λX_A and of Y, λY_A. Using λ per cent of the total supply of each factor in the techniques at A means $(1 - \lambda)$ per cent of them are available for the techniques at B and hence output from these factors would be $(1 - \lambda)X_B$ of X and $(1 - \lambda)Y_B$ of Y. Given this division of factors, total output of the economy is

$$X = \lambda X_A + (1 - \lambda)X_B \quad \text{and} \quad Y = \lambda Y_A + (1 - \lambda)Y_B$$

If $\lambda = 1$, $X = X_A$ and $Y = Y_A$ and if $\lambda = 0$, $X = X_B$ and $Y = Y_B$. Eliminating λ from the two equations yields

$$X = \left[X_B - \frac{Y_B(X_A - X_B)}{Y_A - Y_B} \right] + \left[\frac{X_A - X_B}{Y_A - Y_B} \right] Y \tag{1}$$

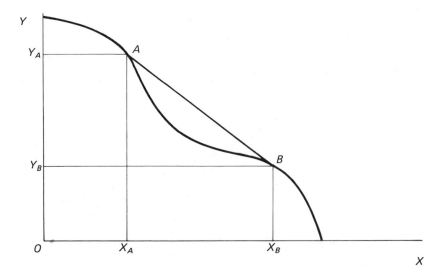

Figure 11.11

Remembering that X_A, X_B, Y_A, Y_B are constants, (1) can be seen to have the form of a linear equation, which as we have seen passes through A and B. Other values of λ therefore bring the economy to points along the straight line AB.

A11.11 **FALSE.** We have ruled out the production possibility frontier being anywhere convex to the origin, but not proved that it is concave, as in figure 11.12(a) as opposed to linear as in figure 11.12(b).

Figure 11.12(a) is the usual case and to investigate further, an Edgeworth production box, analogous to the exchange box, may be drawn up (figure 11.13). Its length shows the total amount of labour available to the economy and its height is total capital. O_X is the origin for the X industry and O_Y the origin for the Y industry. Points on the production possibility frontier show the maximum amount of Y that can be produced for given levels of X production. This requires that the marginal rate of substitution of labour for capital be the same in both industries, for example at the tangency point C, output of Y is maximised given that X_0 of X is produced. The locus of such efficient factor allocations is shown by $O_X C O_Y$. Movements along this 'contract curve' correspond to movements round the production possibility frontier. Movement from O_X towards O_Y increases X output and reduces Y.

The contract curve has the property that it can never cross the diagonal of the exchange box. To prove this note that along the diagonal the capital/labour ratio of the two industries is identical and equal to the economy's overall endowment ratio. It has already been noted (Chapter 5, Q5.13) that with a constant returns production

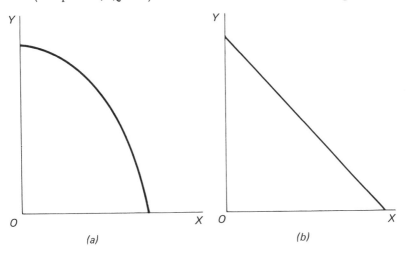

(a)   (b)

Figure 11.12

function the marginal product of each factor depends only on the capital/labour ratio. As the slope of an isoquant equals the ratio of marginal products it follows that the slope of the isoquants also depends only on capital/labour ratios and is constant along a ray through the origin. Now suppose the contract curve did cross the diagonal. At that point the slopes of X and Y isoquants are the same. But these slopes must also be the same at every other point along the diagonal. Thus the contract curve must be identical to the diagonal, in contradiction to the initial assumption. It follows that the contract curve can never cross the diagonal and that if one industry uses a factor more intensively than the other at one output level, it must do so at all outputs. In figure 11.13 the X industry is capital intensive.

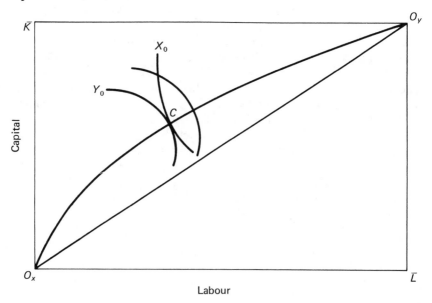

Figure 11.13

Now consider the implications if the economy limited itself to production along the diagonal and so as it varied its output mix it kept factor intensities in the two industries constant. Since there are constant returns we should have $X = aL_X$, $Y = b(\bar{L} - L_X)$, (with $\bar{L}$ total labour supply) and thus $Y = b\bar{L} - X/a$. In other words a linear relationship between Y and X output emerges as shown in figure 11.12(b). But in general it is not efficient to produce along the diagonal of the exchange box and it follows that in moving from the diagonal to the contract curve more of one output can be produced without any loss of the other. In other words the production possibility frontier must lie outside a straight line connecting its two intersections with the origins. Only when efficiency requires that the two industries use factors in the same proportion will the production possibility frontier be linear as in figure 11.12(b). Otherwise it will be concave to the origin as in figure 11.12(a).

A11.12 **TRUE.** Write the production function $X = f(L_X, K_X)$. It follows that

$$dX = \frac{\partial f}{\partial L_X} dL_X + \frac{\partial f}{\partial K_X} dK_X \tag{1}$$

In other words, as a result of a small change in labour input and capital input the change in output is given by the marginal product of labour times the change in labour plus the same for capital. Similarly for Y, if $Y = g(L_Y, K_Y)$

$$dY = \frac{\partial g}{\partial L_Y} dL_Y + \frac{\partial g}{\partial K_Y} dK_Y \tag{2}$$

Dividing (2) by (1)

$$\frac{dY}{dX} = \frac{(\partial g/\partial L_Y)dL_Y + (\partial g/\partial K_Y)dK_Y}{(\partial f/\partial L_X)dL_X + (\partial f/\partial K_X)dK_X}$$

$$= \frac{\partial g/\partial L_Y \left[dL_Y + \dfrac{\partial g/\partial K_Y}{\partial g/\partial L_Y} dK_Y \right]}{\partial f/\partial L_X \left[dL_X + \dfrac{\partial f/\partial K_X}{\partial f/\partial L_Y} dK_X \right]}$$

$$= \frac{\partial g/\partial L_Y}{\partial f/\partial L_X} = \frac{P_X}{P_Y} \tag{3}$$

The third equality of (3) follows from the second, since the fixed factor supplies mean that each unit increase in labour usage in X reduces labour usage in Y by the same amount, i.e. $dL_X = - dL_Y$ and $dK_X = - dK_Y$. Furthermore, on the production possibility frontier the marginal rate of substitution of labour for capital is the same in both industries, i.e. the ratio of marginal products is equal in the two industries and so $(\partial g/\partial K_Y)/(\partial g/\partial L_Y) = (\partial f/\partial K_X)/(\partial f/\partial L_X)$. Hence from (3) we have the slope of the production possibility frontier (the rate at which X trades off for Y) equal to the marginal product of labour in Y divided by its marginal product in X. But in a profit maximising equilibrium the wage rate equals the marginal product multiplied by the price of output and thus the fourth equality of (3) holds, which is our result that the slope of the trans-formation curve equals the price ratio.

A11.13(a) **TRUE.** Since the production possibility frontier is con-cave to the origin (remember factor intensities in the two industries differ) an expansion in Y output must be accompanied by an increase in the relative price of Y (the slope of the production possibility frontier becomes gentler as Y output expands). We now establish a relationship between commodity prices and factor prices. In figure 11.14, X and Y isoquants are drawn. Given the initial relative factor prices, as shown by the slope of AB, it costs the same to produce X_0 of X as Y_0 of Y (since both isoquants lie on the same isocost line). As competition has been assumed, prices equal production costs so X_0 of X must also exchange in the market for Y_0 of Y.

Now suppose there is an increase in the relative price of labour as shown by the slopes of the isocost lines CD and EF. As CD lies to the right of EF it now costs more to produce Y_0 of Y than X_0 of X, and so the relative price of Y must have increased. Increases in the wage rate raise the relative price of the labour intensive good. Reversing the relationship, an increase in the relative price of Y, the labour

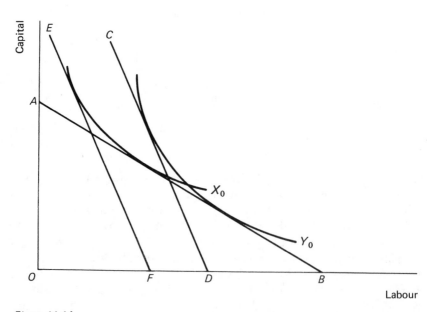

Figure 11.14

intensive good, raises the wage of labour relative to the rental on capital.

(b) **TRUE.** Profit maximisation requires that $w = MP_L^X \, P_X$, or, $w/P_X = MP_L^X$. The value of the wage in terms of purchasing power over X therefore equals the marginal product of labour in X. From figure 11.14 the increase in the relative price of Y increases the wage relative to the rental on capital and, as can be seen, this causes industry X (and Y) to become more capital intensive in production. The marginal product of labour in X rises as more capital per unit of labour is used there and hence the wage in terms of X must rise. Similarly, the wage in terms of Y equals the marginal product of labour in Y. As Y has also become more capital intensive the wage must rise when measured in terms of Y also.

(c) **FALSE.** Measured in terms of Y the wage can be written

$$\frac{w}{P_Y} = \frac{w}{P_X} \frac{P_X}{P_Y}.$$

Since w/P_X has risen but P_X/P_Y has fallen it follows that w/P_Y must rise by a smaller percentage than w/P_X.

(d) **TRUE.** The wage measured in terms of the rental on capital can be expressed

$$\frac{w}{r} = \frac{MP_L^X}{MP_K^X}$$

The numerator of the right hand side is the marginal product of labour in X which equals the wage measured in terms of X and it has been shown to rise by a higher percentage than the wage measured in terms of Y. The denominator is the marginal product of capital in X, and as X has become more capital intensive this has fallen. Hence w/r must rise by a higher percentage than does MP_L^X and it follows that

$$\frac{\widehat{w}}{r} > \frac{\widehat{w}}{P_X} > \frac{\widehat{w}}{P_Y} > 0 \tag{1}$$

where the hats indicate percentage changes. Inequality (1) is known as the Stolper–Samuelson relationship. If the relative price of the labour intensive good rises, the wage increases by the highest percentage in terms of capital, the next highest percentage in terms of the capital intensive output and rises by the lowest percentage in terms of the labour intensive good itself.

A11.14   An equilibrium is unstable if a rise in the relative price of X leads to a rise in excess demand for X. The rise in the price of X will lead to an increase in the supply of X as the economy substitutes round its production possibility frontier. The rise in the relative price of X will also cause, for all consumers, a substitution effect against X. However, the rise in the price of X will cause an increase in the real income of the factor employed intensively in X. If the recipients of labour income have a higher marginal propensity to consume this good than do the recipients of capital income, who will be worse off, it is possible that there will be a net increase in demand for X. An unstable equilibrium is therefore possible if the factor employed relatively intensively in an industry also consumes that good relatively intensively.

A11.15 **FALSE.** By the Stolper–Samuelson relationship, if the price of a good rises (whether caused by tariff or any other demand effect) then the return to the factor employed intensively in the production of the good increases in terms of either output.

A11.16 **FALSE – wages will be unchanged, output of the labour intensive good rises and the capital intensive good falls.** From the answer to Q11.13 it follows that there is a one to one relationship between commodity prices and factor prices. Since commodity prices are set in the world market and are unaffected by the growth in the domestic labour force it follows that factor prices must also be unchanged. As factor prices have not altered, this in its turn means that production techniques in the two industries are the same. Given the original endowments of the economy $O_X \bar{K} O_Y \bar{L}$ is the production box of the economy in figure 11.15.

The production point is A and the slope of ray $O_X A$ shows factor proportions in the capital intensive good X and $O_Y A$ that in the labour intensive good Y. When the supply of labour to the economy is increased by $\bar{L} - \bar{L}'$ but the capital stock is unchanged, the dimensions of the box become $O_X \bar{K} O'_Y \bar{L}'$. Since factor prices are unchanged it follows that factor proportions in the two industries must stay the same. Production of X must therefore still take place along ray $O_X A$ since the X origin is unchanged. The Y production point will, however, lie along $O'_Y C$, parallel to $O_Y A$, so preserving factor proportions in Y. The only factor allocation satisfying both these conditions is at B. As B lies closer to the X origin than A it follows that output of the capital intensive good has fallen. On the other hand it is easily seen

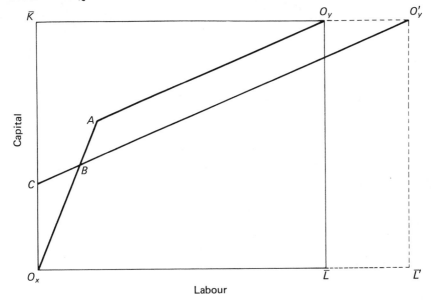

Figure 11.15

that $O'_Y B$ is longer than $O_Y A$ and so output of the labour intensive good rises. This is known as the Rybcynski Theorem.

A11.17(a) **Y is exported.** Full employment of labour requires

$$6X + 2Y = 50 \tag{1}$$

and of capital

$$4X + 2Y = 40 \qquad \cdot \tag{2}$$

Solving (1) and (2) yields production levels $X = 5$, $Y = 10$. As X and Y are consumed in equal proportions the economy exports Y.

(b) **UNCERTAIN.** The full employment equations now become

$$6X + 2Y = 50 \quad \text{(labour)} \tag{3}$$

$$4X + 2Y = 60 \quad \text{(capital)} \tag{4}$$

with solution $X = -5$, $Y = 40$. But a negative output of X is economic nonsense. Either (3) or (4) must hold as an inequality and production functions be of the fixed proportion variety. If this were

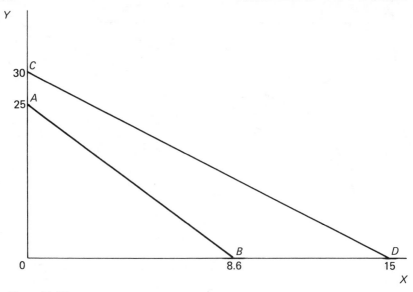

Figure 11.16

not so a zero price of the unemployed factor would induce sufficient substitution to make input coefficients consistent with full employment of both factors. Plotting (3) and (4) as AB and CD in figure 11.16, labour supply can be seen to be the binding constraint on the economy's production. The economy's production possibility frontier is therefore AB. Two equilibria are possible. If on the world market $PX/PY > 25/8.6$ then the economy will specialise in X production, import Y, achieve full employment of labour but have 25.6 units of capital unemployed (to produce 8.6 units of X requires 8.6×4 units of capital). Conversely, if $PX/PY < 25/8.6$, the economy will import X, still have full employment of labour but now have 10 units of capital unemployed.

PART II

12

'New' Theories of Consumer Behaviour

(A)(i) THE DEMAND FOR CHARACTERISTICS

Traditional economic theory regards the consumption of goods and services as an end in itself. Goods appear directly in the utility function of individuals because they are desired for themselves rather than for what they yield. However, in the 1960's an alternative and seemingly more realistic treatment emerged (Lancaster is usually credited as the pioneer of this approach). The general perspective of this 'new' view is that every good provides a complex bundle of characteristics or attributes. Consequently, market goods may be regarded as inter-mediate inputs in the 'production' of the more basic attributes in-dividuals really want. The demand for goods and services is therefore more properly considered as a derived demand. For example, the lamp on the table as we write yields light and decoration, both of which we regard as desirable characteristics. Other lamps that could have been bought also provide light and decoration, though in different proportions and at different cost. The 'new' theory of consumer behaviour is therefore able to provide a basis of comparison between obviously related goods which the traditional theory cannot do. It extends the theory of production into consumption decisions by enabling discussion of whether a particular pattern of goods con-sumption is 'efficient' in providing the characteristics upon which consumers' welfare actually depends.

To be explicit, suppose each good yields two characteristics, X and Y and the quantity of characteristics obtained is directly proportional to the amount of the good consumed. In other words doubling con-sumption of a good doubles the quantity of X and Y obtained. If all income were spent on good 1 the quantity purchased would provide the characteristic mix shown in figure 12.1 at (1). Now suppose all income is spent on a different good, 2. Each unit of this good yields more of characteristic Y relative to X than does good 1, and spending

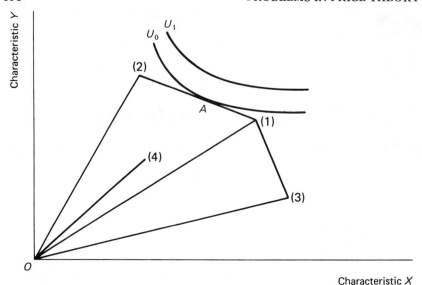

Figure 12.1

all income on good 2 yields characteristic mix (2). Points (1) and (2) are clearly feasible consumption points. However, by buying combinations of both goods other feasible consumption points are obtained. For example, if half of total income is spent on good 1 and half on good 2 the characteristic bundles obtained will be half way between (1) and (2) as shown by A. Other mixes of expenditure yield further points along the straight line connecting (1) and (2). (This is another example of the property of linear combinations demonstrated in Chapter 11, Q11.10.)

Now let there be a third good which yields characteristics combination (3). Points along the straight lines (1)-(3), (1)-(2) and (2)-(3) are now all feasible. However, since the lines (1)-(2) and (1)-(3) lie outside (2)-(3) they yield more of both characteristics than could be obtained by consuming goods 2 and 3 alone. Thus the consumption possibility frontier is (2)-(1)-(3). If a fourth good yielded point (4) then it can be seen that a combination of good 4 with any of the other three goods would lead to a characteristics mix inside (2)-(1)-(3) and hence good 4 would never be consumed. With the four goods shown here the consumption possibility frontier is (2)-(1)-(3) and with the preferences (defined over characteristics) drawn, utility is maximised at A. This involves spending half of total income on each of goods 1 and 2. Note that, however many goods are available, with only two characteristics desired the number of goods consumed will never exceed two. This result leads to the general conclusion that the number of goods consumed will never exceed the number of characteristics desired.

References

Becker Lecture 10. Laidler Chapter 10. Lancaster pp. 253-256. H. John Green pp. 156-165.
     The original Lancaster paper is 'A new approach to consumer theory' (*Journal of Political Economy*, April 1966) and a less technical version is 'Change and innovation in the technology of consumption' (*American Economic Review*, May 1966).

In the questions below, for simplicity it is assumed that all goods yield the same two characteristics in proportions which are fixed but differ between goods.

Questions

Q12.1 A housewife hardly varies her purchase of Cheshire cheese as its price rises. However, when its price exceeds a certain threshold she ceases to buy altogether and switches to some other type of cheese. Traditional consumer theory cannot explain this commonly observed behaviour; however, it fits into the characteristics approach without problem.

Q12.2 One advantage of the characteristics approach is dealing with the introduction of new goods when computing price indices. The following question attempts to bring this out. A man derives utility from two characteristics A and B. Every pound spent on good X yields one unit of A and one unit of B whilst a pound's worth of good Y provides half a unit of A and 4/3 units of B. He spends £4 on X and £6 on Y. A new good is then introduced costing £0.80 per unit and yielding 0.75 of A and 1.5 of B.

   (a) On the basis of this information what is the upper bound to the compensating variation associated with the introduction of the new good?
   (b) If the change in the man's real income is computed by deflating his money income by a conventionally computed Laspeyres price index what answer will be obtained?
   (c) What will be the change in his real income if a Paasche price index is used?

Q12.3 If all characteristics are normal then so must be the demand for all goods.

Answers

A12.1 TRUE — we think. Suppose Cheshire cheese yields two characteristics, carbohydrates and vitamins (both assumed to be desired).[1]
Other cheeses also provide these characteristics, though in different
proportions. In figure 12.2 points A, B and C show the characteristics
bundles obtained if a given sum is spent on Cheddar, Cheshire and
Lancashire cheese respectively. By dividing expenditure between
cheeses, any characteristic combination on the straight lines connecting the specialised consumption points A, B and C may be
achieved. Thus the individual's consumption possibility frontier in
terms of characteristics is ABC. Given the preferences shown, Cheddar
and Cheshire cheese are bought. Now suppose the price of Cheshire
rises. As it does the characteristics bundle obtained from the given
expenditure on Cheshire cheese falls. Suppose price rises so much
that when the given expenditure is spent on Cheshire the characteristic
bundle obtained is B'. This lies inside the straight line connecting A
and C. Thus the consumption possibility frontier becomes AC and
no Cheshire cheese will be consumed since to do so would involve
less of one or both characteristics being obtained as compared to

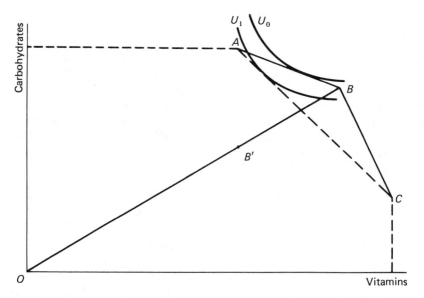

Figure 12.2

1. Of course carbohydrates and vitamins could be regarded as inputs into even
   more basic characteristics such as health.

other feasible consumption points generated by purchasing Lancashire and Cheddar only. The threshold price is that at which the Cheshire cheese ray terminates at the AC intersection and at this price it can be seen that a good deal of Cheshire is still bought. If there is a further price increase no Cheshire is bought at all.

In the conventional analysis a rise in the price of Cheshire may eventually cause purchase of it to suddenly cease if it were a perfect substitute for Cheddar. However, if this were so, whenever Cheshire is bought Cheddar never would be which violates the observed behaviour.

A12.2 (a) −£2.66. By initially spending £4 on X the man obtains 4 units of A and 4 of B and the £6 spent on Y buys $3A$ and $8B$. Thus his total consumption of characteristics is $7A$ and $12B$.

We know that with two characteristics the consumer need never buy more than two goods. Suppose he buys good X and the new good (call it Z) in quantities just sufficient to obtain his original combination of characteristics. To obtain $7A$ it follows that equation (1) must hold

$$X + 0.75Z = 7 \tag{1}$$

and to obtain $12B$ requires

$$X + 1.5Z = 12 \tag{2}$$

(1) and (2) solve to give $Z = 20/3$, $X = 2$. The cost of buying these quantities is $0.8(20/3) + 2 = £7.33$. Repeating the same procedure if Y and Z are bought, the quantities that must be purchased to obtain the original characteristics bundle must solve

$$0.5Y + 0.75Z = 7 \tag{3}$$

$$1.33Y + 1.5Z = 12 \tag{4}$$

The quantities which do this are $Y = -1/3$, $Z = 16/3$. But a negative consumption of Y is impossible. The closest to this solution is to buy no Y. Then 14 units of Z must be purchased to provide the $7A$ even though this yields more than enough B (21 units). The cost of $14Z$ is £11.20 which exceeds the cost if X and Z are bought. Thus the old level of welfare can definitely be replicated at a cost of £7.33 which is a saving of £2.66. So if the new good is introduced and income falls by £2.66 the individual cannot be worse off and this is the maximum compensating variation possible. Since the introduction of the new good will normally change the consumption pattern in terms of

characteristics, the compensating variation will actually be less than
− £2.66.

(b) The introduction of the new good may be treated as a reduction in its price from infinity to £0.80. A Laspeyres price index
weights prices by original consumption levels. Since none of the new
good was consumed originally and the prices of X and Y have not
changed the Laspeyres price index will not change. On this basis it
would be concluded that no change in real income has occurred.

(c) The Paasche index weights prices by current consumption
levels. Since the price of the new good was originally infinite the
Paasche index will show an infinite fall and real income a correspond-
ing infinite rise.

A12.3 **FALSE.** In figure 12.3 the initial characteristics frontier is
AB and the consumption point is C. Suppose a rise in income then
shifts the frontier to DE with the result that the consumption point
changes to F involving more of both characteristics. However, at F
consumption of the X_1 intensive good is unchanged (it is at the same
point on ray OB). Thus a new consumption point a little to the north-
west of F, involving consumption of more of both X_1 and X_2 than
at C, but less purchase of the X_1 intensive good, is quite feasible. (For
further reference see R.G. Lipsey and G. Rosenbluth. 'A contribution
to the new theory of demand: a rehabilitation of the Giffen good',
Canadian Journal of Economics, Vol. 4, No. 2, 1971.)

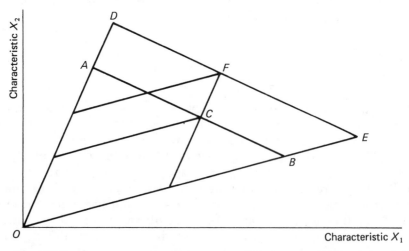

Figure 12.3

(A)(ii) PORTFOLIO CHOICE

The problem we shall be considering is how to invest a given sum of money. Many kinds of assets are available in the market and the investor's objective is to construct an investment portfolio which maximises his utility. What sorts of things should he look for in each asset? Other things equal the higher the expected return to an asset, the more desirable it will be. However, as we saw in Chapter 4 the more variable is the possible return the asset offers, i.e. the riskier it is, the less will it appeal to a risk averter. Broadly speaking then, each asset has two characteristics — expected rate of return and risk. Investors' utility depends on these two characteristics. The problem facing an investor deciding how to allocate a given wealth between different assets can therefore be regarded as an application of the Lancaster approach to consumer behaviour. Each 'good' (asset) offers two characteristics (risk and return) and the task is to choose the consumption pattern (the asset mix of the portfolio) to maximise utility which depends on these two characteristics. The budget constraint is the wealth available to be invested.

An initial problem is how to measure risk. The measure we shall use is the standard deviation. For the record this is found by taking each possible return the asset may yield, deducting from it the average return the asset offers, squaring the result, multiplying by the probability that this payoff will occur and summing this expression over all possible payoffs. Finally, the square root of the whole thing is taken. It is not very important that you are familiar with this measure, which written out like this certainly appears formidable. However, for those who are interested, relevant formal proofs are given in an appendix (p. 213).

Now does the standard deviation measure all aspects of risk which are relevant to an investor? There are two instances in which it definitely does: if all assets have a normal distribution of returns or if the investor's utility function is quadratic. In other cases the use of standard deviation only approximates the measure of risk that is relevant for the individual. However, we shall assume in what follows that the utility of a portfolio can be expressed in terms of its expected return and its standard deviation.

Let us now return to the asset holding strategy of an individual. In deciding whether to include an asset in a portfolio, the effects of its inclusion on the expected return and risk of the whole portfolio must be considered. Just because a particular asset, viewed on its own, is very risky does not mean it is not worth including in the portfolio. Holding the asset may actually reduce the risk of the portfolio since it may have high payoffs when the other assets do badly. Shares in ice-cream factories and umbrella factories may be individually risky but when combined in a single portfolio turn out to be rather safe since the risk of one tends to offset that of the other. Risk is therefore unlike the characteristics analysed in the Lancaster approach in so far as combining equal values of two assets does not necessarily yield a risk which is the mean of that of the two assets. Rather, since risks may be offsetting, the combined risk may be less than that of either asset. Thus we shall have to abandon the simple additive property of characteristics.

We shall analyse a world in which there is one safe asset (say money) and many kinds of risky asset. One rather remarkable result to be shown is that, as long as utility depends only on expected return and standard deviation, the ratio in which an individual will hold risky assets, one to another, will be independent of the particular form of his utility function. Thus different investors, so long as tax rates and transaction costs do not vary between them and if they form the same expectations concerning the riskiness of various assets, will hold the same ratio of the one risky asset to another, even though they may differ in the ratio in which they hold risky to safe assets.

References

The standard reference for economists on the material to be covered is J. Tobin, 'Liquidity preference as behaviour towards risk' (*Review of Economic Studies,* February 1958) and W. Sharpe, 'Capital asset prices: a theory of market equilibrium under conditions of risk' (*Journal of Finance,* September 1964). You may find the exposition in C. Goodhart, *Money, Information and Uncertainty,* (Macmillan) pp. 30–42 helpful and a fuller expository account is to be found in M. Bromwich, *The Economics of Capital Budgeting,* (Penguin).

Questions

Q12.4 Suppose I invest $100 in shares in an umbrella factory. If the year is rainy, profits are high and if I collect the dividends and sell the share I receive $150. But if it is sunny, profits are low and at the end of the year sale of the share and collection of dividends raises only $75. Were I to invest $100 in an ice-cream factory I make $50 if it is sunny and lose $25 if it rains. How much risk will I face if I invest $50 in each factory?

Q12.5 A man has £100 to invest. There are two assets available. The first is risky but has a high expected return. £100 invested in this asset yields the risk–return combination shown by point A in figure 12.4. The second asset is safer but has a lower expected return. Its

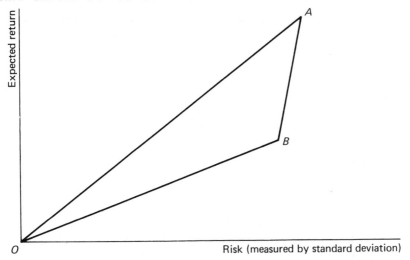

Figure 12.4

risk—return mix is shown by point *B*. Applying the simple characteristics approach the investor's consumption possibility frontier (or
henceforth risk—return frontier) is *AB*. What is the fallacy?

Q12.6 Now suppose one asset is cash which, in the absence of inflation, offers a zero rate of return with complete certainty. The
other asset is both risky and offers a positive expected rate of return.
Draw the consumption frontier for this case.

Q12.7 Draw the risk—return frontier if two risky assets and cash are
available.

Q12.8 Suppose the only characteristics of assets that matter to investors are their expected returns and their standard deviation.
Different investors have different preferences with respect to these
two characteristics but share the same views as to the actual risk and
expected return offered by any particular asset. Show that the ratio
in which different risky assets are held one to another will be the
same for different investors and only the ratio of cash to risky assets
as a whole will vary between them.

Q12.9 Local authority bonds offer a positive return, effectively with
no risk (at least in money terms; and although of course there is a
risk because the future rate of inflation is not known with certainty,
we ignore this). Construct the risk—return frontier if such an asset is
available.

206 PROBLEMS IN PRICE THEORY

Q12.10 Assume the only risk free asset is cash. Analyse the effect on an individual's demand for money of an equi-proportional increase in the return offered by all risky assets.

Q12.11 How would you test the theory of portfolio equilibrium outlined above?

Q12.12 Summarise the assumptions which if violated will invalidate the theory.

Answers

A12.4 **NONE.** There is no risk. When it is sunny I make $25 on the ice-cream factory and lose $12.50 on the umbrella factory giving a net return of $12.50. Rain earns me $25 on the umbrella factory and loses me $12.50 on the ice-cream factory. Whatever happens I earn $12.50. The important lesson is that if the risks of the two assets are at least in part offsetting, the combined risk will be less than the weighted sum of the risks of the assets considered individually.

A12.5 Connecting B to A by a straight line has the following implication: if £50 is invested in the first asset and £50 in the second, the total risk on the whole £100 so invested is the average of the risk associated with investing all £100 in the first asset and investing all £100 in the second asset. But as illustrated in the previous question, this is not necessarily the risk of the mixed portfolio. As long as the risk of the two assets is at least partly offsetting (see Appendix for proof that this simply requires the returns of the two assets to be perfectly positively correlated), the risk—return frontier available must be better than AB, as shown in figure 12.5, for example, as ACB.

The proof that ACB is smoothly concave to the straight line AB is as follows.[1] Consider any point on the frontier generated by mixing the two basic assets in some proportion. Regard the resulting mixed asset as a new composite asset. Do the same for a second point on the frontier. We know that the consumption possibility frontier for the two composite assets must lie to the left of the straight line joining them. Since the two composite assets have been 'manufactured' from the basic assets offered, the overall frontier must also lie to the left of this connecting line. Thus the frontier $A'B'$ in figure 12.6 is impossible since the frontier can never pass to the right of any straight line such as ED connecting two points on it.

---

1. Strictly speaking it is shown that the frontier is concave or a straight line. The straight line comes about if there is no offsetting risk between the two assets.

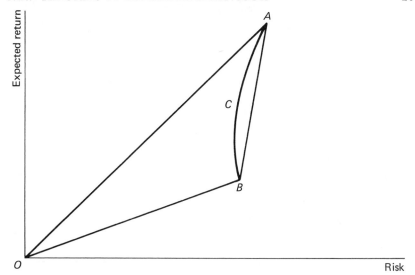

Figure 12.5

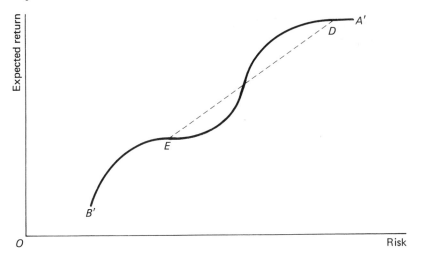

Figure 12.6

A12.6 £100 in cash would put the investor at the origin, O, in figure 12.7, and £100 in the other asset at point A. Now the return to cash is neither positively nor negatively correlated with the return to the other asset. If he puts half his portfolio in cash the investor gets exactly half the expected return and half the risk from putting it all in the other asset. The movements in the rate of return to each can never offset the movements in the rate of return to the other asset

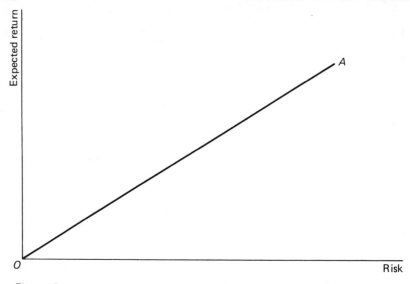

Figure 12.7

since the return to cash is always zero. Thus it is correct to construct the risk–return frontier by joining O and A by a straight line.

A12.7 In figure 12.8 *ADCB* is the risk–return frontier if just the two risky assets are available. Consider a point on it such as C. It is obtained by combining the two risky assets in a certain proportion. Suppose there was an asset which directly offered the risk–return mix at C. By combining this asset with cash all the points along OC become available. And since from the two basic assets a new asset

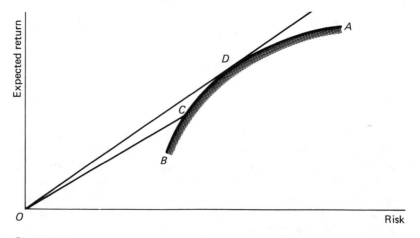

Figure 12.8

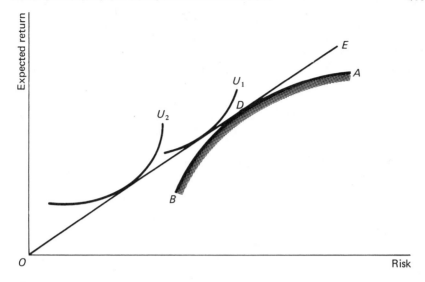

Figure 12.9

with the risk–return characteristics of C can in effect be manu-factured, points along OC are indeed available to the investor. Now the further to the north-west is the frontier, the better off is the investor. The best constraint is achieved by the ray through the origin which is just tangential to $ABCD$. The overall risk–return frontier is therefore ODA.

A12.8 Every investor faces the same investment risk frontier ODA (figure 12.9). U_1 and U_2 are the indifference curves of two investors. (Remember risk is a 'bad' and preferences increase to the north-west – note therefore the similarity with the income–work analysis where income is measured on the vertical axis and hours of work on the horizontal.) Investor 1 has a greater tolerance for risk than does investor 2, but both end up along OD. Any point on OD is achieved by taking the composite asset at D and splitting the total portfolio between this composite asset and cash. However, to find how the basic risky assets must be combined to yield the risk–return charac-teristics of D requires knowledge of the assets themselves but not of investors' preferences (this is known as a 'separation' theorem). The composite asset obtained at D is known as the market portfolio since all investors hold risky assets in the ratios implicit at D and for overall equilibrium the ratios of assets held at D must, of course, equal the ratio in which they are available in the market. If one of the consumers was enough of a risk-lover to be on the DA section of the constraint the theorem would, of course, fail (remember that to be on the DE extension of OD implies the investor holds negative

amounts of cash; this is possible only if he can issue IOU's on which
no interest is paid and this possibility is assumed away).

There is one other qualification to this analysis. Suppose there
exists an asset with exactly the same risk (standard deviation) as the
market portfolio. In market equilibrium the price of this asset would
adjust so as to offer the same expected return as does the market
portfolio. Investors would therefore be indifferent between holding
this asset or the market portfolio. The same kind of result holds if a
portfolio can be found different in composition from the market
portfolio but which offers the same risk. Under these circumstances
the efficiency frontier of risky assets is linear over part of its range
and all investors need not hold the same risky portfolio. However,
the initial assumption that one group of assets could have exactly
the same risk characteristics as another is implausible. Some risk is
always firm specific, for example the risk that a manager will em-
bezzle funds or perhaps die, and this means that if one asset is
dropped from a portfolio it is never possible to exactly preserve its
risk characteristics. However, with firms in the same industry the
pattern of returns will be rather similar (they will tend to belong to
a single risk class) and it may not matter much whether shares in
only one oil company are held rather than shares in all oil companies.
Nevertheless the pure theory does seem to suggest that full optimality
normally requires that all investors hold the same risky portfolio
(see Sharpe (1964) p. 435, footnote 19).

A12.9 The frontier in figure 12.10 is $OrDA$, where r is the rate of
return on local authority bonds.

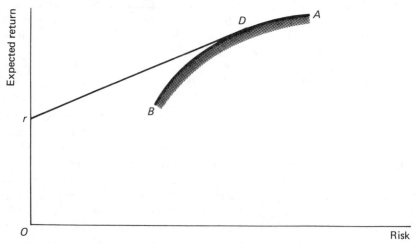

Figure 12.10

A12.10 Initially the consumer is at F in figure 12.11, holding FD/OD of his portfolio in cash. If the return to both assets increases by the same percentage the efficiency locus becomes $A'B'$ and the new consumption frontier is $OD'A'$. [To check that D' is vertically above D proceed as follows. Write the equation of AB as $r = Af(\sigma)$, where r is the expected rate of return and σ is a measure of risk. To find the level of risk at D requires solution of $d(r/\sigma)/d\sigma = 0$ the necessary condition for which is $\sigma f'(\sigma) - f(\sigma) = 0$ (1) and is independent of A. Thus if all assets increase their return by the same percentage then for a given risk, the return on the risky portfolio increases by the same percentage. In other words A rises, but this does not affect the σ which solves (1).] Moving from OD to OD' creates a substitution effect pushing the investor away from the origin and, assuming expected return is a normal good, an income effect which works in the same direction. Thus $F'D'/OD' < FD/OD$ and a lower proportion of the portfolio will be held in cash. However, it has been implicitly assumed that the size of the investor's portfolio remains the same when the rate of return changes. In fact if the investor was initially holding long dated securities and the rate of interest falls he will suffer a capital loss (this is the risk associated with such assets). So even if a higher proportion of the portfolio is held in cash, if the portfolio is of a smaller size this does not mean demand for cash will rise. (The distinction drawn here is between analysing the effects of there being a different rate of interest in the initial position and examining the effects of a change in the rate of interest, cf. Laidler p. 72–73.)

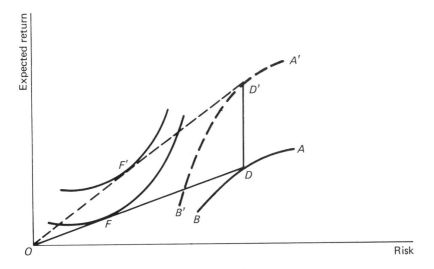

Figure 12.11

A12.11 The most striking prediction of the theory is the result derived in the answer to Q12.8 that all investors hold risky assets in the same ratio one to another. At first sight this prediction is sufficient to refute the theory. However, it should be remembered that by holding unit trusts (mutual funds) there may be a fair degree of uniformity in the ratio in which private investors hold risky assets.

It may also be shown that a further implication of the theory is that in overall market equilibrium the return offered by any particular asset depends on the degree to which it changes the riskiness of the market portfolio. In effect

$$r_i = a + bS_i \tag{1}$$

where r_i is the rate of return of asset i and S_i is the increase in the risk on the market portfolio generated by holding an extra pound in asset i. The coefficients a and b are the same for all assets. This means that the risk—return trade off is the same for all assets. To see why this is so, note that the market portfolio, being efficient, can be found by choosing the amounts of the various assets $A_1 \ldots A_n$ so as to maximise the expected return on the portfolio, subject to the given total value of the portfolio and that its standard deviation takes on some specified level $\bar{S}$.

Thus the Lagrangian is

$$L = \Sigma r_i A_i - a(\Sigma A_i - \bar{A}) - b[S(A_1 \ldots A_n) - \bar{S}]$$

where r_i is the expected return on asset i, $\bar{A}$ is the total value of the portfolio and a and b are Lagrangian multipliers. First order conditions for a maximum are then $r_i = a + b\partial S/\partial A_i$, as required. For the riskless asset $\partial S/\partial A_i = 0$, and so a is the return on the riskless asset.[1]

Seeing whether equation (1′) can be successfully fitted to all assets thus provides another test of the theory (there is a problem in doing this, however, if it has to be assumed that past returns and risk represent the anticipated values of these characteristics).

A12.12 (a) The only asset characteristics investors are concerned with are mean and standard deviation. Alternatively, although investors are concerned with additional characteristics, such as further

---

1. Measuring risk by standard deviation, a non-trivial amount of manipulation allows (1) to be written $r_i = r^* + (\bar{r}_m - r^*) \, \text{cov}(im)/\text{var} \, m$, where r^* is the return on the safe asset, $\bar{r}_m$ is the expected return on the market portfolio, cov (im) is the covariance between the returns if all funds are invested in the market portfolio and the returns if asset i is bought instead, and var m is the variance of the market portfolio. Whilst the above formula, or a variant of it, is frequently used by portfolio analysts, the simple derivation in the text is sufficient for our purpose, which is to show that the return to every asset must conform to the same linear equation.

risk parameters, these additional characteristics do not differ between assets.

(b) All investors have the same view of the riskiness and return of each asset.

(c) There are no fixed transaction costs involved in buying and selling assets. If there were, portfolio composition would depend in part on the wealth of the investor. Only the rich would find it worthwhile buying assets with high transaction costs.

(d) All investors face the same marginal tax rates. If not, some assets may be more attractive to some investors than others for reasons of tax saving. For example, capital gains may be more attractive than dividends for some investors as compared to others.

APPENDIX ON THE PROPERTIES OF THE PORTFOLIO STANDARD DEVIATION

Definitions

The probability that state of the world i will occur is P_i and if it does and the investor puts all his funds in asset X, he obtains a return of x_i. If there are n possible states of the world $\sum_{i=1}^{n} P_i = 1$, the expected return offered by the asset is $\sum_{i=1}^{n} P_i x_i = \bar{x}$. The variance of the returns is $V_x = \Sigma P_i (x_i - \bar{x})^2$ and the standard deviation $S_x = V_x^{\frac{1}{2}}$.

Theorem I
The standard deviation of a portfolio is less than the weighted sum of the standard deviations of the individual assets, where the weights are the shares of the assets in the total portfolio.

Proof
If an investor holds λ per cent of his funds in asset X and the remaining $(1 - \lambda)$ per cent in asset Y then his return, if state of the world i occurs, is $\lambda x_i + (1 - \lambda)y_i$. The variance of the whole portfolio is therefore

$$V_{x+y} = \Sigma_i P_i [\lambda x_i + (1 - \lambda)y_i - \lambda \bar{x} - (1 - \lambda)\bar{y}]^2$$

$$= \Sigma_i P_i [\lambda(x_i - \bar{x}) + (1 - \lambda)(y_i - \bar{y})]^2$$

$$= \lambda^2 \Sigma P_i (x_i - \bar{x})^2 + (1 - \lambda)^2 \Sigma_i P_i (y_i - \bar{y})^2$$
$$+ 2\lambda(1 - \lambda)\Sigma_i P_i (x_i - \bar{x})(y_i - \bar{y})$$

The correlation coefficient between x and y is defined as

$$r_{xy} \quad = \frac{\Sigma P_i(x_i - \bar{x})(y_i - \bar{y})}{[\Sigma P_i(x_i - \bar{x})^2 \Sigma P_i(y_i - \bar{y})^2]^{\frac{1}{2}}}$$

Thus

$$V_{x+y} = \lambda^2 V_x + (1 - \lambda)^2 V_y + 2\lambda(1 - \lambda)V_x^{\frac{1}{2}} V_y^{\frac{1}{2}} r_{xy} \qquad (1)$$

If the returns to the two assets are perfectly positively correlated $r_{xy} = 1$ and if they are perfectly negatively correlated (offsetting risk) $r_{xy} = -1$. We wish to show that the standard deviation of the whole portfolio is never more than the weighted sum of the standard deviations of the individual assets where the weights are the shares of the assets in the whole portfolio, that is that $V_{x+y}^{\frac{1}{2}} \leqslant \lambda V_x^{\frac{1}{2}} + (1 - \lambda)V_y^{\frac{1}{2}}$. Call the right hand side of this inequality W. The least promising case is if $r_{xy} = 1$. We shall show that in this instance $W = \lambda V_x^{\frac{1}{2}} + (1-\lambda)V_y^{\frac{1}{2}}$ does equal $S_{x+y} = V_{x+y}^{\frac{1}{2}} = [\lambda^2 V_x + (1-\lambda)^2 V_y + 2\lambda(1 - \lambda)V_x^{\frac{1}{2}}V_y^{\frac{1}{2}}]^{\frac{1}{2}}$. This is easily done by noting from (1) that when $r_{xy} = 1$, $W^2 = V_{x+y}$. Hence $W = S_{x+y}$ when $r_{xy} = 1$. If $r_{xy} < 1$ it follows from (1) that V_{x+y} must fall and so the mixed portfolio is less risky than linear combinations of the individual assets. This is the basis of the result that the efficiency frontier is dome shaped.

Theorem II
If asset Y is cash then the standard deviation of the whole portfolio is proportional to the fraction of it which is held in the risky asset, X.

Proof

This is obvious from (1). If $S_y = V_y = 0$, then $V_{x+y} = \lambda^2 V_x$ so $V_{x+y}^{\frac{1}{2}} = S_{x+y} = \lambda S_x$.

(B) THE ALLOCATION OF TIME

The standard theory of the consumer considers income as the only limiting factor on the individual's choice. However, equally important is the fact that consumption takes time, which is also in limited supply. In fact, all activities, whether they be paid employment, housework, or leisure pursuits require time as an input. Orthodox theory is strangely schizophrenic in recognising this. Whilst the opportunity cost of time spent in paid work is treated as leisure time forgone, the fact that different consumption activities require different inputs of time as well as money is not explicitly recognised. Hence the influence of time on consumption choice is ignored. A further apparent omission in the standard analysis is that all time not spent in paid employment is treated as leisure time. In reality it may be devoted to home production, that is to creating outputs which could be bought in the market but which are instead 'produced' domestically (e.g. cooking at home rather than going to a restaurant).

Becker's analysis allows us to add time as a further constraint on individual choice along with non-labour income and the wage rate. The crucial point about time is that it is always strictly limited in any one day and its availability does not rise with economic growth as does non-labour income and the wage rate.

To allocate time amongst competing ends requires knowledge of its value in alternative uses. When an individual works in the labour market the cost of time is usually taken as the net of tax wage rate. This measure is only correct to the extent the individual is free to vary his hours of paid employment. However, granted this assumption, the wage rate does provide a useful measure of the opportunity cost of time, so that an indication can be obtained of the cost of activities such as cooking a meal or travelling to work. As different activities involve different mixes of the two inputs time and goods, any rise in the wage rate will tend to alter the relative prices of different activities. In the conventional analysis a rise in the wage rate simply leads to a substitution effect tending to reduce hours spent on non-market activities and an income effect tending to increase them. The Becker approach incorporates substitution effects away from time-intensive commodities or activities in general and an income effect which may or may not favour them. On this view, substitution effects tend to increase market work and income effects are ambiguous.

As an application of this analysis, note that since time is in fixed supply, material progress tends to be associated with a rise in the relative cost of time and therefore of time-intensive consumption activities. This in turn creates a substitution effect reducing the consumption of time-intensive activities. It would therefore be quite wrong to conclude that such activities are inferior, even though consumption of them may fall as real wages rise. Conversely, the rapid growth of fast food outlets, particularly in the US, should not be taken to mean that such establishments provide 'luxury' goods, despite it being affluence that has fostered their growth.

Further, the decision of whether or not to enter the labour market will depend upon the productivity of time spent in non-market activities as opposed to time spent in the market. People who do not work in the market do not necessarily have a strong preference for leisure but may allocate their time in this way because their productivity in non-market activities exceeds that in the market. For example, the total resource cost of producing a meal at home may be less than that of buying it in the market if an individual is more productive at cooking than at a labour market activity. To illustrate, suppose a woman can earn £0.50 an hour and a meal costs £2 to buy in a restaurant and takes an hour to eat. The total time-inclusive cost of buying the meal in the market is therefore £2.50. Suppose also that the cost of the food and other non-time inputs required to produce the meal at home is £1.50, and it takes ¾ of an hour to prepare and an hour to eat, so the total cost at home is £2.375. Thus the woman should produce the meal at home. However, if the wage rate were to double then she should stop cooking and increase hours of work.[1]

As the wage rate and hence the price of time rises so we would expect to observe individuals not only substituting away from time-intensive consumption activities, but also substituting away from time as a productive input into a particular activity and towards goods. Thus, as the female wage rate has increased the extent to which various kinds of household equipment have been substituted for time has risen. This analytical perspective also implies that any change in the price of non-time inputs used in the production of home commodities will affect the number of hours an individual is willing to supply to the labour market. Alterations in the productivity of individuals employed in the home will have similar effects. The relationship between the hours supplied to the labour market and the wage rate will therefore not be independent of the price or efficiency of goods such as washing machines and power drills.

To summarise, the Lancaster approach treated goods as yielding a variety of characteristics upon which utility depends. It could therefore be regarded as an extension of production theory into the sphere of consumption. The in many ways parallel analysis of Becker analyses the production of each attribute as requiring a variety of inputs, notably market goods and time. Thus the final consumption activity of eating uses as inputs food and the time involved in eating

---

1. It has been implicitly assumed here that the consumption value of the meal is the same wherever produced, and the disutility involved in homework is the same as that in market work. These assumptions are not important in so far as our main concern will be in predicting the direction of the effects of changes in wage rates.

and in preparing the food or travelling to a restaurant. Becker therefore has a theory involving multiple inputs producing single outputs and Lancaster a theory of single inputs yielding joint (multiple) outputs. The two approaches could clearly be combined, but here we concentrate on the Becker approach. The new approach allows us to explain differences in behaviour by looking at the factors which influence both the choice of technology used in the 'production' of final consumption activities and the demand for these various activities. It eschews, as far as possible, reliance on differences in tastes as an explanation of behaviour.

References

The original Becker paper is 'A theory of the allocation of time' (*Economic Journal*, September 1965). An updated and somewhat simpler exposition is R.T. Michael and Becker 'On the new theory of consumer behaviour' *(Swedish Journal of Economics*, 75, No. 4, 1973). Both the above are reprinted in Becker's *The Economic Approach to Human Behaviour* (University of Chicago Press 1976). Also worth looking at is R. Gronau 'Leisure, home production and work — the theory of the allocation of time revisited' *(Journal of Political Economy* 1977). In Becker's *Economic Theory* the allocation of time is dealt with in lectures 10, 33 and 34.

Questions

Q12.13 If it were observed that those in highly paid jobs work much longer hours than those in poorly paid jobs this would suggest that time devoted to recreation is an inferior commodity.

Q12.14 As higher paid people engage in more wasteful 'convenience' consumption than the poor it must therefore be the case that the demand for such 'convenience' goods is normal.

Q12.15 Since rich people on average tend to travel by rail while the poor travel by motor-bus it follows that the latter is an inferior good.

Q12.16 A rise in the price of tickets for the theatre will increase the number of hours an individual is willing to work.

Q12.17 If the government were to raise income tax together with excise taxes on goods used in time-intensive activities whilst also lowering taxes on other goods so that real income remained unchanged, it is quite possible that the number of hours worked would remain unchanged.

Q12.18 As compared to golf courses, squash courts are relatively busier during the week than at weekends. This is because preferences are different at the weekends.

Q12.19 Shops are open later at night in bedsit (rooming house) areas than in suburbia. This is because late night labour is cheaper and more available in bedsit areas.

Q12.20 The traditional analysis of work—leisure choice implicitly assumes that an individual's productivity in the home is always below that in the market place.

Q12.21 Suppose an individual derives utility from consumption of goods and leisure time. The only difference from the traditional analysis is that goods may be obtained by home production as well as by spending wage income. If goods produced in the home and goods purchased in the market are perfect substitutes then a rise in the wage rate must reduce the amount of time spent working in the home.

Q12.22 If goods produced in the home and in the market are perfect substitutes then a rise in the wage rate which increases hours of leisure must reduce the number of hours spent working in the market.

Q12.23 Let there be a rise in productivity in the home such that any given period of time spent in home production now yields 10% more output than before. Whether time spent in home production rises depends on income and substitution effects.

Q12.24 If an individual is engaged in both home and market work and leisure is a normal good, an increase in income derived from financial assets will reduce his market work but will have no effect on the amount of time spent in home production.

Q12.25 Traditional theory does not allow us to derive the result that chicken and motor cars are unlikely to be close substitutes. However, once one allows purchased goods to be inputs into more basic commodities, it is possible to make predictions about the likely cross-price elasticities between various inputs.

Q12.26 Poor people typically hold smaller stocks of food relative to their daily consumption than do the rich. This must be because the poor have less favourable access to capital markets and so have greater difficulty financing stockholding.

Answers

A12.13 **FALSE.** Conventional analysis suggests the answer is true. However, it is quite consistent that as the wage rises hours of market work increase *and* so does recreation time. Suppose, for example, that a cleaner can be hired at £2 per hour. If the net of tax wage rate of a householder is below £2 per hour the cleaner is clearly not worth hiring but will become so if the householder earns more than this. Thus, if the net of tax wage rises from £1 to £4 per hour the householder by putting in an extra ½ hour at work can reduce the time he spends cleaning by 1 hour. Hence his recreation time can be increased even as his market work rises. Clearly, the availability of various kinds of labour-saving consumer durables and non-durables which can be substituted for hours of homework will have similar effects.

It should be noted that an alternative explanation of why high wages could be associated with longer hours of work is that employers make all or nothing offers. But Q2.9 in Chapter 2 indicated that even then there will be incentives for employers to choose the working hours employees prefer. Nor is it clear why employers should desire longer hours for the higher paid worker than the lower. Alternatively, it is possible that since well paid jobs are more enjoyable than poorly paid jobs this is why hours of work at them are longer.

A12.14 **FALSE.** As people with high wages can sell their time at a relatively higher price than those with low wages it follows that time for them is much more expensive. Since it takes time to engage in any activity we should find that an activity requiring both time and goods as inputs is more expensive for the rich than the poor. If this hypothesis is correct, we should observe the rich trying to save on time by buying pre-cooked meals or eating in restaurants. Thus such 'wasteful spending' could be a direct result of higher priced time, and need not imply that the pure income elasticity of demand for such goods is positive.

A12.15 **FALSE.** A commodity is inferior if, and only if, given its relative price, the quantity consumed declines as income increases. The mode of transport is only one input into the commodity called travel. There is also an input of time which, as we have already seen, will in general have a non-zero price. Thus, if it takes longer to travel any given distance by bus than by train, the time cost of the former will be greater. The effective price of travelling by the two modes will differ with income level in so far as the price of time rises with income. Given the possibility that it is cheaper for the rich to travel by train when both aspects of the total (time inclusive) price are

taken into account, nothing can be said about the relationship between travel mode and income unless this price variation has been
allowed for.

A12.16 **FALSE.** By now it must be clear that one can identify two
basic inputs into the production of any one commodity. For instance,
the commodity called 'watching a play' requires as input a theatre
ticket, which costs say $3, and three hours of time, whilst the
commodity 'eating a meal' may absorb $6 of food and one hour of
time. So we can say that watching a play is relatively time-intensive
whilst eating a meal is relatively goods-intensive. Now if the price of
theatre tickets rises one would expect an individual to substitute in
favour of other commodities. But given the level of his real income,
and the fact that he will tend to be substituting in favour of less time-
intensive commodities, the only way that his consumption of these
commodities can increase is if he expands the amount of work in the
market. Thus, a rise in the price of goods which are used in the
production of time-intensive commodities could lead to an increase
in labour market activity. Such a substitution effect would be
reinforced if we take into account the fall in real income, always
assuming that time-intensive commodities are not inferior. In using
the traditional analysis we would have to approach this problem via a
rise in the price of theatre tickets leading to a fall in the real wage
rate with a consequent income and single substitution effect with no
way of identifying the kind of good for which price changes will have
the most effect on hours of work. The advantage of an analysis
involving the time intensity of consumption is that it does enable
something to be said about the kind of price change which will have
the greatest impact on market working time.

A12.17 **TRUE.** The answer to this question is a direct application
of the result suggested by the last answer. A rise in income tax reduces the opportunity cost of time, which lowers the relative price of
time-intensive commodities. Offsetting this effect is the rise in the
relative price of time-intensive commodities which results from the
excise taxes on the goods used intensively in their production. Hence
if the prices of various inputs are adjusted so as to leave the relative
price unaltered then as far as substitution effects are concerned,
there will not be any incentive to adjust consumption mix. Thus a
rise in income tax accompanied by compensating changes in commodity taxes need not lead to any change in the amount of work
undertaken in the market place.

A12.18 **FALSE.** The opportunity cost of time varies through the week. On working days wage income is forgone or important home production must be left undone if recreation is to be increased by an hour. At the weekend, with no market work taking up the day, the opportunity cost of time is much lower. Golf is a very time-intensive game and squash much less so. It is therefore to be expected that the demand for squash will be relatively greater during the working week when the opportunity cost of time is higher.

A12.19 **FALSE.** An obvious alternative explanation is as follows. Bedsit areas are dominated by single person households. For them the opportunity cost of shopping during normal working hours is high since to shop at such times means wage income may be lost and/or promotion prospects damaged. Thus in bedsit land there will be a large number of people prepared to pay more for late-night opening. In suburbia it is typically the case that the wife is at home throughout the day and the opportunity cost of her time is actually lower then than outside the normal working day when the rest of the family is around. Thus in suburbia most of the shopping demand will be during the day and there will be relatively few people prepared to pay more for late-night opening.

A12.20 **TRUE.** This must be the case because the traditional analysis assumes that people are utility maximisers and does not appear to suggest that they spend any time in home production. The latter can only follow if the wage rate always exceeds the productivity of time in home production.

A diagrammatic presentation of the market work versus home work versus leisure decision is sometimes helpful. Figure 12.12 is based on Gronau, 'Leisure, home production and work — the theory of the allocation of time revisited' (*Journal of Political Economy*, December 1977). *OT* is the total time available. Leisure time is measured from the origin *O* and time spent in home production from origin *T*. The difference between the two is time devoted to market work. The total quantity of commodities consumed is measured along the vertical axis. For simplicity it is assumed that goods produced at home or purchased in the market are perfect substitutes. The transformation curve *TZX* shows the quantity of goods obtained from a given number of hours spent in home production. Thus with *TN* hours in home production, *OG* goods are produced. Being concave to the origin the curve exhibits diminishing marginal productivity. In addition to home production, goods can be obtained by market

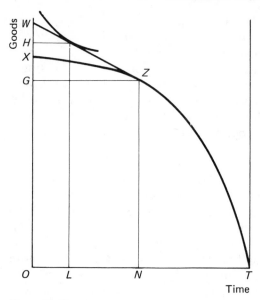

Figure 12.12

work. Thus if LN hours are devoted to market work, HG additional goods are obtained. If the wage rate is constant so is the market trade-off between goods and leisure time. Efficiency in goods production requires that time is devoted to household production until its marginal productivity there falls to that in market work. Beyond this point goods production is undertaken by working in the market. In the diagram the point at which market work takes over is where the slope of the home production transformation curve equals the constant slope of the market work transformation curve (i.e. the wage rate) and occurs at Z. Thus the overall 'efficient' transformation curve is WZT. The individual's utility depends on his consumption of goods and services. With the preferences shown, optimality involves OL hours of leisure, LN hours of market work and NT hours of home production. So under normal circumstances we shall have tangency at a point like Z with time allocated to home and market work as described. But in the traditional analysis tangency is implicitly at the point T, with no distinction between home work and leisure.

A12.21 TRUE. As can be seen from figure 12.13, with a higher wage the equality between the marginal productivity of time in home and market production occurs with less time devoted to home production. The rise in the wage reduces time spent devoted to home production from TN to TN'.

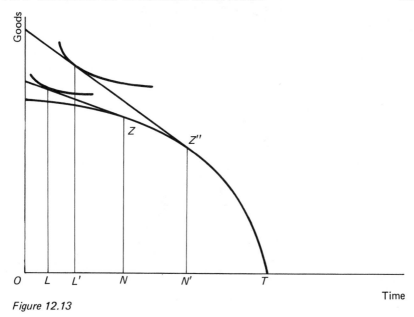

Figure 12.13

A12.22 **FALSE.** From figure 12.13 it is seen that time spent in home production falls. With the rise in the wage rate the opportunity cost of leisure has increased so the substitution effect works towards less leisure. On the other hand the increase in real income will tend to result in more leisure being taken. In figure 12.13 on balance more leisure is taken, but hours of work have also increased from LN to $L'N'$ because of the fall in home production. Thus this analysis suggests the market labour supply curve is much more likely to be positively sloped than does the standard model in which, whenever leisure rises, hours of work fall.

A12.23 **FALSE.** In figure 12.14, AT is the original transformation curve which when shifted upwards by 10% for every level of time input becomes BT. It can be seen that the point of tangency between the wage line and the transformation curve shifts to the left. Thus as long as the individual continues to work in the market, time devoted to home production rises by $N_1 - N_2$ whatever his preferences.

A12.24 **TRUE.** The effect of an increase in non-labour income is to increase the quantity of goods that can be consumed for any given level of time input. Thus in figure 12.15 the goods available at all levels of time input increase by OX_0. So without doing any work whatsoever the individual has a consumption possibility of OX_0.

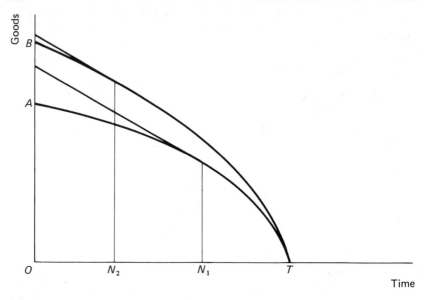

Figure 12.14

Hence any transformation of time into goods will start from a base of OX_0 rather than zero. However, the increase in income has no effect on the production possibilities, which means that the shape of the transformation curve does not change. As the wage rate is also unchanged the new point of tangency will be at a point directly above the old. Thus, so long as the individual spends some time in the market the amount of time used in home production will remain at NT. Only if the individual drops out of the market would home production time be diminished. Since leisure is a normal good, time spent in the labour market will be reduced from L_1N to L_2N, as leisure increases from OL_1 to OL_2.

A12.25 **TRUE.** Let the basic commodity Z_i be produced using the inputs X_i and Y_i. As the share of X_i in the total cost of Z_i must be less than one, a 10% rise in the price of X_i will lead to a less than 10% rise in the cost of Z_i. The cost of input X_i relative to Y_i will therefore have risen by a greater percentage than the cost of Z_i relative to final commodity Z_j which uses as inputs X_j and Y_j. Given that the substitution possibilities in production are similar to those in consumption, it must follow that the change in price of X_i will have a smaller impact on the demand for X_j used in the production of Z_j than on the demand for Y_i. Thus if Z_i is a meal and Z_j a journey we can say that the cross-price elasticity between

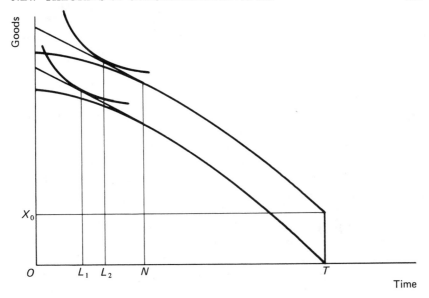

Figure 12.15

chicken (X_i) and ham (Y_i) will be greater than the elasticity between chicken (X_i) and motor cars (X_j).

A12.26 **FALSE.** The advantage of holding large stocks is that shopping trips need be less frequent. A major cost of such trips is the time they involve, and time is generally more valuable for the rich. It follows that the rich have greater incentives to hold stocks and so economise on shopping trips even if they can borrow and lend at the same interest rate as the poor.

(C) FAMILY DECISION MAKING

Economic theory has generally analysed the consumption and labour supply decisions of individuals in isolation from the family unit to which the majority of people belong. This deprives us of a number of interesting insights. The purpose of this section is to consider the influence of the family on the behaviour of its members.

Sociologists typically view the family as a complicated network of interpersonal relations. However, it is not clear that any testable propositions emerge from this approach. In contrast, the most straight-forward economic model focuses on the differences in comparative advantage between the various family members. For example, because

of the pattern of relative wages in the labour market it has certainly
been true in the past that men had a comparative advantage in market
work and women in home work. If the wife went out to work and the
husband stayed at home, the family would have fewer of both types
of good. A Pareto efficient allocation of activities, as always, permits
every family member to be better off, and our hypothesis is that the
family will behave in a Pareto optimal fashion. Hence as the market
opportunities available to women improve, so their traditional role
as housewives will tend to change. Furthermore, the advantage to
marriage will fall, for if men and women face similar opportunities in
the home and in the market, then there is a smaller gain from the one
specialising in home work in exchange for the receipt of market goods
from the other. Thus as the wages of women rise relative to those of
men, so we would expect to see the marriage rate decline.

The above analysis is based simply on the proposition that families
will select Pareto optimal alternatives. However, it does not answer
such questions as to how much market and home work the family
will engage in, merely who will do which type of activity. To enable
investigation of wider issues, it would be useful if the family could be
treated as if it behaved according to a single transitive utility function.
Most economists have found this a dubious assumption, probably
basing this view on analysis of the type employed by Samuelson.[1]
However, Gary Becker has provided an ingenious if controversial
rationale for the single utility function assumption. Suppose there
exists a 'head' of the family in a sense to be subsequently defined.
The head cares for the welfare of all family members. His or her
utility function may therefore depend, amongst other things, on the
amount of leisure he has, the quantity of goods the family enjoys in
common, the quantity of goods that he alone consumes, and the
welfare of each of the other family members. Their welfare depends
in turn on their own leisure and consumption levels. The constraints
facing the family are the rates at which the leisure hours of the
various family members can be transformed into the different kinds
of home produced goods and into money income and how money
income can be spent to provide the goods desired by the different
family members. Given all these constraints there will be some allocation of the time of the different family members and expenditure
pattern of money income that maximises the utility of the head.
However, why should this describe how the family will actually behave? The reason, as will be shown, is that the head is taken to be
the person who makes net transfers of resources to all the other
family members.

1. 'Social indifference curves' (*Quarterly Journal of Economics*, February 1956.)

Let us for simplicity suppose the transfer is in terms of purchasing power over market goods and services (though it need not be). Assume a family activity allocation is established which maximises the head's utility and one of the family members, say the son, has the opportunity to engage in an action which raises his income by the equivalent of £5 and reduces the head's by £8. Now, the head would have initially been transferring income to the son such that the marginal utility from his own consumption equals the marginal utility the head enjoys from the son's consumption. When the son's income rises by £5 and his own falls by £8, the head would find that his marginal utility from his own consumption would be higher and that from his son's consumption be lower than previously. Thus the head would transfer fewer pounds to the son. How much less would the son receive? Well, if transfers were cut by £5 then the income of the son would be the same but that of the head be lower than before. The marginal utility of the head's consumption would therefore exceed the son's and so the head would cut transfers by even more than £5. Consequently, by taking the specified action, the son ends up worse off than before and so has no incentive to behave in this fashion. It follows that if the family has a head who cares about the welfare of the other family members who receive net resource transfers from the head, then the family will behave according to the head's consistent utility function. Becker calls this the 'rotten kid' theorem. The basic assumption of this analysis is that each family has a head or central figure who cares about other members. There is no need to think of the head in the sense of a Victorian patriarch who imposes his wishes on other members. In fact all members can potentially act independently of the wishes of the head, but as it turns out only at a cost to themselves. Indeed, family members linked by a head have an incentive to act in the interests of all, even if they have no direct interest in each other. The 'rotten kid' theorem is important because it allows the family to be treated as if it behaved according to a single consistent and transitive utility function.

References

The approach taken here was pioneered by Gary Becker, particularly in 'A theory of social interactions' (*Journal of Political Economy*, 82, No. 6, 1974); 'Altruism, egoism, and genetic fitness: economics and sociobiology' (*Journal of Economic Literature*, September 1976) and 'A theory of marriage: the economics of the family' (*Journal of Political Economy*, 81, No. 4, 1973). All the above and other relevant papers are reprinted in G. Becker, *The Economic Approach to Human Behaviour* (University of Chicago Press 1976).

Questions

Q.12.27 An increase in the wage of women relative to that of men will increase the divorce rate.

Q12.28 An increase in the wage of women relative to that of men will tend to increase the number of hours wives work in the market and reduce the number of hours men work in the market.

Q12.29 The behaviour reported in Q12.28 implies that wives are worse off when their wage rises.

Q12.30 The participation rate (per cent of the population seeking paid employment) of both old and young men has shown a continuous decline through time. Over the same period the participation rate of women has risen along with average family income. This must imply that the consumption of leisure by married women is an inferior good to the family unit whilst that of men is a luxury.

Q12.31 The extent to which different family members participate in home production depends only on the relative market wage of the various family members.

Q12.32 Suppose as a result of improved education the productivity of women rises by the same percentage both in the market place and in the home. There will in consequence be no change in the division of labour within the household, but both members are now likely to supply fewer hours of market labour.

Q12.33 Men with working wives are more likely to have positively sloped labour supply functions than those whose wives spend all of their time in the home.

Q12.34 The reduction in the number of children per family and the increase in the demand for nursery education is a direct result of the rise in the absolute wage rate of women employed in the labour market.

Q12.35 Farm families are larger than city families because of the invigorating effect of country air.

Q12.36 The harder it is to divorce a spouse and the greater the penalties for doing so, the lower will be the proportion of the population married at any one time.

Q12.37 People who have a particular preference for good food and housing are, other things equal, more likely to marry or live together.

Answers

A12.27 **TRUE** — or at least the present analysis suggests that this is likely to happen. Marriage could be viewed, at least in part, as an exchange of market goods, in the production of which the husband has a comparative advantage, for household production in which the wife has a comparative advantage. The gains from this exchange are shared between the two partners. When the wife's wage rises, the difference in comparative advantage narrows and so therefore do the potential gains from exchange. Thus the tendency is for marriages to dissolve as the mutual benefits they yield fall.

A12.28 **TRUE.** An increase in the wage of women will make the family better off (at least if the wife goes out to work before or after the rise). This income effect will tend to reduce the hours of work of all family members. However, the increase in the wage of women will have a substitution effect, increasing their hours of market work and this effect will not be present for other family members.

A12.29 **FALSE.** With a caring 'head' the increase in the family's welfare will be shared out amongst all its members. If women work longer hours in the market they will enjoy a reduction in home work, or an increase in market goods, or some other 'reward'.

A12.30 **FALSE.** As the family becomes better off then, other things equal, we should expect all family members to reduce their hours of work. In the case of the young and old who both typically earn low wages and so their market work yields less benefits to the family unit, this may involve dropping out of the labour market altogether. For the young, this effect is reinforced to the extent that the return to education has increased. As for women, the rise in their real wage rate will induce a substitution effect in favour of their market participation, their home work in part perhaps being replaced by that of the young and old. So the observations in the question can certainly be rationalised by the substitution effects of a rise in the women's wage rate, perhaps reinforced by income effects on young and old men's participation rates, but without recourse to the assumption that the leisure of women is inferior to the family unit.

A12.31 **FALSE.** The wage rate which can be earned by family members only provides information about the productivity of each member in the market place. This wage rate represents the opportunity cost of using the family member in the home but it does not provide any information about productivity in the home. To decide who does what, the opportunity cost in terms of forgone market earnings of an individual must be compared to his or her productivity in the home. For instance, even though a wife could earn twice as much as a husband in the market she will not seek employment if her productivity in the home is three times that of the husband.

A12.32 **TRUE.** If the only change was an increase in the wife's market wage then we would observe substitution away from her time in the production of home commodities. However, as her productivity in the home has increased by the same percentage as the wage, the per unit opportunity cost of the goods that she produces in the home remains the same. Thus there will be no change in the activity allocation of the family. But as family income has risen, we will expect to observe an increase in the consumption of all normal goods including leisure, and this will reduce work hours of all kinds. So although both family members would work less, the wife would tend to undertake the same proportion of housework.

A12.33 **TRUE.** An increase in the wage rate of men increases the comparative advantage of the husband in market activities. This induces a substitution effect tending to increase the husband's market work. In the case of a husband with a wife who also works in the market the substitution effect can work in two ways. Firstly, market goods will be substituted for the husband's leisure. But it also becomes efficient to substitute the husband's home work by that of the wife, who will consequently reduce the number of hours she supplies to the market. This latter substitution effect is absent if the wife does not engage in market work.

A12.34 **TRUE.** At least on the basis of the simple theory explored here. It seems reasonable to assume that the primary input into the production of children is the wife's time. So as the wage rate of women has risen, the cost of children has increased. This will encourage both a substitution effect away from having children and a reduction in the input of 'mother time' per child. The means by which the latter can be reduced is by the purchase of more market inputs, such as nursery services.

A12.35 **POSSIBLY.** But the economic approach concentrates on the differences in the costs and benefits of having children in the two locations. Firstly, it is probably cheaper to bring up children on the farm since the cost of accommodation and play space is much lower, as is the cost of food. On the other hand the benefits of children tend to be higher on the farm since they can provide useful labour which city children cannot to the same extent. Also, it may be relevant to note that transport costs may make consumption activities other than having children relatively more expensive on the farm. The larger farm families should not therefore be surprising.

A12.36 **UNCERTAIN.** The proposition in the question certainly could be true since the greater the difficulty of breaking up a marriage that proves unsuccessful, the longer we should expect individuals to spend searching for the right spouse, and this effect tends to reduce the proportion of the population that is married. On the other hand, once a marriage is entered into it is much more difficult to break up and since the partners have been more carefully selected there will be less desire to dissolve it. This clearly increases the proportion of married people.

A12.37 **TRUE.** In so far as there are economies of scale in preparing food and in the use of living accommodation, this suggests that the incentive for such people to marry, or live together, and so enjoy economies in the provision of what are in effect public goods for the family, is relatively great. Of course the most obvious public good involved in marriage, and one which requires joint inputs of partners' time, is procreation. The jointness of the inputs into this long lived non-market good probably explains why the relatively indissoluble marriage contract is so popular. Since women engaged in child rearing normally forego labour market investment opportunities, this may also explain the attractiveness of a contract which at least partially specifies financial provisions should the relationship break up.

13

Searching for the 'Best' Price

Introduction

In very few markets do all transactions take place at the same price. Examples are ready to hand in everyday experience. Housewives prepared to shop around can often find significant price differences both for food and consumer durables. The buyer of a new car may be able to negotiate a different price from every dealer he approaches. Similarly, not all firms pay the same wage rate for jobs requiring the same skills.

The fact of such price dispersion raises a problem for the textbook model of the market in which all goods of a single type are sold at an identical price. Examination of how consumers, workers and firms behave in the presence of price dispersion may provide clues as to whether in the long run markets adjust to equilibrium with a single price. At all events economic theory cannot ignore the presence of price dispersion. In the text of this chapter, optimal consumer behaviour in the presence of price dispersion is outlined. Questions follow and then the model is adapted to explain labour market search. Some of the implications of the analysis explored in the text and subsequent questions include rationales of the short- and long-run Phillips curve and a discussion of the effects of incomes policy on unemployment.

Reasons for Price Dispersion

The most obvious explanation of price dispersion is that the goods and services traded are not really homogeneous. A grocery store selling outside usual business hours is offering a service its competitors do not, even if its produce is physically identical. The same is true of a hi-fi shop providing a particularly good after-sales service. In the labour market, many grades of skill exist each of which is rewarded

232

with a different wage rate. In all these cases, like is not being compared with like. Perhaps much of what superficially passes for price dispersion can on closer examination be explained by such considerations.

Another possible rationale of price dispersion occurs in a product market in which a monopoly is able and willing to practise price discrimination. This, by definition, gives rise to price dispersion since different groups of customers pay different prices. Whilst the foregoing reasons for price dispersion are of interest in their own right, they are not the subject of this chapter. Here we are specifically concerned with the role of information and the costs of its acquisition.

(A) PRODUCT MARKET SEARCH

The first step in the analysis is to build a model which will describe how individuals faced by price dispersion decide how much information to acquire before buying. It is assumed that the consumer has some prior knowledge. Specifically, he knows how many shops are selling at each price, but does not know the price charged by any particular shop. In other words, he has information about the distribution of prices across all shops but no information about which shop charges which price. Search will take place if he wishes to find out the prices charged by specific shops.

To search requires time and probably transport, both of which are costly. As more and more shops are visited so the lowest price found will tend to fall (it cannot rise). Once having entered the market, the problem for the individual is to decide how much information to acquire before buying. The solution depends on the expected gain from an additional search, which is the expected fall in price resulting from the additional search, less the cost of undertaking it. So having decided to search on the basis of the cost and gain, the consumer will use these two factors as a guide to when he should stop. However, choosing the correct search strategy is not as simple as at first sight it might appear. There are at least two possible approaches. The first follows Stigler (1961).

Stigler's Decision Rule (Fixed Sample Size Rule)

Stigler viewed search as a process of selecting a random sample of the right size from a distribution of prices known with certainty. The consumer decides how many shops to visit and then buys from the one charging the lowest price. The problem is therefore to decide the optimum number of shops to visit. The criterion for making such a decision is familiar from many other areas of economics. As long as the gain from an additional search exceeds the cost, one should continue to increase the size of the sample. The rule is derived from the proposition that an activity should be continued up to the point at which the marginal benefit is equal to the marginal cost.

Having selected the sample, the price that will be paid is the lowest of that sample. Before search takes place it is not known what the minimum price actually found will be. All that is known is the expected minimum price, which will decrease as the size of the sample drawn from a particular distribution is increased. (Explanation: if the sample size is increased by one, the extra observation may well be lower than any yet encountered, in which case the minimum price has fallen. Alternatively, it may be the same or higher in which case the minimum price will not have fallen. Since in general there is a finite probability that the first outcome will occur, the minimum price must be expected to fall as the sample size is increased.)

The gain from increasing the size of the sample is the fall in expected minimum price. A property of all price distributions is that this gain increases at a declining rate as the sample size is increased. Thus, marginal revenue from search is always declining.

To make matters concrete we shall derive a very simple equation. Let the expected minimum price obtained after n searches be $\bar{E}(P_n)$ and after $n + 1$ searches $\bar{E}(P_{n+1})$. Then, assuming the consumer wishes to buy one unit only of the good, Stigler's rule may be formulated as selecting that size of sample which results in the reduction in the expected price being equal to the marginal cost of visiting one more shop. That is,

$$\bar{E}(P_n) - \bar{E}(P_{n+1}) \; = \; C \tag{1}$$

where the marginal cost, C, of an extra search is the cost of time and transport involved in visiting a shop and is assumed to be constant.[1] As a cost is incurred each time a shop is added to the sample, it may be the case that a further cost is incurred once the minimum price has been found. That is, both time and transport costs must be paid to return to the shop with the minimum price, unless it happens to be the last shop visited. This cost is known in the literature as the cost of recall. For the present we shall ignore the cost of recall in the

---

1. Those with an eye for detail will note that since the number of searches must be integral, the defining characteristics of the optimal number of searches should really be stated in terms of inequalities as follows;

$$\bar{E}(P_n) - \bar{E}(P_{n+1}) \leqslant C$$

$$\bar{E}(P_{n-1}) - \bar{E}(P_n) \geqslant C$$

calculation of the optimum number of shops to visit. The implications of its inclusion are explored in question 13.9.

The problem with Stigler's rule is that it ignores information obtained while searching. Such information could alter the shopper's optimal decision. Suppose that the first price observed is the lowest one in the market place. Stigler's rule would advise noting the offer and continuing searching until the initial plan had been fulfilled. Once having obtained the complete sample the consumer would return and accept the first price that had been offered. However, since the lowest price possible was offered at the first shop visited, it is absurd to continue searching.

The Sequential Decision Rule

A more sensible procedure than the Stigler rule would be to stop after each search, review the information acquired so far and then ask whether it is worth continuing. If the gain from an additional search exceeds the cost then undertake the search. This is an example of a sequential decision procedure.

To find the form of the solution let us proceed as follows. As before the cost of each search is C, the consumer only wants to buy one unit of the good and, given his income and preferences, the maximum price he will pay for it is P_m. Given this upper bound to the prices which are acceptable, the consumer can calculate the average price of all those shops selling at or below P_m.

The distribution of prices across all shops is depicted in figure 13.1. Let the shaded area to the left of P_m be termed α. This area is the probability of finding a price less than or equal to P_m. Now, P_m is the maximum price that the consumer is prepared to pay, so the gain from entering the market and searching could be thought of as a reduction in price below this level. The probability of obtaining such a

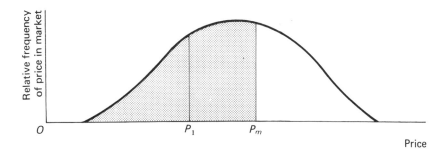

Figure 13.1

reduction is equal to $\alpha(P_m)$ and the expected value of all the prices below P_m is $E(P_m)$, so

$$E(G) = \alpha(P_m) [P_m - E(P_m)] \tag{2}$$

is the expected gain from the first search when the maximum acceptable price is P_m. If this gain is greater than C (and the consumer is risk neutral) then the first search is worthwhile; if it is less, the cost outweighs the benefit and it is not worth entering the market. But if it is worthwhile making a first search the question is should search activity continue? Suppose the first search yielded a price above or equal to P_m. This information is of no value, and hence the expected gain from the second search is the same as from the first search. If the first search yielded a price below P_m, say P_1, the value of the second search must be less than that of the first. This is because gains will only be made if the second search brings a price below P_1, and even then the gain from such prices will be lower than on the first search by $P_m - P_1$. It therefore follows that the expected gain from another search can never be greater than the expected gain from the preceding search.

In general, let us define $\alpha(P)$ as the probability of finding a price below P and $E(P)$ as the mean value of all prices below P. There will be some P that solves

$$\alpha(P) [P - E(P)] = C \tag{3}$$

This P, let us call it P_R, the reservation price, is the price which equates the expected gain from an additional search to the cost. If the individual finds a price which is equal to or less than P_R he should stop searching, as at this price the expected gain of an additional search will be equal to or less than the cost. So before search begins one fixes P_R and proceeds to search by refusing all prices in excess of P_R and terminating when a price is found below or equal to it.[1] This procedure is described in the flow chart (figure 13.2).

Since the number of firms in the market is limited it will not usually be possible to find an actual market price which exactly solves equation (3). Nevertheless a market price for which any offer below or equal to it should be accepted, and any above rejected, can always be found. The method of solving for P_R defined in this way is

1. The above discussion has been for an infinite number of shops. With a small number of shops the probabilities would change significantly after each search and so, therefore, would the reservation price — see Q13.7. In particular, unsuccessful searches eliminate low-price shops and so the reservation price tends to rise through time.

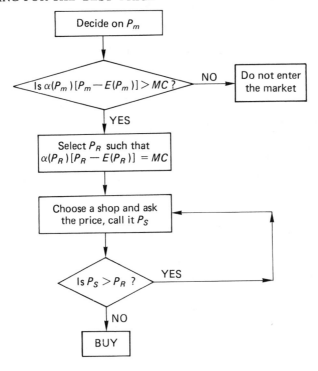

Figure 13.2

as follows. First, order the available prices from highest to lowest. Then insert prices, taking the highest first, in the right hand side of (3) until the first price is reached at which C is greater than expected gains. This price is the reservation price. Some economists, even in the case of a discrete distribution, would define the reservation price as that which solves (3). Such a price will always exist although it may not be a price that is offered in the market. Either this approach or the one specified above will lead to a correct operational rule for the consumer. However, in the questions attached to this chapter, all of which involve discrete distributions, the convention of choosing as a reservation price one actually offered in the market, has been followed. This saves a calculation and, as noted, still leads to optimal behaviour.

Note that the number of shops the consumer will expect to visit is $1/\alpha(P_R)$. For an explanation see the answer to question 13.1.

References for this section are combined with those on labour market search at the end of section B since most of the analytical issues raised are the same.

Questions

Q13.1 The maximum price a consumer is willing to pay for a good is £6. His search costs are £0.50 per shop visited. There are a large number of shops and he knows that $^2/_3$ of all shops charge £4, and $^1/_3$ charge £4.50 but does not know which shops charge which price.

(a) Assuming he wishes to buy one unit of the good and follows a sequential search rule, what will his reservation price be?

(b) How many shops will he expect to visit before finding one selling at or below his reservation price?

(c) What price will he expect to pay?

(d) Suppose his search costs were £0.20. Re-answer question (a), (b) and (c).

(e) If search costs are £0.20 and the consumer follows a Stigler rule, how many shops will he search and what will be the expected price he will pay?

(f) Compare the expected gain from search using the sequential decision rule with that from using the Stigler rule.

(g) Suppose that the consumer is misinformed and all shops charge £4.50. Comment on the merits of the Stigler versus the sequential rule under these circumstances.

Q13.2 In a certain market $^2/_3$ of the shops charge $4 and $^1/_3$ charge $4.50. Half the customers have a search cost of $0.50 and the rest of $0.20 (pehaps the second group have a lower cost of time). What percentage of the total custom will the $4.50 shops expect to receive assuming each customer follows an optimal sequential search rule?

Q13.3. Suppose the lowest price offered in a market characterised by price dispersion is $1. Consumers differ in their search costs but for no consumer are costs less than $0.10 per search. If one of the shops charging $1 were to raise its price to $1.10, what would happen to its sales? What are the implications of your answer for the existence of an equilibrium price dispersion?

Q13.4. In a market characterised by repeat purchases and imperfect information, at least in the short run stores are likely to face kinked demand curves at their current price.

Q13.5 Show that for sequential search the expected total cost of acquiring a good (expected price plus expected search costs) equals the reservation price and therefore that it is worth entering a market if and only if the use value of the good, P_m, exceeds the reservation price, P_R.

Q13.6 A landlord owns a property which on average tenants occupy for one year. When the premises fall vacant he expects to have to wait one week before finding a replacement tenant if he sets a rent of £10 per week; two weeks if the rent is £11; and four weeks if the rent is £11.15. Assuming the landlord wishes to maximise his long-run returns, what rent does he charge? (Problems of discounting may be ignored.)

Q13.7. A consumer knows that there is an equal chance that any shop will sell a certain good at £4 or £4.50 (perhaps shops periodically offer 50p discounts). There are three shops he can potentially visit. The first is reached after a 10 minute walk, the second after a 20 minute walk along the same road, and the third after a 22 minute walk along the road (i.e. 2 minutes further than the second shop). If the consumer attributes a 1.5 pence cost to each minute spent walking, and values the good at £4.55, is it worthwhile going shopping for the good and what is his optimal strategy?

Q13.8 In all the previous questions it has been assumed that the searcher knows the distribution of prices with certainty. It is, of course, relevant to enquire how he obtains this knowledge without also knowing which shop offers which price. Perhaps the consumer visits a new town which he assumes has the same distribution of prices as that in his home town. Alternatively, he may buy a good which he assumes will have a similar distribution of prices to one previously purchased (e.g. the price distribution of washing machines may be similar to that of spin dryers.) However, it is plausible that a searcher does not know for certain what the price distribution is, although the process of search may influence his view of what the true distribution is likely to be. Suppose as a special case, that a consumer believes the distribution of prices is either that all firms offer a price of $13 or else that 99% of firms offer a price of $10 and 1% of $12. His search costs are less than $1. What is his optimal strategy?

Q13.9 How must the Stigler decision rule be amended if costs of recall (the cost of returning to the shop which has the minimum price) are included?

Answers

A13.1 (a) **£4.50.** If the consumer makes one search, the price he will expect to pay is $\frac{1}{3} \times 4.50 + \frac{2}{3} \times 4 = £4.16$. Since the good is worth £6 to him and the costs of search are only £0.50, it is clearly worth his while entering the market. Now, suppose that on the first search he finds a price of £4.50. Is it worth his while to search again? If he does, the chance that he will find the lower price is $\frac{2}{3}$ and he will then make a gain of £0.50. Thus his expected gain is £0.33, which is less than the cost of search, so his reservation price is therefore £4.50.

(b) **One.**

(c) **£4.16.** As a result of his single search he will expect to have to pay a price of $\frac{1}{3} \times 4.50 + \frac{2}{3} \times 4 = £4.16$. (Note that this is below the reservation price. By definition, the price the searcher will expect to pay can never be above the reservation price and will normally be below it.)

(d) **The answer for reworked (a) is £4.** If the consumer has already found a price of £4.50 the expected gain from an additional search is once more £0.33. But now this exceeds his search costs and he will continue searching until he finds a price of £4.

The answer for reworked (b) is 1.5. The probability he will find a £4 shop on his first search is $\frac{2}{3}$. The probability that he will find a £4.50 shop on his first search and that only on his second search does he find a £4 shop is $\frac{1}{3} \times \frac{2}{3}$. The probability he goes to n shops before finding a £4 shop is $\frac{2}{3} (\frac{1}{3})^{n-1}$. Thus the expected number of shops he must visit is

$$S_n \underset{\lim n \to \infty}{=} 1(\tfrac{2}{3}) + 2(\tfrac{1}{3}) (\tfrac{2}{3}) + \ldots + n(\tfrac{1}{3})^{n-1} (\tfrac{2}{3}) \tag{4}$$

(i.e. where the summation is for n tending to infinity).
This looks a little formidable but actually requires limited manipulation to evaluate. From (4)

$$S_n = \tfrac{2}{3} [1 + 2(\tfrac{1}{3}) + 3(\tfrac{1}{3})^2 + \ldots + n(\tfrac{1}{3})^{n-1}] \tag{5}$$

$$\tfrac{1}{3} S_n = \tfrac{2}{3} [0 + (\tfrac{1}{3}) + 2(\tfrac{1}{3})^2 + \ldots + (n-1) (\tfrac{1}{3})^{n-1} + n(\tfrac{1}{3})^n] \tag{6}$$

Subtract (6) from (5)

$$\tfrac{2}{3} S_n = \tfrac{2}{3} [1 + \tfrac{1}{3} + (\tfrac{1}{3})^2 + \ldots + (\tfrac{1}{3})^{n-1} - n(\tfrac{1}{3})^n] \tag{7}$$

$$S_n = [1 + \tfrac{1}{3} + (\tfrac{1}{3})^2 + \ldots + (\tfrac{1}{3})^{n-1} - n(\tfrac{1}{3})^n] \tag{8}$$

$$\tfrac{1}{3} S_n = [\tfrac{1}{3} + (\tfrac{1}{3})^2 + \ldots + (\tfrac{1}{3})^n - n(\tfrac{1}{3})^{n+1}] \tag{9}$$

Subtract (9) from (8)

$$\tfrac{2}{3} S_n = 1 + n(\tfrac{1}{3})^{n+1} \tag{10}$$

As n tends to infinity, $n(\tfrac{1}{3})^{n+1}$ tends to zero, thus

$$\tfrac{2}{3} S_n = 1 \text{ and } S_n = \tfrac{3}{2}$$

The expected number of shops visited is 1½. As a general result, if α is the probability that price is equal to or lower than the reservation price then $1/\alpha$ is the expected number of searches required before such a price is found.

The answer for reworked (c) is £4.

(e) **He will visit one shop. £4.16.** If one search is made the expected minimum price found is $\tfrac{2}{3} \times 4 + \tfrac{1}{3} \times 4.50 = £4.16$. Should two searches be made the chance that both will yield a price of £4.50 is $\tfrac{1}{3} \times \tfrac{1}{3}$. Thus, the chance of at least one of the searches yielding a price of £4 is $\tfrac{8}{9}$ and the expected minimum price is $4 \times \tfrac{8}{9} + 4.50 \times \tfrac{1}{9} = \dfrac{36.5}{9} = £4.055$. The expected gain from a second search is therefore £0.11 and so it is not worth extending the sample to two. Expected price is £4.16.

(f) **Sequential search yields an expected gain of £0.066 over the Stigler rule.** Under Stigler expected price is £4.1666 and search costs are £0.20. Under sequential search expected price is £4 and expected search costs are $1.5 \times 0.2 = 0.3$. Thus, the expected gain from the sequential procedure is £0.0666.

(g) With the sequential search procedure the reservation price the consumer sets is £4.0. He would never encounter such a price and so search for ever. In practice he may revise his expectations. But since the Stigler rule limits search to one, it may be a safer rule of thumb when the price distribution is not known with certainty.

A13.2 $\tfrac{1}{6}$. From the answer to question 13.1 we know that the reservation price of the $0.50 search cost customers is $4.50 and of the others is $4. Thus the only customers the $4.50 shops get are those with

$0.50 search costs. However, although this group will buy from a $4.50 shop, on average $\frac{2}{3}$ of them arrive at a $4 shop first. Thus the $4.50 shops expect to make only $\frac{1}{3} \times \frac{1}{2} = \frac{1}{6}$ of the total sales.

A13.3 The rise in the firm's price will not affect the flow of customers coming to ask its price. But will any customer who bought at $1 now refuse to buy at $1.10? We know all customers have a search cost of at least $0.10. Therefore the benefits of their continuing to search to find a shop offering $1 must be equal to or less than the cost. So if the firm increases its price it will lose no custom and obtain higher profits. All firms will tend to act in a similar fashion and therefore the initial price distribution will not persist through time.

What will happen? Suppose all consumers place a use value on the good of P_m. No shop would charge more than this, for if it did it would lose all sales. Since the earlier reasoning shows that, this constraint aside, the lowest priced shops will be continually raising their price, a final equilibrium must emerge in which all shops charge P_m, the monopoly price. However, at this price no consumer would be enjoying any surplus and if it is costly to reach the market, no one will find it worth setting out. Thus the market collapses.

If instead of assuming that all consumers wish to buy only a single unit of the good, they are assumed to face downward sloping demand curves then, as before, the monopoly price will be established. But now the consumers will be left with some surplus, which may be sufficient to cover the costs of getting to market. Hence the market may survive. Price dispersion nevertheless disappears in equilibrium. One way of preserving price dispersion is to suppose that marginal costs differ between shops. Alternatively, if there exists a group of consumers with zero search costs then, should a low price shop raise its price, it will definitely lose sales. An equilibrium in which some shops charge high prices and others low prices is then possible. On this model see S. Salop and J. Stiglitz, 'Bargains and ripoffs: A model of monopolistically competitive price dispersion' (Review of Economic Studies, October 1977) and on the earlier monopoly result P. Diamond, 'A model of price adjustment' (Journal of Economic Theory, June 1971).

A13.4 TRUE. Suppose price is raised. Existing customers of the store will find out immediately and rather than return to the store will search for lower prices elsewhere. However, if price is cut it will take time for the customers of competing stores to discover this, and so there will be little expansion of sales in the short run. Interestingly, in the usual kinked demand curve oligopoly model, the inelastic portion of the demand curve is generally explained by customers being so well informed that competitors are forced to follow speedily any price cut.

A13.5 The expected total acquisition cost (A) of the good with reservation price P_R is

$$A = E(P_R) + C/\alpha(P_R) \tag{11}$$

where the first term is the expected price that will be paid and, remembering $1/\alpha$ is the expected number of searches, the second term is expected search costs. The reservation price is chosen to satisfy

$$a(P_R) [P_R - E(P_R)] = C \tag{12}$$

Substituting (12) in (11) yields

$$A = P_R$$

which is the result that reservation price equals expected acquisition costs.[1] On entering the market and searching optimally the expected total acquisition cost of the good equals P_R. Since this is what must be expected to be forgone in obtaining the good it is only worth entering the market if the use value, P_M, is at least equal to this amount. Making use of this criterion in deciding whether to enter the market, the flow chart for optimal product market search can be presented in the alternative form shown in figure 13.3.

A13.6 The problem may be formulated as one of maximising the average weekly return from the property. If a rent of £10 per week is charged, the property is expected to be vacant one week and let for 52 weeks, and the average weekly return is 52 × £10/53 = £9.81. At a rent of £11 average return is 52 × £11/54 = £10.59, and at £11.15

---

1. Of course, the result only holds when reservation price is defined by eq (12) rather than by the actual market price immediately above it. There is a more direct way of showing that the reservation price must equal expected total acquisition cost. Suppose, in contradiction, that $P_R > A(P_R)$. Then it would be sensible to refuse to buy at P_R, for continuing to search would yield an expected gain of $P_R - A(P_R)$. However, if P_R is rejected, it cannot be the optimal reservation price. Conversely, if $P_R < A(P_R)$, then continuing to search when a price of P_R is found yields an expected loss of $P_R - A(P_R)$. It follows that rejecting a price just a little below P_R would also yield a loss, as compared with continuing to search. Again, this is in contradiction to P_R being the optimal reservation price. Thus the only possibility is $P_R = A(P_R)$.

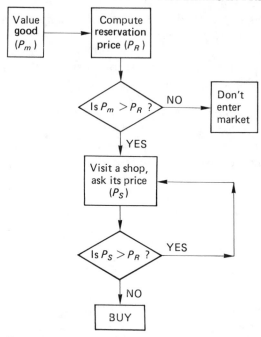

Figure 13.3

average return is $52 \times £11.15/56 = £10.35$. Thus over a long stretch of time returns are maximised if a rent of £11 is charged and the property is vacant on average $2/54 = 3.7\%$ of the time.

A13.7 Enter the market, buy from the first shop to charge £4 and pay £4.50 at last shop only if neither of the others charges £4. To decide whether to enter the market it is first necessary to compute the expected total costs of acquiring the good if an optimal strategy is followed. This cost should then be compared to the value of the good in order to determine whether to enter the market.

The search strategy comprises a set of rules which tell the consumer what to do once the price a particular shop charges is known. However, to formulate such a rule it is necessary to know what happens if the good is not bought from the shop in question. Thus suppose the first shop along the road charges £4.50. Should the second shop be visited? One advantage of going to the second shop is that a third is very close by and so this is in some sense part of the payoff of the journey to the second shop. The way to solve the problem is, therefore, to look at last things first. If the consumer arrives at the second shop and it charges £4.50 should he go to the third shop? This helps us decide whether he should go to the second shop. In its turn the answers to both these questions are required to determine whether to enter the market in the first place.

To implement this methodology, suppose first, that the customer has actually arrived at the second shop and found that it charges £4.50. Would it then yield an expected gain to go on to the third shop? The expected cost saving is 25p and the cost of the 4 minute walk (2 minutes there and 2 minutes back) is only 6p so it is clearly worth making the journey. Now suppose the consumer arrived at the first shop and it charged £4.50, would it be worth going on to the second shop? If he did there is a ½ chance it would charge £4, in which case the good would be bought there, and 20 minutes extra walking be incurred at a cost of 30p. Should the second shop charge £4.50 we have seen that it is worthwhile going on to the third shop. The probability that the customer deciding to go to the second shop will end by buying from the third shop and paying £4, is therefore ½ X ½ = ¼ which is also the probability of paying £4.50 at the third shop. Thus if the consumer goes to the second shop and then, on the basis of the price quoted, makes an optimal decision as to whether to go on to the third shop the expected price he will pay is ½ X 4 + ¼ X 4 + ¼ X 4.50 = £4.125, giving an expected price fall of 37.5p from the £4.50 asked at the first shop. The expected extra walking costs are ½ X 30 + ½ X 36 = 33p. Hence if the first shop asks £4.50 it is worth going to the second shop. The expected price paid for the good is therefore ½ X 4 + ½ X ½ X 4 + ½ X ½ X ½ X 4 + ½ X ½ X ½ X 4.50 = £4.06 (the probability of buying at the first shop at £4 is ½, the probability of buying at the second shop at £4 is ½ X ½, whilst if he arrives at the third shop he will buy at whatever price is asked). The expected walking cost involved is ½ X 30 + ½ X ½ X 60 + ½ X ½ X 66 = 46.50p. Total expected costs are therefore £4.525. As this is less than the value of the good to the consumer it is worth entering the market and continuing along the road until a £4 shop is found and paying £4.50 only if no shop charges £4.

A13.8 There is no reservation price. If the first shop visited offers a price of $13 then the searcher knows that the correct distribution is that all shops charge $13 and hence will buy from the first shop. But suppose he visits a shop charging $12, then he knows the second distribution is the correct one and if he makes an additional search is almost certain to make a gain of $2. Therefore it is worth continuing to search until a price of $10 is found. Thus there is no reservation price because there is no price below which any price will be accepted and above which all prices will be rejected.

A13.9 There are two factors here. Firstly, if n shops are visited the probability that the last one visited will offer the lowest price is $1/n$. Thus the probability of having to pay a cost of recall is $(n-1)/n = 1 - (1/n)$. This clearly rises as n increases. In fact this argument is too simple since it is only sensible to pay the cost of recall if it is less than the difference between the last price found and the lowest price. Nevertheless, the presence of a cost of recall still tends to reduce search activity. Secondly, as the number of shops visited is increased it is likely that in returning to the lowest priced shop a long journey must be made. For both reasons, expected recall costs rise with n. Thus marginal search costs will tend to rise with n. Remember that with the sequential rule the consumer never has to go back to a shop so costs of recall play no role.

(B) LABOUR MARKET SEARCH

If an unemployed worker believes that there exist a number of potential employers, each of whom may offer contracts of differing attractiveness, then labour market search may be worthwhile. That is, the first job the individual is offered may not be the best available in the market. It may therefore be sensible to reject it and wait for a better offer to materialise. In the meantime the income that would have been earned had the job been accepted is lost. Whether waiting and searching for a better job will prove advantageous clearly depends both on the length of time that is expected to elapse before a better job is found and on the wage it will pay once found. It is notable that a small percentage increase in wages may justify a considerable waiting period. For example, if a worker expects to be in a job for only a year then one month's unemployment pays off if it raises the wage he receives by 10%.

The formal model of job search is analytically analogous to that of product market search. The workers optimal strategy is to fix a reservation wage such that he accepts the first offer he receives of a wage in excess of this amount. To set about determining the reservation wage consider the gains from additional search if a wage offer of w has been received. If he rejects the offer and waits one period before receiving a higher offer of say $\hat{w}$, what is the gain? Well, in every period after the search, the wage he receives is higher by $\hat{w} - w$. Suppose the individual has an infinite life and will work in any job he takes for the rest of his life. Then the present value of an annual payment of $\hat{w} - w$ starting next period, is $(\hat{w} - w)/r$, where r is the appropriate discount rate (it will in practice depend on the individual's access to capital markets). Hence, when an offer of w is received, the expected gain from a search taking one period is

$$E(G) = \frac{\alpha(w)}{r} \ [\ E(w) - w] \tag{13}$$

where $\alpha(w)$ is now the probability of finding, during the search period, a wage in excess of w, and $E(w)$ is the expected value of the best wage offer in excess of w received after one period of search.[1]

Having found the gain from search, what are the costs? The main cost is the loss of wage income for the current period. Offsetting this loss, in part, may be unemployment benefits (U) which are paid whilst searching for a job. Costs of attending for interview and so on may also be involved, but these will be ignored. It follows that the reservation wage is defined by

$$\frac{a(w_R)}{r} \ [E(w_R) - w_R] = w_R - U \tag{14}$$

for at w_R the expected gains from another period of search just equal the costs.

Two points should be made about equation (14). It might seem from our discussion that it assumes that an individual who rejects an offer in one period can go back to it if he wants to in the next period. The reason why this may appear to be so is that we have considered a gain from search as occuring if a higher wage is found next period but not identified a loss when a lower wage is discovered. Certainly, there would be no loss if the individual could go back to the first job. However, even if this option is unavailable, search according to the reservation wage rule of equation (14) would never require returning to a job since it is the first job offering a wage above w_R that is accepted.[2] As the option to go back to a job is never taken, it is therefore irrelevant whether an individual can in fact return to a job after rejecting it.

Secondly, it is sometimes said that search theory is ideologically loaded since it implies that all unemployment is voluntary. Whether or not this is a valid form of criticism, the theory does not imply that unemployed workers must have job offers they could accept if they wanted to. We have assumed that it takes one period to make a

1 Note that whilst in reality individuals have finite life expectancies and the longer they spend searching for a job the shorter the time spent in it and earning, this will make hardly any difference to our equation. This is due to the power of compound discounting, the effect of which is that the loss of a period of wage income as close as 10 periods in the future has a small present value (only minor changes are needed to take this consideration into account directly).

2. The reader should consider what changes in the assumptions of the model would make the option of returning to a job important.

search. Possible job advertisements appear only once in a period or it may take that long to arrange an interview. But it does not follow that having gone for interview the searcher will actually receive an employment offer (no offer could be regarded as finding a wage of zero). In our equation $\alpha(w)$ is the probability that one period of search will yield a wage offer in excess of w. It therefore certainly takes account of the possibility that no offer is received. Some individuals may therefore have been unemployed for a number of periods without having had any offers.

Another criticism of the model outlined above is that it assumes that the worker finds it more efficient to search whilst unemployed. If, as much evidence suggests, job search is at least as effective when an individual is employed as unemployed then surely the optimal strategy would be to take the first job offered and then continue to search for a better job whilst employed. It therefore appears that search theory cannot explain unemployment (Tobin 1972). However, this view overlooks the fact that psychic and monetary costs may be involved in accepting a job and quitting it after a short period of time. Thus workers entering the labour force for the first time or losing their existing jobs may not find it worthwhile accepting a low paid job when they expect to quit it not long after. Indeed, a record of frequent quitting may not be conducive to getting offers of higher paid employment. Furthermore, applying for a high paid job whilst employed in a low paid one may be taken as an adverse 'signal' (see next chapter) by the employers offering the better paid jobs. They believe the candidate cannot have the attributes for a high paid job if the best he can find so far is a poorly paid job. Counteracting the last effect is the possibility that employers may take long durations of unemployment as an adverse signal of quality. Nevertheless, it can be seen that there are strong arguments for suggesting that an unemployed individual will find it more effective to carry out his search whilst unemployed rather than taking the first job that comes along and then searching whilst employed. The model would appear capable of saying something about unemployment.

Labour Market Search when a Job is Already Held

Suppose a currently employed worker finds that since accepting the job the distribution of wages in the market has changed though not the wage paid in his own job. The employer may be sluggish in raising his wages as compared to other firms, or the employee may feel that his acquired skills are presently unrecognised and would earn higher wages elsewhere. The problem he faces is in deciding whether to search for a new job, and if so whether to do this by quitting his existing job or searching whilst still employed. What are the advantages of search whilst employed? The most obvious is that it does not involve the loss of wage income over the search period. As against this, search could be less efficient than if the individual is unemployed since he has less freedom as to when to attend for interview, visit employment exchanges and so on. Search whilst employed also eats into leisure time when much of the search activity must take place. Whether it is worth quitting and searching, possibly receiving unemployment pay and having more leisure time available, but losing the current wage instead of searching whilst retaining the job, is clearly an open issue. However, it is not surprising that it is often more advantageous to search whilst employed when a job is currently held. If this is the search method chosen, it follows that the worker will quit only when an acceptable job has been found, and that no unemployment will be involved. Note, however, that the worker will not necessarily move to the first job which offers him a better wage than the one he is currently earning. If even higher wage rates could be found without too much difficulty then the costs of changing jobs may be sufficiently great that it is not worthwhile moving to a job which will only be held for a short period before something better materialises.

The Phillips Curve

A.W. Phillips (1958) found evidence that high rates of change of money wages were associated with low levels of unemployment. Recent inflationary experience has not fitted this picture. Rapid increases in wage rates have been accompanied by rising unemployment. It seems that whereas in the short run high rates of increase in money wages and low unemployment go together in the longer run unemployment returns to its original ('natural') level and wage increases do not moderate (the long-run Phillips curve is vertical).

One explanation of the distinction between the long- and short-run Phillips curves is provided by search theory. Firstly, we suppose that whatever the state of unemployment in the economy there are always some firms with vacancies arising from the unexpected losses of workers, expansion in the demand for their particular products or from innovations. Secondly, there is a pool of unemployed workers searching for jobs on the basis of something like equation (13). In the past, wages have been growing at some steady rate which workers have become accustomed to. They therefore accurately judge the market distribution of wages in setting their reservation wage. However, suppose there is a sudden increase in the rate of change of money wages. Unemployed workers do not realise this has happened and thinking that the market distribution of wages is unchanged do not alter their reservation wage. However, since money wages have in general risen this means that the number of firms offering a wage above any given level has increased and so, therefore, has the probability the worker will on any search find a wage in excess of his reservation level. On average, workers will consequently be accepting jobs after a shorter waiting period. The level of unemployment will therefore fall.

In the longer run, workers begin to realise that the true market distribution of wages has changed. If they know that all wages are λ per cent higher than the original expectations, then by equation (13) the reservation wage will also rise by λ per cent (this assumes unemployment benefits also increase by λ per cent). Thus the percentage of jobs offering a wage in excess of any particular worker's reservation level will return to its original level, as will the level of unemployment.

The rise in the rate of increase of money wages was therefore associated with a fall in unemployment in the short run though in the long run unemployment returns to its original level. The return to the natural level would be rapid if those who mistakenly accepted jobs immediately quit them when they realise the true wage distribution. Fixed costs of quitting slow this process, and if those with jobs search whilst employed, this has the same effect. Under these circumstances unemployment rises, as those remaining unemployed, or laid off from declining sectors, or entering the labour market for the first time, revert to their old search behaviour. Thus, suppose in equilibrium unemployment in each period is 100 and there are 100 vacancies. At the end of the period, 50 people accept jobs and are replaced by 50 new entrants and 50 new jobs appear, so that at the start of the next period, unemployment and vacancies are once again 100. But this period, because of inflation illusion, all the unemployed accept jobs. In the following period, unemployment would be down to the 50 new entrants and if they search as before, by the end of the period 25 find jobs. Consequently, the next period starts with 75 people unemployed and 75 vacancies. In the period after, unemployment would be 87.5 and gradually reverting to its equilibrium level. However, it is important to note that the rise in unemployment has not been associated with rising quits.

It should be noted that the above is only one possible rationale for the long- and short-run Phillips curve. For a survey see Santomero and Seater (1978).

References

Alchain A., 'Information costs, pricing and resource unemployment' in *Micro-economic Foundations of Employment and Inflation Theory* by E. Phelps *et al.*, Macmillan 1970.

Gronau R., 'Wage comparisons — a selectivity bias', *Journal of Political Economy*, November /December 1974.

Holt C., 'Job search, Phillips' wage relation and union influence: theory and evidence' in Phelps *et al.*, *op. cit.*

Lippman S. and McCall J.J., 'The economics of job search: a survey', *Economic Inquiry*, Part 1, June 1976, Part 2, September 1976.

McCall J.J., 'Economics of information and job search', *Quarterly Journal of Economics*, February 1970.

Mortensen O.T., 'Job search, the duration of unemployment and the Phillips curve', *American Economic Review*, June 1971.

Phillips A.W., 'The relation between unemployment and the rate of change of money wage rates in the United Kingdom, 1861–1957', *Economica*, November 1958.

Nelson P., 'Information and consumer behaviour', *Journal of Political Economy*, March/April 1970.

Rothschild M., 'Models of market organisation with imperfect information', *Journal of Political Economy*, November/December 1973.

Samtomero A.M. and Seater J.J., 'The inflation—uemployment trade-off: A critique of the literature', *Journal of Economic Literature*, June 1978.

Stigler G.J., 'The economics of information', *Journal of Political Economy*, June 1961.

Stigler G.J., 'Information in the labour market', *Journal of Political Economy*, suppl., October 1962.

Stiglitz J.E., 'Equilibrium in product markets with imperfect information', *American Economic Review* Papers and Proceedings, May 1979.

Tobin J., 'Inflation and unemployment', *American Economic Review*, March 1972.

Questions

Q13.10 There is a probability of ½ that after one period of search the best wage offer received by an unemployed individual is £10. The probability that the best wage will be £15 is ¼, and there is ¼ chance that no employment offer will be received. Assume the individual has an infinite working life, that no unemployment benefit is paid and that, for the reasons discussed in the text, it is inefficient to search whilst employed.

   (a) If future income is discounted at the rate of 10% ($r = 0.1$) what will be the searcher's reservation wage, expected duration of unemployment and expected wage?

   (b) Another unemployed individual is like the first in all respects except that he is more impatient and discounts future income at the higher rate of 20% (perhaps he faces less favourable borrowing opportunities). Find his reservation wage, expected unemployment duration and expected wage.

Q13.11. An economic upswing tends to increase vacancies and therefore the probability of getting a job offer paying any specified wage. At least initially, this increases the probability that a period of search will yield a high wage offer and reduces the probability that no offer will be received. Suppose the upswing changes the probabilities of question 13.10 such that there is now a probability of 0.5 that the best wage yielded by a period of search is $15, the probability that the best wage offer received is $10 rises to 0.4 and the probability of no offer is now only 0.1. Find the change in the expected duration of unemployment generated by the upswing for the individual with the discount rate of $r = 0.1$ and also for the individual with $r = 0.2$.

Q13.12. (a) Suppose there are two types of job an individual can apply for. All the firms offering each type of job pay the same wage, job A commanding a wage of £40 and job B of £60 per period. When applying for a job it is not known with certainty whether an employment offer will be made. In the case of an A job the probability of getting the job is $\frac{4}{5}$ and that for a B job is $\frac{2}{5}$. Assume that each period he is unemployed the individual can, if he wishes, apply for an A job and a B job (one of each is advertised). Is it worth the individual applying for an A job if he is currently unemployed and $r = 0.1$? What is the expected duration of his unemployment?

(b) An individual who is less well skilled than the one in part (a) has only a 0.5 chance of landing an A job and a 0.1 chance of being offered a B job. What strategy should follow and what is the expected duration of his unemployment?

Q13.13 A particular individual can search one firm per period. The market distribution of wages inclusive of non-pecuniary income is as below:

Wage rate	30	40	50	60	70
Number of firms	20	20	20	20	20

To ease computation we assume $r = 1$. The individual is currently unemployed. There are no psychic costs of search but for every period spent searching unemployment pay of 28 is paid. However search activity and work both absorb non-market time which is valued at 30.

(a) Is search worthwhile?

(b) What will his reservation wage be?

(c) Is the reservation wage equal to the wage the individual will expect to earn if he follows an optimal strategy?

(d) What is the expected duration of search for the individual?

Q13.14 Suppose every firm in the market increases the wage it offers by a third from those in the previous question. However, in the short run the searcher does not realise this has happened. How will the duration of his labour market search change? Does the theory of search provide an explanation of the difference between the long- and short-run Phillips curve?

Q13.15 It is sometimes claimed that a mean preserving rise in the variance of wage offers increases both the reservation wage and the expected duration of search unemployment. Consider the three wage distributions A, B and C below. All three distributions have mean 50 but B and C have a higher variance than A.

wage		30	40	50	60	70
	A	20	20	20	20	20
Number of	B	30	10	20	10	30
firms	C	50	0	0	0	50

Suppose the initial distribution is A, that $r = 1$, there is an unemployment benefit of 9 but time has no value in non-market activities. The wage distribution then changes to B. Compare the variances of A and B and find the effect of the change in distribution on the reservation wage and the expected duration of unemployment. Do the same if the distribution changes from A to C.

Q13.16 An incomes policy which allows flat rate wage increases will not lead to an increase in the duration of search as the variance of the distribution remains the same. However, a uniform percentage rate increase will increase the variance and thus lead to a rise in the duration of search. Assess this proposition assuming in both cases that unemployment benefits do not increase with wages.

Q13.17 Given the existing distribution of wage offers, government subsidised job centres reduce the costs of search and therefore must increase the average duration of unemployment .

Q13.18 The provision of job centres will tend to increase the number of people who experience a spell of unemployment in any year.

Q13.19 The finding of an American survey that over 80% of people who change jobs do so without a period of unemployment show that most individuals do not bother to search.

Q13.20 An individual knows he will live for three periods. He is unemployed and faces the distribution of wage offers shown below. Whilst out of work and searching for a job he receives unemployment benefit of £5 and forgoes non-market activities he values at £6. Each period he can visit one firm. If he accepts a job he holds it for the rest of his life. The individual suffers no psychic costs from search or from work.

Wage rate per period	Number of jobs
7	100
10	100
16	100

(a) Assuming an optimal strategy is followed, will the individual enter the labour market and what will his expected lifetime income be?

(b) What is the expected duration of unemployment?

(c) Suppose the value of non-market activity is increased to £9. Find the new optimal search strategy and associated lifetime income. In particular what should be done if at the end of period one an offer of £7 is received?

(d) How far do you think this analysis could be used to explain why people drop out of the labour market? What other explanations may be offered?

Answers

A13.10 (a) **Reservation wage £15, expected duration of unemployment 4 periods, expected wage £15.** Suppose a wage offer of £10 is held. If another search is undertaken there is a ¼ chance that the higher wage of £15 will be found. If the £15 wage is discovered the expected annual gain is ¼ × 5 = 1.25 which has present value 1.25/0.1 = £12.50. As this exceeds the loss of the wage of £10 during the search period it is worth searching till a wage of £15 is found.

The expected length of search will depend upon the probability of finding an acceptable wage. The higher the probability of finding an acceptable wage the shorter the time spent searching. In fact, the expected period of search is the inverse of this probability. This was shown in the answer to question 13.1 (iv).

In this case the probability of finding a wage equal to or in excess of the reservation level is ¼. Hence the expected duration of unemployment is 4 periods and the expected value of the wage is of course £15.

(b) **Reservation wage £10, expected duration of unemployment 1.33 periods, expected wage £11.66.** When a wage of £10 is held the expected present value of search is (¼ × 5)/0.2 = £6.25 and hence further search does not recoup the loss of current income. The reservation wage is therefore £10. The probability that a period of search will yield a wage equal to or in excess of the reservation level is ½ + ¼ = ¾ and hence the expected duration of unemployment is 4/3 = 1.33 periods. Since there is twice the probability that the highest wage found will be £10 rather than £15 the expected wage is ⅔ × 10 + ⅓ × 15 = £11.66.

A13.11 **For r = 0.1 expected search duration falls and for r = 0.2 it rises.** With the initial probabilities and $r = 0.1$ the reservation wage was $15 and the expected duration of unemployment 4 periods. With the new probabilities the reservation wage clearly remains at $15 but as the probability of receiving such a wage has risen to 0.5 the expected duration of unemployment is now only 2 periods.

When $r = 0.2$ the reservation wage was $10 and the expected duration of unemployment 2. But with the new probabilities the expected gain from a period of search when an offer of $10 is held is $(0.5 \times 0.5)/0.2 = \$12.50$. Hence the reservation wage now rises to $15. Since the probability of finding this wage is 0.5 the expected duration of search rises to 2.

A13.12 (a) **A jobs are not worth applying for and the expected duration of search is 2½ periods.** Suppose the best offer the individual has is from an A job. If he rejects this and searches for another period there is a $\frac{2}{5}$ chance he will find a B job, in which case the expected present value of the gain is $(\frac{2}{5} \times 20)/0.1 = £80$. As this is greater than the wage foregone of £40 it is worth searching until a B job is found. Thus it is never worth applying for an A job and the expected duration of search is $\frac{5}{2} = 2\frac{1}{2}$ periods.

(b) **Apply for both jobs but do not wait for a B if only an A is offered. Expected duration of unemployment 1.47.** If an A offer is held the expected present value of another period of search is $(0.1 \times 20)/0.1 = 20$ and thus is not worth undertaking. Hence both jobs will be applied for. If an A job is offered but not a B, the A job will be accepted. The probability that no job is found is the product of the probability that an A job is not found and that a B job is not found (the two events are assumed to be independent). This is $4/5 \times 2/5 = 8/25$. Consequently the probability of an acceptable offer is $17/25$ and the expected duration of unemployment $25/17 = 1.47$.

A13.13 (a) **Search for a job.** The individual who is unemployed can stay in the home where, in effect, a wage of 30 is earned. If search turns up a wage in excess of 30 it has yielded a benefit and the expected gain is $0.2 (10 + 20 + 30 + 40) = 20$. The cost of the search is the loss of the 30 of non-market time less the unemployment benefit of 28 giving a net cost of 2. Hence the benefits of 20 exceed the costs of 2 and search is worthwhile.

(b) **40.**

In the present case the reservation wage is equal to 40, since

$$E(G) = \frac{4}{5} (55 - 40) = 40 - 28 = 12 = C$$

where 55 is the mean of the wages in all jobs paying at least 40. Any wage rate in excess of 40 would result in the expected gain from an additional period of search being less than the cost.

(c) **NO.** If the worker accepts any offer equal to, or greater than, 40 the expected wage must be in excess of this amount and is 55.

(d) **1.25.** The probability that a search will yield a wage equal to or in excess of the reservation level is 4/5 and the expected number of searches is $5/4 = 1.25$.

A13.14 If the individual does not know about the changes in the wage distribution his reservation wage must remain at 40. But when all wages increase by $\frac{1}{3}$ the lowest wage offered is 40. Thus the individual will accept the first job offered. His expected duration of search will therefore fall from 1.25 to 1. If everybody acts in like fashion unemployment will therefore fall.

This is exactly what the short-run Phillips curve relationship predicts. As the rate of change of money wages increases, so unemployment falls. However, in the longer run we should expect workers to learn that wages in general have risen and thus re-adjust the reservation wage. In the present case assuming the unemployment benefits and the value of non-market activities also rise by $\frac{1}{3}$ the reservation wage will likewise increase by $\frac{1}{3}$ and the average duration of unemployment return to its original level.

In this example we have taken a once and for all change in money wages and found that in the long run there will be no change in unemployment as workers come to learn of the new wage distribution. But even if the rate of change of money wages were to be maintained we should expect workers to learn of this higher rate of change. Thus, they would be able to predict correctly the wage distribution in any period and consequently set the correct reservation wage. With a sustained and hence anticipated rate of inflation there is no reduction in the average duration of search. Therefore in the long-run the Phillips curve is vertical.

A13.15 **Variance A = 200, B = 260, C = 400. Reservation wage is 40 for A, 30 for B and 70 for C. Unemployment durations 1.25, 1, 3⅓ respectively.** Distribution A has mean 50. The variance is found by subtracting the mean from each wage, squaring the result, multiplying by the probability of that wage occurring and summing over all possible wages. In the case of A the variance is $0.2 \times 20^2 + 0.2 \times 10^2 + 0.2 \times 10^2 + 0.2 \times 20^2 = 200$. At wage 30 the expected gain from search is $0.2 (10 + 20 + 30 + 40) = 20$ and the cost is $30 - 9 = 21$. If a wage of 40 is held the expected gain from search is $0.2 (10 + 20 + 30) = 12$ and the cost is $40 - 9 = 31$. Thus the reservation wage is 40 and the expected duration of unemployment is $5/4 = 1.25$.

Distribution B has mean 50 and variance $0.3 \times 20^2 + 0.1 \times 10^2 + 0.1 \times 10^2 + 0.3 \times 20^2 = 260$. At wage 30 the expected gain from a search is $0.1 \times 10 + 0.2 \times 20 + 0.1 \times 30 + 0.3 \times 40 = 20$ and the cost is $30 - 9 = 21$. Hence 30 is the reservation wage and, since the first job found will be accepted, the duration of unemployment is 1. Here we have a case where a rise in the variance of wage offers leads to an increase in the duration of search.

Distribution C has mean 50 and variance 400. At wage 30 the expected gain from search is $0.5 \times 40 = 20$ and the cost 19. Thus the reservation wage is 70 and the expected duration of unemployment is $10/3 = 3\frac{1}{3}$.

A13.16 (a) FALSE. The argument behind the assertion is that in the case of flat rate wage increases the variance of the distribution of wage offers does not change, whilst in the case of a percentage increase it rises. Therefore, the duration of search in the latter case must be increased. This argument is false as it presumes that the reservation wage is an increasing function of the variance which, as we have shown in the previous question, is not true.

Now to answer the question. From the text we have, for a continuous wage distribution

$$a(w_R)\ [E(w_R) - w_R]\ =\ w_R - U \tag{15}$$

With the flat rate wage increase let the rise in all wage offers be equal to d. Now let us see whether a new reservation wage of $w_R + d$ is appropriate. At this wage

$$\bar{a}(w_R + d)\,[\bar{E}(w_R + d) - (w_R + d)]$$

$$= a(w_R)[E(w_R) - w_R] = (w_R - U) < (w_R + d - U) \tag{16}$$

where a bar over a function indicates that it is for the new wage distribution and thus $\bar{a}(w_R + d) = a(w_R)$ and $\bar{E}(w_R + d) = E(w_R) + d$. The right hand side of (16) is the marginal cost of search if an offer of $w_R + d$ is held and the left hand side is the expected gain. Thus from (16) the new reservation wage rate must be less than $w_R + d$. So, as compared to the original situation, the duration of search will decline. This is intuitively reasonable given that the unemployment compensation U has remained unchanged for it means that the opportunity cost of search has increased.

(b) Let the percentage increase in all wage offers be 10%. Now test whether the reservation wage should also rise by 10%. If it did then

$$E(G) = \bar{a}(1.1w_R)\,[\bar{E}(1.1w_R) - 1.1w_R] = 1.1a(w_R)\,[E(w_R) - w_R] \tag{17}$$

Thus, with the new wage distribution, if an offer of $1.1w_R$ is held the expected gain from search has risen by 10%. However the cost of search, $1.1w_R - U$, has increased by more than 10% as the unemployment benefit remains fixed. It follows that the new reservation wage must be less than 10% higher than the old, and as compared to the original situation the duration of search will fall.

Hence under either kind of incomes policy less search is undertaken. Note, however, that if unemployment benefits rose in the same way as wages then the expected duration of search would remain unchanged in each case.

A13.17 **FALSE.** By centralising information, job centres have the general effect of reducing the time taken to search a firm. Thus if it took one period to search a firm before, it may now take only half a period and so the time cost of a search would be halved. Therefore, the number of firms searched must be expected to increase. However, the duration of unemployment would only increase if the number of firms searched were to double. Though this might happen there is no reason why it must happen. Indeed, as job centres offer a large number of jobs in a single visit and since their pre-employer interview screening raises the chance of receiving an offer once transport costs are incurred to visit an employer, we would expect the duration of search unemployment to fall.

A13.18 **TRUE.** The lower price of search, given the rewards, must increase the number of people for whom it is now worthwhile to look for a new job. As in practice these subsidies are only available during working hours the incentive to become unemployed to search will tend to increase.

A13.19 **FALSE.** Whether it is worth quitting an existing job and becoming unemployed to search depends upon the increased efficiency of specialisation on search activity in relation to the cost of the foregone earnings. If employment agencies are not open after working hours it may be impossible to search while employed. More to the point, a greater number of jobs may be visited in a given period of time if effort is concentrated, rather than spread over a number of periods. So the probability of finding a job in a given period will increase if one becomes unemployed to search. Hence the higher income in the new job will be earned for a longer period. The advantage to specialisation falls to the extent that jobs can be found by newspaper advertisements and employment exchanges open at night. This latter oppportunity is probably more significant in the US than in the UK. Another aspect the searcher must take into account is the possibility that an employer may take unemployment as a signal that the applicant is incompetent. This type of phenomenon is taken up in the next chapter. However, the point is that employees need not quit to search actively and hence the observation in the question does not imply that search is unimportant.

A further important point is that most of the workers who are involuntarily unemployed in the sense that they have lost their job or have only just entered the labour market will be searching since there will almost certainly be some jobs available which they do not consider worth taking. For the reasons discussed in the text it may not be worthwhile for an individual who is unemployed to take the first job offered and then continue to search whilst employed. It therefore does not even follow that the survey evidence means that search theory has nothing to say about unemployment.

A13.20(a) **Search for Work. Expected income £27.66.** The optimal strategy comprises a set of rules which tell the searcher what to do if he receives a particular offer in a particular period. However, whether it is worth accepting an offer at the end of the first period depends on the opportunities available in the second and third periods. Hence to answer the question we must look back from the decision what to do in the third period in order to find the overall set of rules. This is the method of dynamic programming (see question 13.7).

Suppose the searcher has an offer of £7 at the end of the second period. Should he take it? Since the value of non-market time is only £6 it is clear that he does better by taking the job. Similarly, if he had an offer of £10 or £16 he would accept.

Now let us go to the end of the first period. If the best offer he then has is £7, should he accept? The answer this time is no. If the job is accepted £14 is earned over the remaining two periods of life. Should the job be rejected and period 2 be spent searching, £5 unemployment benefit will be received and in period 3 the expected wage will be £11 and thus total expected income over the two periods is £16. The £7 job should therefore be rejected. Applying the same reasoning, if at the end of the first period he is offered a £10 or £16 job he should accept.

Choosing to enter the labour market therefore yields the following expected lifetime income. In the first period he will search and receive unemployment pay of £5. If he receives an offer of £10 or £16 he accepts and spends the rest of his life in work. The probability of this is $\frac{2}{3}$. If at the end of the first period he receives a £7 offer he searches during period 2, receives another £5 unemployment pay and then stands a $\frac{1}{3}$ chance of each of £7, £10 or £16 during period 3. The probability of spending period 2 searching is $\frac{1}{3}$, thus expected lifetime income is

$$5 + [\tfrac{2}{3} \times \tfrac{1}{2}(20 + 32)] + \tfrac{1}{3}[5 + \tfrac{1}{3}(7 + 10 + 16)] = 27.66$$

If the three periods are devoted to non-market activities only £18 is 'earned'. Thus entering the labour market is the superior alternative.

(b) $1\tfrac{1}{3}$. Whatever happens he spends period 1 searching. If he receives an offer of £10 or £16 he then spends the rest of his life in work. The chance he will do so is $\tfrac{2}{3}$. If he receives an offer of £7 at the end of period 1 he searches in period 2 and then accepts any offers made. The chance this will occur is $\tfrac{1}{3}$. Thus the expected duration of unemployment is

$$[1 \times \tfrac{2}{3}] + [2 \times \tfrac{1}{3}] = 1\tfrac{1}{3} \text{ periods.}$$

(c) **Search, but if offered a £7 job in any period drop out of labour market. Expected lifetime income is £28$\tfrac{1}{3}$.** At the end of period 2 an individual searching in the labour market would now reject a £7 job since the value of non-market time is £9. If at the end of period 1 he receives a £7 offer, as before this would be rejected. But instead of spending the second period searching he would drop out of the labour market. This is because search yields an expected income for the remaining two periods of $5 + \tfrac{1}{3}(16 + 10 + 9) = 16\tfrac{2}{3}$, whilst spending the time in non-market activities produces with certainty an income of 18; thus expected lifetime income is now $5 + (\tfrac{1}{3} \times 18) + \tfrac{2}{3} \times \tfrac{1}{2}(20 + 32) = 28\tfrac{1}{3}$.

(d) The previous question and answer show a sequence of two periods of unemployment during which search takes place, followed by a final period in which the worker leaves the market. Thus it provides a possible explanation of the drop-out phenomenon. It is clearly most applicable to those made redundant late in life who do not find it worthwhile searching for another job.

An alternative view is that a worker holds an excessively optimistic view of the distribution of wages. As he learns the truth he may not find it worthwhile continuing the search. It should be stressed that the first explanation depends on a finite working life causing the gains from search to be lower for an older worker, even if he believes he faces the same wage distribution. The second explanation is based on the worker revising his view of the wage distribution as he gets older.

A further set of explanations concerns drop-out as a temporary phenomenon. During downswings the probability of finding any kind of job may become so low that it ceases to be worth searching at all. However, when the upswing arrives work may once again be sought.

Counteracting this 'discouraged worker' effect is the possibility that if the main breadwinner is unemployed other family members may be forced to seek work to maintain family income. Thus this 'added worker' effect works towards increasing the numbers seeking work during downswings.

14

'Lemons', 'Screening' and 'Signalling'

Intoduction

The last chapter focused on one aspect of imperfect information, the problem faced by a consumer searching for prices. With hardly any modification this analysis can be applied to search where there is uncertainty concerning the quality of goods offered. Suppose all shops charge the same price but differ in the quality of goods sold. Consumers know the market distribution of quality but not the characteristics of the goods offered by a particular shop. Assume, however, that quality can be ascertained before purchase by visiting a shop and inspecting the goods. If a monetary value is attached to each grade of a good then an optimal strategy based on the costs and benefits of an additional search can be devised much as before.

Unfortunately this model captures few of the important issues concerning product quality. The unsatisfactory assumption is that customers are able to judge quality before purchase. Typically it is only after having used a good for some time that its characteristics become known. But by then it is generally too late. For example, will a second hand car perform satisfactorily? Even with prior inspection it is difficult to know without using it for some time. In somewhat similar vein, an employer may have difficulty determining an employee's productive potential at the time of hiring, or a worker may be unsure of employment conditions when he accepts a job.

In this chapter we shall be concerned with the operation of markets in which participants are unsure of the exact nature of the goods that are traded. A further complication is that such markets are typically characterised by asymmetric information. One side of the market possesses knowledge the other side does not. Implications include that where customers cannot properly judge quality at the point of sale there is an incentive for the sellers of substandard goods to make false quality claims. And even if customers are prepared to pay for quality if they are certain they are getting it, there is little motivation for a seller to supply high quality items since customers cannot distinguish them from inferior products at the point of sale.

The above description paints a very pessimistic picture. Yet it is clear that in the absence of perfect information incentives exist to improve the situation. Thus, where job applicants have different productive potentials employers will find it worthwhile to try and find out as much as they can about them. That is, they will subject applicants to a 'screening' process. What kind of things may be looked for in a potential employee? Productivity cannot be judged directly but some observable characteristics may turn out to be quite closely correlated with it. Thus possession of a degree may indicate attributes that will prove useful in certain kinds of jobs. Similarly race or sex, whether or not justifiably, may be taken by employers as indicators of on-the-job performance. Any observable characteristic of this kind which conveys information to market participants is known as a 'signal'. From the examples given it may be seen that some signals, such as higher education, may be under the control of individuals and others, such as sex and race, cannot be changed.[1] We shall be considering the equilibrium and welfare characteristics of markets in the presence of screening and signalling. To begin with, a special and interesting class of cases will be examined. These are markets in which price itself serves as a signal of quality.

I THE MARKET FOR 'LEMONS'

The ideas here are based on a stimulating and important article by George Akerlof (1970). The type of markets studied are those in which the sellers of a good know its characteristics better than do potential buyers. It will be shown that in the presence of such an asymmetric distribution of information the functioning of the market is impaired, and that in the limit all trade may cease. In such circumstances a case may be made for government intervention to increase the welfare of all parties.

(a) Used Cars as an Example

Some new cars of a particular make and model are good and some are bad (in the US they are known as 'lemons', in the UK as 'Friday' cars). The bad cars are continually breaking down and subject to all

---

1. In Michael Spence's seminal work (see references) the unalterable signals are termed 'indices'.

sorts of gremlins. If the car is a lemon this soon becomes known to the owner. However, it is difficult for a potential buyer to judge whether the car is a lemon (and the seller will hardly tell him). The buyer may be aware of the average quality of cars traded on the market but will have difficulty ascertaining the characteristics of any particular car.

Consider the second-hand market for three month resales of new cars. This market is subject to a severe problem. Anyone who sells a car after three months' ownership automatically creates a suspicion. Why is he selling? Perhaps because he knows the car is a lemon. Therefore, don't buy.[1]

More generally, the demand for three month resales will depend on price and on the probability of being sold a lemon, which tends to increase as price falls. This is because a reduction in price contracts supply and it will be the owners of the better quality cars who, at the lower price, no longer find it worth selling. Thus the fall in price reduces the average quality of cars offered.

Suppose at the initial price supply exceeds demand. The fall in price contracts supply but increases the probability of being sold a lemon. Demand may therefore also fall. Hence it is not certain that at the lower price excess supply will fall. Whilst no market clearing price may exist it is more likely that the price of each vintage of used car (and particularly the more recent vintages) will be below the price of a new car by a factor greater than can be accounted for by depreciation in use. Owners of good cars will be 'locked in' (unable to trade at a realistic price) and potentially Pareto efficient trades will not take place. Finally, note that the lemons problem is less severe if a used car is bought from a dealer. This is because dealers can offer fairly effective guarantees and, being in the market continuously, will suffer greatly if their reputation becomes tarnished. The result is that dealers are able to sell at significantly higher prices than private sellers because their quality claims are more reliable.

Questions

Q14.1 Equal numbers of four qualities of a certain brand of automobile are produced by a manufacturer. The values placed on each grade of car by two groups of potential consumers are as shown. No consumer wishes to own more than a single car and there are three times as many type 1 consumers as there are type 2 consumers. The

---

1. This seems to be a variant of the Marx (Groucho) problem 'I don't want to be a member of the kind of club that will have me as a member'.

Automobile quality	Value to type 1 ($'000)	Value to type 2 ($'000)
A	20	18
B	18	17
C	15	16
D	11	12

price of a new car is $16,000. All consumers are expected utility maximisers and for simplicity have a constant marginal utility of income. Ignore depreciation during the first three months after a car leaves the factory.

(a) Analyse the market for three-month resales assuming that consumers are only able to judge the quality of a specific car after purchase but that they do know the average quality of cars traded. What kinds of car will be traded and at what price?

(b) If both buyers and sellers know the quality of every second-hand car traded, will all consumers be better off than in the previous case?

(c) What explanation, apart from the 'lemons' phenomenon, can be offered as to why three month cars generally sell at a high discount on the new price?

(d) It sometimes happens that a manufacturer starts production of a new model before having sufficient capacity to cope with demand. Long waiting lists develop and possibly second-hand cars exchange for higher prices than new cars (this has sometimes been the case with Jaguar cars). Under these circumstances why does not the manufacturer raise prices to eliminate the excess demand?

(b) Insurance as an Example

An insurance policy is more valuable to a person the more likely he is to have to make a claim or, from the viewpoint of the insurance company, the more likely he is to be a bad risk. It follows that the higher the premium charged on a policy the more good risks are lost by an insurance company for only bad risks are prepared to pay high premiums. As a result, every individual in the market may be willing to take out 'fair' insurance yet no insurance company can afford to sell a policy because at any price it will attract too many 'lemons'. This problem is known in the insurance context as the problem of 'adverse selection'. A case for compulsory state medical insurance can be established on the basis of this effect.

Questions

Q14.2 The value to a buyer of an insurance policy offering full compensation in the event of loss clearly depends on the probability that such a loss will be suffered. Suppose there are two equal-sized groups of customers in the market. The high risk customers are prepared to pay £212 for the policy and the low risks £180. If a policy is offered to the high risk individuals the expected value of the claim is £200 and for the low risks it is £170. Assume the insurance market is competitive and therefore that in equilibrium the expected cost of a policy equals its price and, crucially, that insurance companies know the proportion of high and low risk individuals in the market as a whole, but not the riskiness of any particular customer.

(a) Assuming that the only policy to be offered is one which offers full compensation, at what price will it be sold?
(b) Now consider an alternative policy which pays only a fraction of costs in the event of loss. This policy is of course less attractive to customers than the first, and bad risks are only prepared to pay £130 for it, whilst good risks, for whom the loss of complete coverage is less serious since their expectation of suffering a loss is lower, are prepared to pay £120. The expected cost of providing the policy to the good risk customers is £119. What equilibrium will now be established in the insurance market? (Assume it is possible to sell both complete and partial policies.)
(c) Suppose a competitive equilibrium were to be established in which individual good risks *can* be directly distinguished from bad risks. What policies would be offered then?
(d) If from the equilibrium in (b) the high risks declare themselves as such, who gains and who loses?
(e) In the circumstances of (b) is there a case for state provision of insurance?

Q14.3 Even if there is no adverse selection problem, insurance firms are often reluctant to offer policies which pay the full amount of loss suffered. Why is this?

(c) The Cost of Dishonesty as an Example

Where buyers cannot distinguish good quality from bad there is a clear incentive for sellers to produce low standard goods (assuming it is cheaper to produce low than high quality goods). As this happens and the average standard of the product offered declines, so demand (for all grades of good) will fall and eventually the market may disappear, even though at the right quality it is well worth producing the good.

Questions

Q14.4 Suppose there are two types of producers of a good. Highly skilled and efficient manufacturers produce an article which customers value at £14, whilst 'cowboy' producers sell a good which is worth £8. At the time of sale customers cannot distinguish a high quality product from a low quality but they do know from experience the average proportions of the two types of good in the market.

(a) If there are equal numbers of both types of producer and both have constant per unit production costs of £11.50 at what price will trade take place?
(b) Will banning low quality sellers (say by forming a trade association which effectively polices quality) yield an actual Pareto improvement?
(c) Now suppose that *each* producer can produce either a high or a low quality good. The high quality costs £11.50 to produce and the low quality £11. In the absence of intervention what will the competitive market equilibrium price be? Will the manufacturers have an incentive to form a trade organisation to ban low quality production?

Counteracting Institutions

This 'lemons' problem tends to disappear in markets characterised by repeat purchases. If a customer buys a poor quality good from a shop he will not return. Thus there is a tendency for the poor quality sellers to loose business and the good quality to gain. Through time poor quality sellers may therefore be driven out of the market and product quality not be degraded. However, it may still be worthwhile for fly-by-night operators to enter, offer low quality goods, make quick profits and move on before their reputation becomes established. Indeed, many goods may not be bought sufficiently frequently for the identity of reputable sellers ever to become known (durable goods, tourist services, etc.). It follows that the 'lemons' problem may still persist, at least unless the market participant can do something to prevent it.

To recapitulate, for goods bought at infrequent intervals, seller reputation may never be established and so the incentive remains for dealers to make a fast buck by degrading quality and perhaps ultimately destroying the market. However, even though individual goods may be bought infrequently, a customer may visit a shop or dealer or buy from a manufacturer often if they stock a wide variety of goods. To establish a reputation for quality and avoid the lemons problem high-quality sellers therefore have an incentive to diversify into many lines of business. All sorts of goods will be sold under single brand names and departmental stores and chain stores will come into being.

Guarantees can also play an important role in signalling quality. Only the better quality sellers will be able to offer comprehensive guarantees (since the expected cost of providing a guarantee is lower for more reliable goods). Thus customers may to some extent be able to discriminate between qualities and so overall standards not be degraded. The problem is that it is difficult for customers to know how effectively guarantees will be honoured.

Similarly, firms may seek ways of convincing customers of their intention to remain in business permanently. The motivation for doing this is that such firms will have to adopt honest marketing policies, if they are to secure the repeat sales and recommendations necessary for long-term survival. Building elaborate premises decorated with expensive sculptures and engaging in prestige advertising can yield a pay-off only in the long run. Therefore, these activities serve as a signal to potential customers that the firms will stay in business in the long run and hence will honour their quality claims.

Finally, note that one interpretation of the lemons problem is as an externality. Low quality sellers reduce the sales of all traders. One way of dealing with this is for the good quality sellers to get together and form an association from which the low quality sellers are banned. This may be done with the help of the state, as for example with doctors, or less effectively by means of a trade association. Hence it is possible that licensing systems and trade groups, which are often the object of obloquy by economists, may actually deal with lemon type problems and be welfare improving even if at the same time they extract monopoly rents.

II NON-PRICE SIGNALS

(a)   Education as an Example

Graduates earn more on average than those who do not have degrees. At least four possible explanations of this observation exist.

1. A degree is not in any way responsible for the earnings differential. It so happens that those with a high earning potential also have a preference for university or college life. The correlation between earnings and degrees is spurious as far as causation is concerned (in the same way as is the reported correlation between storks migrating from Denmark and births in Britain).
2. As a result of artificial and conventional rigidities certain jobs offer high wages. These wages do not respond to the forces of demand and supply. Naturally there is competition to get such jobs. Although employers have no real expectation that the holder of a degree will be more productive, nevertheless since a degree nominally represents a qualification and is a method of choosing from amongst the excess supply of applicants, it is graduates who get the well paid jobs. The degree is therefore a method of rationing and becomes necessary to obtain a well paid job. (Graduates and non-graduates become, in effect, non-competing groups.)
3. Another possibility is that what students learn during their course actually raises their productivity in work. Earnings are related to productivity and hence it is the degree course that is responsible for the higher earnings. This is the human capital approach. Education creates useful skills.
4. A degree course does not raise the productivity of the graduate. However, those people who can successfully complete such a course require aptitudes which will also prove highly productive in work. Employers cannot directly assess the productivity of school leavers but the possession of a degree does serve as a good indicator of ability (i.e. it serves as a signal of high productivity). Therefore, although education does not raise productivity, it acts as a kind of aptitude test (and so is a method of 'screening' applicants). Consequently it yields its possessors a high income.

Though the first three explanations may contain elements of truth, it is the last explanation that will be explored here. In the following questions assume that, in the absence of any signal, firms cannot tell the true productivity of potential employees. Indeed, even after employment, abilities do not become clear until retirement, when it is too late. This assumption is relaxed in the section on internal labour markets but for the moment we wish to highlight one aspect of signalling effects. After the questions we summarise the conclusions they suggest.

Questions

Q14.5   Suppose there are equal numbers of two kinds of people; alphas whose productivity is 15 units and betas whose productivity is 5 units. Production takes place in perfectly competitive firms.

(a) Assume employers cannot assess the productivity of individual workers but do know the average productivity of the work force. What will be the wage rate and, if there are n workers in total, what will be the output of the economy?

(b) Now suppose that at a cost of 2 units of output, alphas can obtain a degree. Betas, however, do not have the particular mental abilities required to pass the exam however much they 'spend' in the attempt. If it is generally known that only alphas can pass the exam, what will be the wage structure, the rate of return to education, and the net output of the economy?

(c) Suppose the cost of the degree is 6. What will wage rates be?

(d) If no individual knows whether he is an alpha or beta examine the possible equilibria. (Assume the cost of taking the course is 2.)

Q14.6 This time there are, as before, two categories of workers, alphas and betas, but now there are two kinds of job, 1 and 2. The productivity of the two types of worker in the two jobs (or production techniques) is as shown.

	Job 1	Job 2
alpha	20	10
beta	10	16

(a) Suppose alphas and betas can be distinguished at no cost. What will be the wage rates and total economy output?

(b) If it is impossible to determine whether any particular individual is an alpha or a beta what will be the wage rate and the output of the economy?

(c) If the same test (degree course) as before is available at a cost

of 2 to determine whether an individual is an alpha or a beta
what will happen to total output? What will be the private rate
of return to education?

Although highly stylised, questions 14.5 and 14.6 should convince
that, in the absence of direct information concerning productivities,
education may well serve as a screening device. If it does so it could
either raise or lower the aggregate real income of the community
though educational signalling will always tend to widen wage dif-
ferentials.

Summary Results on Educational Signalling

1. Signalling may make society as a whole worse off [Q14.5 sections
   (a) and (b)].
2. Signalling may make society as a whole better off [Q14.6
   sections (b) and (c)].
3. Signalling may make the group buying the signal better off than
   if there was no signalling [Q14.5 (a) and (b)].
4. Signalling may make the group buying the signal worse off than
   if there was no signal available [Q14.5 (a) and (c)].
5. The availability of a signal may make the non-signallers worse
   off [Q14.5 (a) and (b)].
6. The signal may make the non-signallers better off [Q14.6 (b)
   and (c)].

A more general model of signalling than in the questions above is
to assume that education can be acquired by everyone, but is less
costly for the more productive. A signalling equilibrium is then
characterised by the return to education being positive for the more
able and negative for the less able. Employers believing that a degree
is a signal of ability would consequently find their beliefs confirmed
and so an equilibrium be established.

(b) Non-Educational Signals

As mentioned in the introduction, not all characteristics that employers use as proxies for productivity may be under the control of
the applicant. It may be possible to decide voluntarily to take a degree.
However, it is not feasible to change sex or race. Yet employers may
judge that either of these characteristics yields information about
productivity. Most plausibly, whether or not justifiably, the attitude
held may be that whilst not all women are less productive than all
men, the proportion of less productive women is higher than that of

men. (Many of the reasons why women workers may be less productive than men have to do with sociological factors — it's always mother who stays home when the kids are sick — rather than any kind of biological or psychological factor.) The following question examines some of the implications of this model.

Question

Q14.7 In a particular job there is an equal chance that a man will have a productivity of either 6 or 9. For women the probability of productivity 6 is 2/3 and the probability of productivity 9 is 1/3. Assume that employers are unable to judge the productivity of individual applicants but do know the average productivity of the group to which they belong.

(a) What will be the wage of men and women?
(b) If equal pay legislation is passed what will happen to wage rates and to the level of employment of women?
(c) Suppose in addition to equal pay it is required that the sexes be hired in the same proportion as they apply for jobs (equal opportunities). What will happen to wages if as many men as women seek jobs?

III INTERNAL LABOUR MARKETS

A common tendency is for large corporations to recruit only the most junior staff outside the firm. Appointment to more senior positions comes about through internal promotion. One explanation for this practice is simply that after a time with the firm, employees develop firm-specific skills and knowledge. Thus the most suitable candidates for promotion are naturally existing employees. Secondly, other things equal, employees prefer to avoid the disruption of a move to another firm. Thus the employer can get an internal candidate at lower rates than an outsider who must be compensated for the transfer. Also, appointments from outside may adversely affect morale in the firm. In fact it may become difficult to make junior appointments if senior jobs are always filled from outside.

Let us, however, concentrate on an alternative explanation. Suppose no acquisition of firm-specific skills takes place. However, individuals only reveal their true characteristics after having been employed by the firm for a period. The firm is then able to make appropriate promotions once it has this knowledge. This explanation of internal labour markets is based simply on the fact that the firm knows the attributes of its own employees much better than those of outsiders. It can therefore slot people into the right jobs more effectively by internal promotion.

One qualification to the above analysis is required. If one firm promotes a person, that acts as a signal to others that he has certain desirable characteristics. Promotion acts as a signal to other employers who will tend to poach the now identified high quality employee. Internal labour markets will therefore tend to break down since information about outside candidates is no longer scarce. This will not happen to the extent that different firms seek different characteristics in employees. Then the fact that one firm promotes someone gives limited useful information to other firms, who will again have an incentive to promote from their own ranks.

Questions

Q14.8 Small firms can discover the attributes of their employees more rapidly than can large firms. People who know they are of above average ability would therefore be well advised to seek their first job in small firms.

Q14.9 Suppose that a firm pays the training costs of its workers. These equal $10. Workers are of two kinds. Both types stay with the firm for at least one period but high turnover workers (possibly women) have a half chance of leaving the firm at the end of the first period whilst low turnover workers, once they have committed themselves to the firm, are certain to stay for two periods (their whole working life). Assume that in firms with no training costs required, the per period wage either kind of worker can earn is $5. If, for simplicity, firms and workers both have a zero discount rate what kind of wage structure and promotion policy will be offered by the firm with training costs?

References

Akerlof G., 'The market for lemons: qualitative uncertainty and the market mechanism', *Quarterly Journal of Economics*, August 1970. Arrow K.J., 'Some mathematical models of race discrimination in the labour market' in A.H. Pascal (ed.) *Racial Discrimination in Economic Life*, Lexington Books 1972. Doeringer P and Piore M., *Internal Labor Markets and Manpower Analysis*, D.C. Heath 1971. Nelson P., 'Information and consumer behaviour', *Journal of Political Economy*, March/April 1970. Spence A.M., 'Job market signalling', *Quarterly Journal of Economics*, 87, 1973. Spence A.M., *Market Signalling: Informational Transfer in*

Hiring and Related Screening Processes, Cambridge University Press 1974.
Stiglitz J.E., 'The theory of "screening" education and the distribution of income',
American Economic Review, June 1975.
See also 'Symposium: The Economics of Information', *Quarterly Journal of Economics*, 1976, pp. 591-696 and 'Symposium on Economics of Information',
Review of Economics Studies, 1977, pp. 389-601.

Answers

A14.1(a) The expected use value of a new car to type 1 consumers is
(in thousands of dollars) $(20 + 18 + 15 + 11)/4 = \$16$, and to type
2 consumers is $(18 + 17 + 16 + 12)/4 = \$15\frac{3}{4}$. Since the price of
new cars is $16, type 1 consumers buy new cars and type 2 consumers
do not. If there are N type 1 consumers and hence $N/3$ type 2 consumers the demand (by type 2 consumers) and supply (by type 1
consumers) of used cars can be summarised as in the table below and
in figure 14.1.

Price	Supply	Average value to type 2 consumers of cars offered	Demand
$11 < P < 12$	$\frac{1}{4}N$	12	$N/3$
$12 < P < 15$	$\frac{1}{4}N$	12	0
$15 < P < 18$	$\frac{1}{2}N$	14	0
$18 < P < 20$	$\frac{3}{4}N$	15	0
$20 < P$	N	$15\frac{3}{4}$	0

$N/4$ cars of quality D are traded at a price of $12. The gain to type 1
traders is $\$N/4$ whilst type 2 traders just pay the maximum they are
prepared to for grade D cars.

There are a number of additional characteristics of this solution
that should be noted. As it turns out that grade D cars sell for $12
the expected value of a new car to type 1 customers is actually
$20 + 18 + 15 + 12/4 = \$16.25$. Thus they will definitely buy new
cars. Type 2 customers, however, still value new cars at $15.75 since
their use value of a D car is $12. Buying a new car at $16 therefore
actually yields an expected gain of $0.25 to type 1 customers. If on
selling a car they expect to be able to re-enter the new market they
will be prepared to sell each grade of car at $0.25 less than shown in
the schedules above. However, it is easily seen that this still leaves the
price at $12 and supply at this price is $N/4$ D cars.

It may also be asked whether this solution will repeat itself period
by period. There is no reason why it should not. After three months

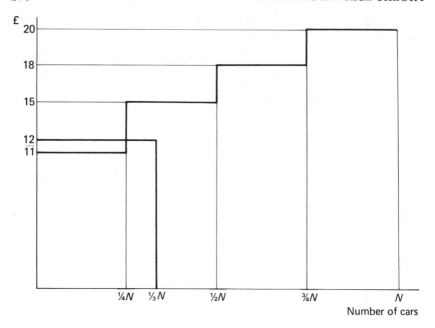

Figure 14.1

$N/4$ type 1 customers will be re-entering the market for new cars. Additionally, there will be owners of both types who have held cars until they are no longer worth using and thus are about to re-enter the market. This outline of market dynamics should suggest that the market can indeed repeat itself period by period.

(b) $P_C = 15$, $P_D = 11$. Both grade D and grade C cars are tradable when the quality of each individual car is known to consumers. Suppose $P_C = 15$ and $P_D = 11$. Type 2 buyers would then be indifferent between the two qualities of cars (the net gain to type 2 consumers from the purchase of either quality of car being $1). At these prices the total number of cars offered is $N/2$ and $N/3$ will be bought. Sellers have no incentive to reduce prices further for then cars would be fetching far less than their use value to the sellers (at selling prices 11 and 15 the expected value of a new car to type 1 consumers equals 16 and so this time no incentive exists to cut prices below these levels in order to enter the new market), and if the price of either grade of car were to be raised (separately or together) competition between sellers would cause prices to fall back to $P_C = 15$ and $P_D = 11$. These are consequently the equilibrium prices. Compared to case (a) type 1 consumers gain $N/3$ and type 2 consumers lose $N/4$. Whilst there is a net gain of $(N/3 - N/4) = N/12$, not all consumers gain.

(c) A common suggestion is that there are prestige and other psychological attractions in buying a brand new as opposed to a second-hand car. Alternatively, the car may be subject to real physical depreciation over the first three months. However, some variant of the lemons analysis and imperfect information effects does seem relevant in explaining much of the depreciation. Would you buy a used car from a man who had owned it for only three months unless he could tell a very good story?

(d) Long waiting lists may serve as a very effective advert for the car. They lead to higher sales in the long-run when capacity is fully adequate since it remains in the public memory that owning this type of car is prestigious and something rather special. If, alternatively, prices were initially high and then cut this may serve as an adverse signal. Potential customers may think there is something wrong with the model if a price cut is needed to maintain sales.

A14.2(a) **£200.** At this price only high risks find it worthwhile to buy and since their expected claims are £200 the insurance companies make zero expected profits. If price were between £200 and £180 then no low risk customers would be attracted and the insurance companies would make losses. Should a price of £180 be charged then the low risks *are* attracted, however the expected claim per policy is ½ × 200 + ½ × 170 = £185 and so again losses are expected.

(b) **Full coverage offered at £200, partial coverage offered at £119.** If high risk customers buy the £200 policy they enjoy a 'consumer surplus' of £12. If they buy the £119 policy their surplus is only £11. Thus they undertake full insurance and the suppliers of such policies just cover their expected costs. That leaves the low risk individuals to buy the partial coverage policy at £119, on which they enjoy a surplus of £1. Once again the providers of this policy just cover expected costs. If any of these firms were to offer a slightly more comprehensive policy it would attract all the high risks and so make a loss. If a less comprehensive policy is offered, all low risk customers would be lost (remember at fair rates the most preferred policy is one which fully covers any loss). The incomplete coverage policy in the question was therefore chosen as the most comprehensive policy which, when offered at a price equal to the expected cost of low risk claims, is just sufficiently expensive that the high risk customers find it better to buy the fully comprehensive policy. Of course, no such policy may exist in which case in equilibrium the only policy offered will be a fully comprehensive one at £200.

This analysis has been based on the very interesting paper by M. Rothschild and J. Stiglitz, 'Equilibrium in competitive insurance markets: an essay on the economics of imperfect information'

(*Quarterly Journal of Economics*, November 1976). Whilst this question gives the spirit of their analysis, by providing a proper foundation in terms of utility theory R and S also show that it is possible (but not necessary) that no equilibrium exists in competitive insurance markets.

(c) **Fully comprehensive at price £200 to bad risks and £170 to low risks.** Remember, as shown in Q4.18, at fair premiums an individual's most preferred policy is one which covers any risk and so equalises income in all states.

(d) Now the solution in (c) is established, so the high risks lose nothing and the low risks gain £9. Insurance companies continue to cover expected costs.

(e) YES. If the government were to provide fully comprehensive insurance free of charge the average benefit per person is (212 + 180)/2 = £196 and the expected cost is (200 + 170)/2 = £185. Hence the average net benefit per person is £11 whilst in the solution to (b) it was only £5.

This is therefore an argument in favour of state provision. But, before recommending such intervention, knowledge both of how state provision works in practice as well as of the efficiency costs of raising taxes to cover the financial losses involved is really required. There is also the 'moral hazard' problem considered in the next question and answer.

A14.3 Suppose if my house burns down I lose $50,000. If my insurance policy pays me $50,000 in these circumstances, then my net losses are zero. Consequently, I have no incentive to take precautions to avoid my house burning down (fire extinguishers, alarms, etc.). These precautions may be efficient in the sense that when they are taken the expected value of the claim falls by more than the cost of the precautions. To provide an incentive to take these efficient precautions the insurance company may refuse to insure up to the full value of the house.

The fact that insurance reduces the incentive to take efficient precautions is known as the 'moral hazard' problem. One way to try and get around it is for the insurance company to stipulate that certain precautions must be taken (fire alarms installed, etc.) before a policy is granted. This often happens. But where the precautions depend on the actions of the insured (such as being careful with matches) it is more difficult to induce efficient precautions to be taken. To some extent an incentive for precaution always remains since the value of the property to the insured is generally greater than the market value, which is the most that a company will normally pay in the event of a loss. But because of the moral hazard problem it is generally optimal for insurance companies to offer policies which pay out less than the market value in the event of a loss. As a very severe example of a moral hazard problem can you see why insurance companies will not offer policies to cover loss of profits?

A14.4(a) **No market.** Both firms are prepared to supply as long as price exceeds £11.5. However with both firms in the market the expected value of a purchase to a customer is only £11. Thus there is no price at which demand is positive and producers cover costs. There can be no market.

(b) **YES.** Depending on the relative number of buyers and sellers price will either be £11.5 or £14 (it may be £14 if there is a limit to the amount each producer can manufacture). If the former, consumers are better off and producers no worse off; if the latter, the reverse is true.

(c) **No trade.** Since customers cannot tell at the time of purchase whether a good is high or low quality all manufacturers will save costs by producing the low quality good because both types sell for the same price (assuming competition, no seller is sufficiently large for his strategy to make an appreciable difference to average market quality). But the cost of producing the low quality item is greater than the market value so no trade will take place. If sellers start producing high quality items they will find that they will be swamped by low quality producers trying to cash in and spoiling the market.

Excluding low quality production, as before, will yield a potential Pareto improvement and allow some sellers to survive, possibly making supra-normal profits if they are limited in number. Thus an incentive to form a producer association exists.

A14.5(a) **Wage = 10. Output = 10n.** The expected productivity of a worker is $\frac{1}{2} \times 15 + \frac{1}{2} \times 5 = 10$. Any employer who offers a wage less than this will be outbid by other firms able to make a positive expected profit from additional employment when the wage is below 10. If a firm offers a wage above 10 it will expect to make a loss.

(b) **Wage of alphas = 15 (net of education cost, 13); wage of betas 5; net output is 9n.** If an alpha spends 2, his true productivity will be identified and he will earn 15. As compared to the solution in (a) this represents a net gain in income of 3 and so all the alphas will be induced to buy education. Those with no education will all be betas earning 5. For alphas the rate of return to education is $(15 - 5)/2 \times 100 = 500\%$. After netting out the cost of education the output of the economy is $5n/2 + 13n/2 = 9n$. Since net output is lower by 10% the social rate of return to education is -10%. As far as this example is concerned, making available higher education seems undesirable since it reduces net output and increases inequality.

(c) **Three equilibria exist.** Suppose last generation no one acquired a degree. The wage rate was therefore 10. If in this generation each person expects the same thing to happen as last generation then each alpha will calculate that by taking the course his income will rise by 5. This will not pay for the cost of education, so nobody will undertake it this generation. We therefore have an equilibrium repeating itself period by period.

Now consider the situation if last generation all alphas were graduates. They would be paid 15 and those without education be recognised as betas and paid 5. It follows that the pay-off to education is 10 and exceeds the cost. All alphas will become graduates and initial expectations be fulfilled. Hence another possible equilibrium is that all alphas become graduates. But in this case the net wage of the graduates (9) is lower than if no education were available.

Finally, consider the case in which 1/5 of all alphas take the course. Then the net income of an individual alpha is 13 whichever strategy he follows. However, this is an unstable equilibrium. If the proportion of alpha graduates is displaced from 1/5, the switch will continue until one of the two previously specified equilibria is established.

(d) Start from the initial equilibrium wage of 10 prevailing if nobody buys education. An individual can then make the following calculations. By taking the course he has a 50% chance of being certified an alpha. His expected return is therefore $\frac{1}{2} \times 5 = 2.5$ (he fails the exam if a beta, but we assume he can pretend he never took the exam). This exceeds the cost of education. However, as taking the course is an uncertain prospect with an equal chance of a net return of 3 or -2, a risk averse individual may not choose to take the course. If everybody acts in a similar fashion then nobody gets educated and this is consistent with the individual's initial assumption.

Alternatively, if last period everybody took the degree course then those passing the exam were paid 15 and those failing it 5, along with people not taking the exam. Under these circumstances the expected return to education for each individual (not knowing his own abilities) is $\frac{1}{2} \times 10 = 5$ giving a net expected return of 3. This may well be sufficient to offset risk aversion in which case everybody would take the course and again the initial expectations be fulfilled. The economy's output falls to $8n$.

A14.6(a) **Wage alphas = 20, betas = 16, total output = 18n.** Employers will allocate alphas to Job 1 where their productivity exceeds that in Job II and betas to Job II, leading to the wages given above. Assuming equal numbers of alphas and betas, output is $\frac{1}{2}n20 + \frac{1}{2}n16 = 18n$.

(b) **Wage = 15, output = 15n.** The expected productivity of a worker in Job I is 15 and in Job II is 13. Employers will therefore allocate all their workers to Job I and pay a wage of 15.

(c) **Wage alphas = 20, net = 18, wage betas = 16, net output = 17n, private rate of return to education = 200%.** Alphas will find it worthwhile taking the degree for then they are allocated to Job I and receive 20 giving a net wage of 18. Betas will then be identified as not having degrees and be allocated to Job II receiving a wage of 16. The private rate of return to education for the alphas is $(20 - 16)/2 \times 100 = 200\%$, remembering that an alpha can now pass as a beta and be paid 16 without the degree. The interesting thing to note here is that as compared to (b) not only is total output higher but everyone is better off. This is because in this model, information is socially valuable in allocating people to the right jobs.

A14.7(a) The expected productivity of men is $\frac{1}{2} \times 6 + \frac{1}{2} \times 9 = 7\frac{1}{2}$, which will be their wage, and of women is $2/3 \times 6 + 1/3 \times 9 = 7$.

(b) **Wages = 7½, all women unemployed.** Suppose the wage is 7½. Employers would then be happy to hire men but not women. One possible solution is that one group of firms employ only men at a wage of 7½ and another only women at wage 7. However, we assume this is not permitted and that all firms must pay the same wage. It then follows that the market wage would be 7½ and no women be employed. Suppose the market wage were 7¼. Any firm could then raise its wage to 7.3, get as many men as in the market and, since their productivity is 7½, increase profits. Only a wage of 7½ is a sustainable equilibrium.

(c) **Wage equals 7¼, full employment.** When a firm employs an additional woman it can also employ another man and so its output rises by $7 + 7\frac{1}{2} = 14\frac{1}{2}$ and so it is prepared to pay, and granted competition actually will pay, 7¼ to both the man and the woman.

A14.8 **UNCERTAIN.** Whilst it may be true that small firms discover worker ability faster than large firms, this does not necessarily mean they are better bets for those of higher ability. Opportunities for promotion arise less frequently in small firms and the variety of jobs they offer tends to be smaller. Hence promotion prospects, particularly for the risk averse, may be less attractive in small firms. Furthermore, promotion in a large firm with an established reputation may be a more marketable asset for getting a job elsewhere. That is, other employers do not know the attributes of small firms and therefore cannot judge whether their apparently successful employees really have desirable characteristics.

A14.9 **Internal promotion with age.** If the offer was of $5 in both periods of a worker's life then some quitters would be attracted, and when they left at the end of the first period the training cost of $10 would have to be paid for their replacements. Suppose instead the firm promised $4 in the first period of work and $6.50 in the second period. Quitters would not accept this offer since they would forego $1 in the first period and have only half a chance of obtaining the $1.50 extra in the second period, thereby reducing expected lifetime income by $0.25. Non-quitters however, are delighted to accept the offer since it raises their lifetime income by $0.50. The firm saves considerably on the training costs of the quitters. Offering this kind of wage schedule therefore induces workers with the characteristics the firm desires to self-select themselves. (See 'Self-selection and turnover in the labour market' J. Salop and S. Salop, *Quarterly Journal of Economics,* November 1976).

To all intents and purposes an internal labour market has emerged — obviously 'promotion' to the higher second period wage will be offered only to workers who have spent the first period with the firm.

Can you see why this wage policy will be less attractive to firms if workers face imperfect capital markets? In such circumstances, if firms providing training are unable to enforce long-term labour contracts, they may offer first period wages equal to those available in non-training firms but higher wages in the second period of the worker's life. The motivation is to reduce turnover costs by diminishing the incentive for workers to quit (see A6.16). Such firms will experience an excess supply of applicants, but of course they will not respond by cutting wages. It may be interesting to look at Q6.12 again in the light of this turnover model.

15

Public Choice

PUBLIC GOODS

Markets are one method of allocating scarce resources. However, a substantial proportion of the economic activity of modern societies is under the direct collective control of governments, whether local or central. One explanation is that the government can do a better job of providing certain kinds of goods than can the market. Notice that this is a strictly comparative advantage proposition. Demonstrating that a particular market does not achieve the conditions necessary for Pareto efficiency is not a sufficient basis for saying that collective provision would represent an improvement. In democracies politicians are voted into office by individuals pursuing their own private interests, the politicians themselves are likely to be motivated (at least proximately) by the desire to maximise their chances of re-election, and government agencies are staffed by persons trying to climb the bureaucratic ladder. There is no guarantee that in the event the government will perform better than the market. Nevertheless there is a class of goods, public goods, in the provision of which it is rather likely that the market will perform badly and for which the case in favour of government intervention is therefore strongest.

A public good is a slippery concept to define. Different authors emphasise different aspects, and this is probably a case where the pursuit of definitional purity is of no particular help when it comes to policy prescription (see Mishan 1971 for a review of the problem). However the general approach is to require of a public good that it satisfy the conditions of 'non-rivalness' and 'non-excludability'.

The non-rival property is that one person's consumption of a good does not reduce the amount available to other people.[1] For example,

1. Distinctions have sometimes been drawn between optional non-rival goods, such as TV programmes which not everyone has to consume at the same level

283

when one ship makes use of a lighthouse this does not reduce the value of the light to other shipping. This is in contrast to a private good such as apples for which the more one person eats the less there is for others. Non-excludability means that the provider of a good cannot prevent people from using it. Once a lighthouse is operated it is impossible to stop all shipping using the route from benefiting. Together, non-rivalness and non-excludability certainly give rise to problems for market economies. The provider of a non-rival good will not necessarily take the benefits it yields to others into account, and certainly has little incentive to do so if non-excludability means they cannot be charged for these benefits (public goods may be regarded as jointly supplying all members of the community with services). Furthermore, there is little reason to provide the good for own consumption. Rather there is a temptation to rely on others to provide it who are then unable to exclude non-payers. This is known as the free-rider problem (it is the major reason public goods are distinguished from externalities).

Non-rivalness or non-excludability even taken individually give rise to problems. If a good is non-rival but excludable (perhaps an uncongested road) then the provider will set a positive price. This will discourage some users, but since the social opportunity cost of allowing their consumption is by definition zero, this is socially sub-optimal.[2] A good which is non-excludable but rival (perhaps an apple tree in a private garden from which the local kids steal apples) cannot be charged for. Hence benefits accrue to some users which the provider does not take into account when deciding how much to produce.

The existence of public goods therefore creates a case for collective provision. The problem is to formulate institutional means of deciding, in the absence of markets, how much government expenditure there should be and how the revenue should be raised to cover costs. We defer the discussion of voting rules until after the questions on public goods.

References

Demsetz H., 'The private production of public goods' *Journal of Law and Economics* 1970. Head J.G., 'Public goods and public policy', *Public Finance* 1962. Mishan E.J., 'The postwar literature on externalities', *Journal of Economic Literature*, March 1971. Samuelson P.A., 'The pure theory of public expenditure', *Review of Economics and Statistics*, Vol 36, 1954.

(you can turn off) and non-optional non-rival goods such as national defence which all must consume at the same level.
2. But see Demsetz and question 15.7 for a case where this problem does not arise.

Questions

Q15.1 In the absence of government intervention a market economy would never produce a public good.

Q15.2 If a good is non-rival but excludable it will never be produced by the private sector.

Q15.3 If a non-rival good is sold in the market its price must exceed the marginal social cost of additional usage. It follows that collective government provision would lead to a potential Pareto improvement.

Q15.4 Suppose a government follows a socially optimal policy of providing an optional non-rival but excludable good. If all users must be charged the same per unit price most users will wish to buy more units than they can and no consumer fewer. (Assume no efficiency costs in raising the revenue required to cover any losses.)

Q15.5 A road is a non-rival good because one individual's use of it does not reduce that of another.

Q15.6 Once a non-rival good is produced it is potentially available to all members of a community. Hence it is wrong to argue that larger communities will tend to consume greater quantities of a particular non-rival good than smaller communities.

Q15.7 If all consumers of an excludable non-rival good have identical tastes, a Pareto optimal solution will emerge in the market if there is competition between suppliers.

Answers

A15.1 FALSE. Consider the example of a lighthouse which is both non-rival and, at first sight, non-excludable. (In fact it may be possible to charge at the port of destination but we presently ignore this.) A shipping company may well have an incentive to provide the lighthouse if it sends many ships on the route the lighthouse serves. The company cannot run the risk that no one provides the lighthouse, and even though once built all users of the route benefit, but cannot be charged, this does not matter. Putting this proposition in a mildly formal manner, the lighthouse will be built by the company if $(1-p) \, V > C$, where V is the value to it of having the lighthouse, p is the probability that if it does not build the lighthouse someone else will, and C is the building cost. It can further be seen that an insurance company has an incentive to build a lighthouse if many of the ships it insures use a particular route. A rather interesting account of the extent to which lighthouses have in practice given rise to public good problems for the market is to be found in R. Coase, 'The lighthouse in economics' (*Journal of Law and Economics,* October 1974).

A15.2 **FALSE.** Since the good is excludable a producer can make usage dependent on paying and thereby may be able to cover his costs. An uncongested swimming pool is an example.

A15.3 **FALSE.** By definition of a non-rival good it costs nothing to admit additional users. However, a private firm must charge a positive price if it is to cover the fixed costs of providing the good, and also any costs of collecting the revenue itself. In general, a positive price will discourage potential users. But it would be wrong to conclude from this that a potential Pareto improvement would necessarily arise if the government were to take over and provide the good at a zero price. The government would thereby incur a loss and have to raise revenue elsewhere. The efficiency costs of doing this *may* offset the direct gains arising from the increased usage of the non-rival good.

There is a further point. Even if government provision optimally pursued could lead to a potential Pareto improvement, it does not follow that when vested with the responsiblity to provide the good the government *will* pursue an optimal policy. Politicians, bureaucrats and officials are all human and will tend to take actions which, given the institutional framework in which they operate, favour their own interests rather than those of society. Markets may be subject to failure but this does not create an *a priori* case for intervention, as governments are also prone to act in a less than 'ideal' fashion.

A15.4 **TRUE.** Suppose in figure 15.1 OC is the cost of providing each unit of the good. Curves A and B show the values two consumers, A and B, place on each unit of the good provided. Since the services of each unit of the good are equally available to the two consumers the social value of a unit of the good is the sum of the values to the two customers. This is given by the vertical summation of A and B, as shown by curve $A + B$. The marginal social value of output equals the marginal social cost at q_0. Both A and B should therefore consume the q_0 units of service of the good available. To induce B to consume q_0 service units price must be P. At this price A would wish to consume q_1 units, which is more than he can. Note further that if consumer A is charged P_1 for the good and B a price of P then both would freely choose to consume q_0 units of the good and total

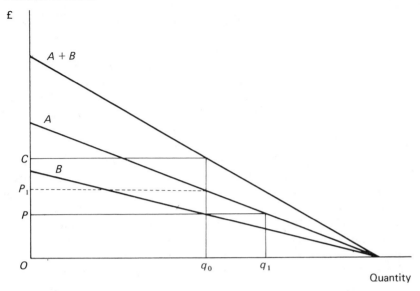

Figure 15.1

production costs are covered. Such an outcome is known as a Lindahl equilibrium. How would it be established? Well, suppose sets of prices (or equivalently tax shares) are proposed which just cover costs. Individuals then record how much of the good they would wish to consume at the various prices. When a set of prices is found at which everyone wants to consume the same amount of the good, the Lindahl equilibrium has been found. Of course, this assumes that individuals truthfully reveal preferences. Can you see why there is an incentive not to do so?

A15.5 FALSE. The statement is only true if the road is congestion free. As more people use a given road we would expect congestion to occur. Once such a level of utilisation is reached there is a definite cost in terms of increased journey time, which new travellers impose on existing users. Thus the road is not non-rival for more consumption by one person does reduce that available to others.

A15.6 FALSE. As the number of people using a particular public good increase so the value of the services provided will rise. That is, when calculating the social value of a unit of a public good we add the marginal private valuation of each member of the group. Thus as the size of the group increases so the value of a marginal unit of the public good will increase. So if both communities have the same costs of producing the public good, the larger community will tend to produce a larger quantity.

A15.7 TRUE. Consider for concreteness the case of video-taped television programmes. The programme itself is a non-rival good in so far as additional viewers do not reduce the amount of the programme available to existing watchers. Whilst it is true that the cassette in which the programme is 'delivered' is a private good, this does not affect the non-rival characteristic of the programme.

In figure 15.2(a) the cost curves of a representative firm are drawn. The curve DF in (b) shows the demand curve of each of the identical consumers net of the cost of the cassette. The vertical summation of these curves is EF and so if there are n consumers, EF will be n times higher than DF. With identical firms the industry supply curve is SS'. A social optimum requires that q_1 programme be produced and they each be viewed by all n consumers. This is exactly what emerges under competition. Suppose the price a consumer is charged to view a programme is P_1. Then since there are n consumers the producer will receive $nP_1 = OS$ per programme. If the number of producers is large no one producer can affect the market price of programmes and so each producer maximises profits by selling q_1/n programmes and just covers costs. When the total output of q_1 is sold the market clearing price is P_1. Note that we assume that whereas each programme is different, they are similar in the sense that consumer welfare is

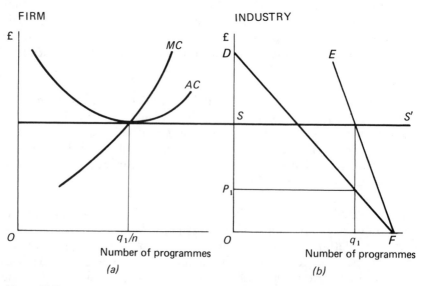

Figure 15.2

affected equally whichever of the programmes is withdrawn from the market. If each producer adds only, say ½%, to total supply then this will hardly affect the marginal valuation of the consumers and so the price taking assumption is justified.

How important is the identical tastes assumption? All the foregoing was based on the Demsetz paper (see references) and he goes on to show that where tastes differ but can be distinguished by sellers, optimality is once again achieved (normally, competition prevents price discrimination but not here). In practice, tastes probably do differ and cannot be directly identified by sellers, hence the conventional problem of some potential buyers being inefficiently excluded by a market does remain. Nevertheless, apart from the attraction of its ingenuity, Demsetz's analysis does suggest that the market distribution of non-rival goods may not be as inefficient as is often thought.

II VOTING SYSTEMS

Granted that everyone is agreed that some amount of collective provision together with associated taxation is desirable, how much should be undertaken? Decisions of this kind must be taken through the political system. One possibility is that a policy is acceptable only if everyone in the community votes in favour of it (a unanimous decision rule). An alternative rule is that a policy is accepted if a majority of the community vote in favour of it. Further twists are introduced when, instead of voting directly for policies, the community vote for politicians who, broadly speaking, represent policy packages (combinations of policies on, say, defence expenditure, educational expenditure and many other items). The consequences of these different methods of taking social decisions and why some rules may be preferred to others by the community is explored in the questions below.

References

Black D., The theory of Committees and Elections, Cambridge University Press, 1958. Bowen H.R., 'The interpretation of voting in the allocation of economic resources', Quarterly Journal of Economics, November 1943. Buchanan J.M., 'An economic theory of clubs', Economica, February 1965. Davis O.H., Hinich M.J. and Ordeshook P.C., 'An expository development of a mathematical model of the electoral process', American Political Science Review, June 1970. Mueller D.C., Public Choice, Cambridge University Press 1979. Oates W.E., Fiscal Federalism, Harcourt Brace, 1972. Tullock G., The Vote Motive, Institute of Economic Affairs 1976.

Questions

Q.15.8 If a community has a public expenditure—tax mix which is Pareto optimal, then it will be impossible to alter the policy if any change must receive a unanimous vote in favour.

Q15.9 Any policy change which is passed by a unanimous voting rule must result in an actual Pareto improvement.

Q15.10 If only a majority of votes in favour are required before a policy is put into effect, then although any change need not be an actual Pareto improvement, it must be a potential Pareto improvement.

Q15.11 Since a majority voting rule permits policy changes which are not potential Pareto improvements whilst the unanimous rule does not, the latter must be superior on efficiency grounds.

Q15.12 Suppose a community has to decide on the level of public expenditure. Different voters favour different levels. It is possible to rank the voters in order of the level of public expenditure they would most like, from smallest to largest. The median voter is the voter who appears halfway down this list, i.e. there are as many voters who favour a higher level of expenditure than he does as there are voters who favour a lower level. It follows that in a majority vote the level of expenditure favoured by the median voter would defeat any other policy.

Q15.13 Suppose a single issue is to be decided. In a two-party system in which the party receiving the majority of votes gets elected, then both parties will adopt the policy favoured by the median voter. (Assume single peaked preferences as explained in A15.12.)

Q15.14 In a three-party system, no party will duplicate the policy of any other.

Q15.15 (a) Now suppose that two issues are to be decided. Let us say the rate of income tax and the proportion of tax revenue spent on defence as opposed to education. Combinations of policies may be plotted in figure 15.3. The most preferred policy mixes of the three equal sized groups of voters are shown as A, B, and C. There are two parties and everyone votes for the party closest to his most preferred policy. The problem is where will the parties locate. Four

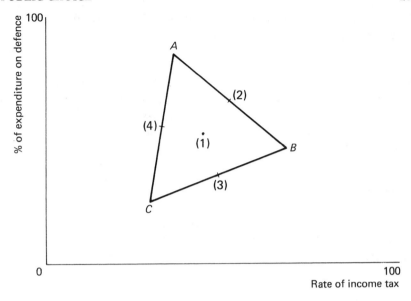

Figure 15.3

possibilities are illustrated as (1), (2), (3) and (4). Would any party choose location (1)?
(b) If 60% of the voters were at A, what positions would the parties take?

Q15.16 Suppose voters' preferred policy mixes were spread uniformly within the circle in figure 15.4. What outcome would emerge with two parties?

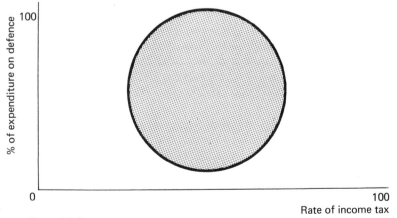

Figure 15.4

Q.15.17 Why do communities not have a referendum on each policy issue instead of voting for politicians who represent collections of policies?

Q15.18 In a general election the probability that any individual vote will decide which party gets elected is virtually zero. Since it requires effort to get to the polling station it follows that the costs of voting outweigh the benefits for the individual and therefore it is irrational' to vote. Why therefore do people vote?

Answers

A15.8 **TRUE.** By definition of a Pareto optimum, any change from it must make at least one person worse off. Hence, at least one person will vote against the change and this is sufficient to prevent the policy from passing.

A15.9 **TRUE.** From the definition of an actual Pareto improvement, nobody is made worse off whilst at least one person is better off by the policy change. Clearly, if a policy were to make somebody worse off he would not vote for it and thus the policy would not pass with a unanimous decision rule.

A15.10 **FALSE.** With majority voting, policy changes need not represent actual Pareto improvements. If A and B benefit from a policy but C is harmed, then a majority rule would pass the policy (assuming each voter looks only to his self-interest) even though C is made worse off. There is no need that a winning policy be a potential Pareto improvement either. Suppose A and B gain £10 each and C loses £30 if the policy passes. The majority rule would ensure that the policy does pass even though the gainers could not compensate the losers. (Although C should then propose that the policy be abandoned and A and B receive £12 if such transfers are possible.)

Incidentally, there is another very well known problem with majority voting, identified by the Marquis de Condorcet in 1785. Let there be three voters, 1, 2 and 3 with preferences over the three alternative policies, x, y and z. Voter 1 most prefers x, then y, then z; voter 2 ranks the policies y, z, x; voter 3 orders them z, x, y. It follows that with a majority voting rule, policy y defeats z on the votes of 1 and 2, policy x defeats y on the votes of 1 and 3, but z defeats x on the votes of 2 and 3. Hence, if voting were to continue until a policy is found which defeats all others, no decision would ever be reached. (Though all individuals have transitive preferences, social decisions are intransitive and so lead to cycling.) Alternatively, if the winner of the second vote is the accepted policy, then the final policy depends on the arbitrarily chosen order of voting.

A15.11 **FALSE**. To find policy packages which make everyone better off is in practice almost impossible. With a unanimous voting rule in force, policy would hardly ever change from its current state. Majority voting means however that many policy changes would be passed which are potential Pareto improvements. Sometimes, particular individuals may lose from these changes but other times they will gain. If every change had to make everybody better off society would forgo many opportunities which would yield overall benefits. Although policies may sometimes be passed which are socially costly, it is nevertheless quite possible that on balance everybody would be better off if decisions had only to be supported by a simple majority. This is particularly so since, as we shall see, those policies actually adopted will tend to reflect the views of the median voter and on the whole those policies passed may therefore represent potential Pareto improvements.

The above is, of course, not a proof that a majority voting rule is superior to an unanimous rule. What it attempts to do is show that arguments exist which would make it preferable to have a majority rule. However, there is certainly no reason why the simple majority rule should be optimal. It could be that a 60% rule would be better, but pure theory cannot come up with a particular number.

A15.12 **FALSE**. In figure 15.5(a), voter II is the median voter and the level of expenditure he most prefers is B. Suppose that level of

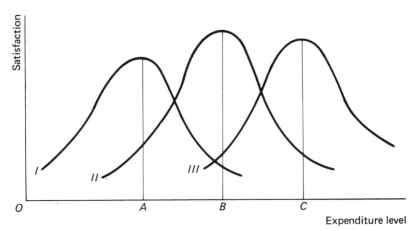

Figure 15.5(a)

expenditure A were to be proposed and a vote taken as to whether it
is A or B that is preferred. Both individuals II and III prefer B to A
and so B is passed on a majority vote. Similarly B would defeat any
other proposal, such as C.

Now turn to figure 15.5(b). Unlike figure 15.5(a), voter III has
more than one peak (turning point) to his utility function. In figure
15.5(b), B is the policy preferred by the median voter where the
ranking is according to voters' 'most desired' outcome. But this policy
will be defeated by A (which attracts voters I and III). Policy A will
in turn be defeated by C and C can be defeated by B. This is the
Condorcet problem outlined in A15.10. Single peaked preferences
are sufficient to eliminate this problem and do seem more plausible
than multiple peaks.

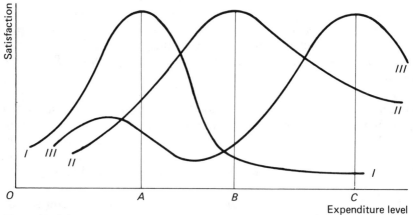

Figure 15.5(b)

A15.13 TRUE. The politician wishing to get elected has the problem
of choosing a policy. Suppose the opposition selects some policy
which is not B in figure 15.5. Then by choosing B, victory is certain,
for B defeats all other policies. Now suppose the opposition choose
B. All other policies will be defeated and hence the best thing to do
is select B also and presumably face a 50/50 chance of being elected.
Whatever the opposition does, it pays to aim policy at the median
voter and hence both parties will end up adopting B, at least assuming
they can correctly identify the preferences of the median voter.

Note that with the multiple peaked preferences of figure 15.5(b),
the party choosing policy last would be the winner. Presuming the
electorate believes the incumbent party will maintain its policies, it
will therefore be defeated and the parties will regularly alternate in
power.

A15.14 **TRUE.** Suppose there are n voters. If initially all three parties adopt the policy favoured by the median voter, they will receive $n/3$ votes. Now suppose one of the parties adopts a policy which offers just a little more public expenditure. It will capture all the votes of that half of the population which favours more public expenditure than does the median voter. Thus, that party will have $n/2$ votes and the other two parties will be left with $n/4$ votes each. The defecting party will therefore certainly win if the other two parties stay where they are. Consequently, neither of the other two parties will wish to maintain their policies either. If initially the three parties were all adopting some policy other than that favoured by the median voter then the conclusion follows, though more forcefully than before, since a defecting party by changing its policy in the correct direction can now capture more than 50% of the vote if the other parties stay where they are.

The argument above shows that in a three-party system, no two parties will wish to get caught adopting the same policies. No answer seems to be forthcoming as to what policies will actually be adopted. In a three-party system the parties will continually be trying to change their positions in response to changes by other parties who will in turn react to these changes. No predictions can easily be made about the outcome of this progress and our actual experience of pre-election party political jockeying for position should suggest how complex the game is.

A15.15 (a) **Location (1) will never be occupied.** Suppose one party chose (1) and another (2). Since (2) is closer to A and B than is (1), this must be a winning position.

Now consider the fate of a party which adopted (4). If the other party occupied a position a little to the northwest of (2) it would capture all the A voters from (4) and still retain the B voters and so win the election. But if a party did occupy such a position, then it is open to the other party to move a little to the north east of (3), capture all the B votes and also the C votes and so win the election. This kind of process will continue and in this situation we might expect considerable pre-election jockeying for position. No definite predictions can be made except that platform (1), which minimises the total distance from the most preferred positions and so may well be a Pareto optimum, will never be chosen.

(b) **Both parties would take up positions at A.** If one party were at A and the other elsewhere, the party at A would get 60% of the vote and so win.

A15.16 **Both parties would adopt the policy at the centre of the**

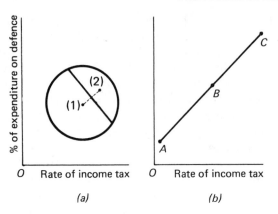

Figure 15.6

circle. Suppose in figure 15.6(a) one party were to adopt policy mix (2). Then by choosing policy mix (1) the other party would capture all votes to the left of the chord drawn and hence win the election. Both parties would be forced to choose policy (1).

It is easily seen that if voters' preferences are distributed such that all lines dividing the area into two equal parts meet at a single point then, with two parties, a centre clustering result will always emerge. However, with three parties this will not happen.

Also, note in passing that with the three voters A, B and C with preferences as illustrated in figure 15.6(b) then with two parties a centre clustering result will once again emerge.

A15.17 From the previous questions and answers we may expect that if policies are voted on individually, the outcome will more closely reflect the preferences of the electorate than if politicians must adopt policy packages. However, there are clearly costs in having frequent votes. Apart from the actual time involved in the process of voting, there is the effort required on the part of the electorate to master the issues and, where rapid decisions are necessary (e.g. in war), a general vote is obviously inefficient. Particularly where most people share the same preference or at least where median voter type results obtain, the efficiency of having specialists taking decisions and being elected at infrequent intervals is evident.

A15.18 After at least 2½ hours of discussion the authors failed to reach a consensus on this question!

Index